UNITY LIBRARY & ARCHIVES
Kabbalistic aphorisms.
BM 526 .S7 1971

KABBALISTIC APHORISMS

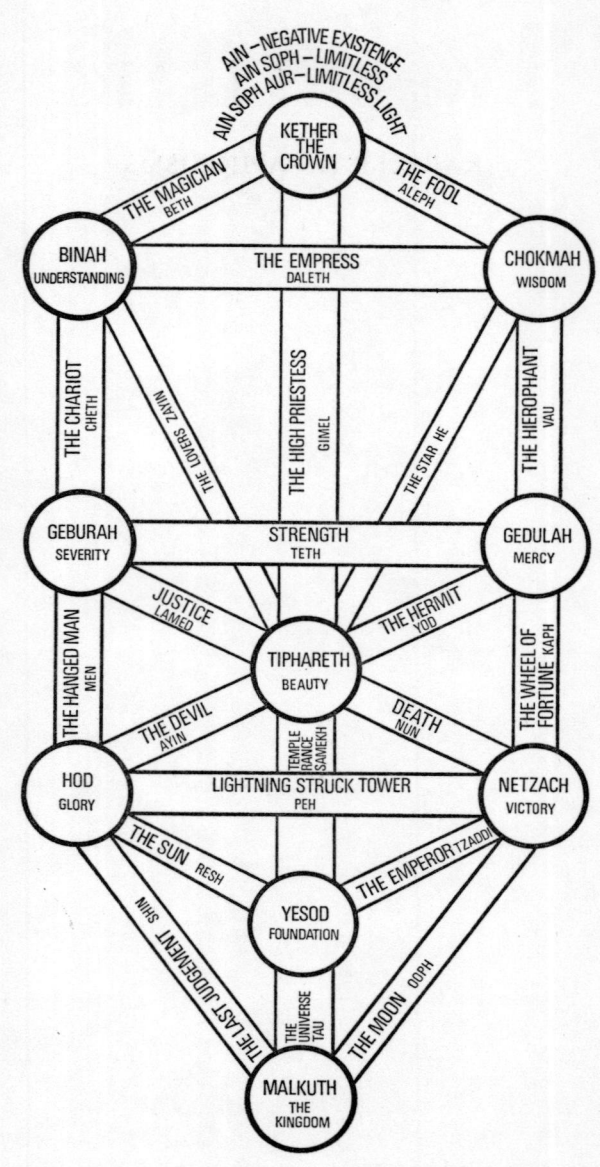

KABBALISTIC APHORISMS

by

JAMES STURZAKER

THEOSOPHICAL PUBLISHING HOUSE LTD.
68 Great Russell Street, London WC1B 3BU
ADYAR: MADRAS   WHEATON ILL., U.S.A.

© James Sturzaker

First printed 1971

ISBN 7229 5226 0

*Printed in Great Britain by Richard Clay (The Chaucer Press), Ltd.,
Bungay, Suffolk*

CONTENTS

BOOK I

Section 1	Concept	*page* 1
Section 2	The Ain	7
Section 3	Kether	10
Section 4	Chokmah	13
Section 5	Binah	16
Section 6	Gedulah	19
Section 7	Geburah	22
Section 8	Tiphareth	25
Section 9	Netzach	28
Section 10	Hod	31
Section 11	Yesod	34
Section 12	Malkuth	37
Section 13	The Divisions of the Soul	40

BOOK II

Section 1	General	43
Section 2	The Fool	46
Section 3	The Magician	50
Section 4	The High Priestess	53
Section 5	The Empress	57
Section 6	The Star	60
Section 7	The Hierophant	63
Section 8	The Lovers	66
Section 9	The Chariot	69

Section 10	Strength	72
Section 11	The Hermit	75
Section 12	The Wheel of Fortune	78
Section 13	Justice	82
Section 14	The Hanged Man	85
Section 15	Death	88
Section 16	Temperance	91
Section 17	The Devil	94
Section 18	The Lightning-struck Tower	97
Section 19	The Emperor	100
Section 20	The Moon	103
Section 21	The Sun	107
Section 22	Judgement	110
Section 23	The Universe	113
Section 24	General	117

EXPLANATORY NOTES

The Mystical Kabbalah is a glyph or symbol system which consists of the Tree of Life and the twenty-two Major Arcana of the Tarot cards or, to give the cards their correct name, the Book of Thoth.

Many books have been written on the subject but all have expressed the mystical and occult side of this teaching of the Ancient Wisdom. The Kabbalah is more than that, however; it is a teaching as old as the hills, just how old no one can truly say, but it certainly goes back more than two thousand years, yet it is as relevant and modern today as it was long ago.

Here is a common meeting ground for the present day physical scientist and the metaphysician. The Kabbalah is a science in itself and can be used for many purposes. The mathematician, the biologist, physicist or housewife will find it as practical and useful as the mystic or occultist.

Contained within this glyph are the basic qualities that make and keep life moving. All life operates through the basic principles of Positive, Negative and Balance, so does the Kabbalah.

Force and Form are components of Life, they are part of the Tree of Life.

Light and its breakdown into colour, which is an integral part of Life, is also an integral part of Kabbalah.

A Universe, the human body or a single atom can be understood by scientist and layman alike when related to the Kabbalistic glyph.

The psychologist can penetrate into hidden depths and the philosopher lose himself in the contents of the most amazing psychological and philosophical symbolism ever to be given to Man.

The tycoon who is concerned with running a successful business could save the high fees of consultants by studying the organization and administration as expressed by the Kabbalistic glyph. Even the more mundane domestic tasks can be more successfully carried out.

The advantage of the Kabbalah lies in its simplicity for those who require the simple method and its complexity for those who want to attempt to understand and unravel the secrets of Life.

This book of Kabbalistic Aphorisms has been compiled to suit the needs of all. Churchman and atheist, materialist and occultist, highly intelligent and not so gifted will find satisfaction by a study of each section of the Aphorisms in relation to the aspect of the glyph with which they are concerned. The superficial will find profound depths and the complex mind will marvel at its simplicity.

Although the need should not arise, the author will always be pleased to assist any reader who has doubts about the interpretations. A stamped addressed envelope is all the author requires.

J. STURZAKER
25 Circle Gardens
Merton Park
London SW19 3JX
England

INTRODUCTION

1. The origin is lost in the dim and distant past and it is unlikely that the truth of where and how this teaching of the ancient wisdom was given to man will ever be known.

2. It has been stated that the Gods gave the teaching to Abraham. This in itself raises a number of pertinent questions.

3. Was Abraham a being of flesh and blood, or was this symbolic figure an aspect of the group consciousness as Adam was symbolic of the human race?

4. Accepting the fact that Abraham was flesh and blood we still do not know when or where the Kabbalah was introduced, because no individual can be certain at what point in time and space Abraham came into physical manifestation.

5. A number of authorities quote this teaching of the ancient wisdom as stemming from one race, but again there is no satisfactory proof.

6. One can say with more certainty that the Jews preserved the Tree of Life and the Bohemians preserved the Tarot cards.

7. Only by combining and understanding both the Tree of Life and the Tarot cards can we hope to glimpse the truth of the ancient wisdom.

8. The two aspects of the Kabbalah for many years were kept apart to such a degree that many people did not realize the Tarot was an integral part of the Kabbalah.

9. Even today most Kabbalistic writers deal with either the Tree or Tarot, but rarely with both.

10. The main use of the Tarot for many generations has been for divination, except for that small band of souls who all down the ages have preserved the true spiritual understanding of the Book of Thoth.

BOOK I

Section 1

CONCEPT

1. The Kabbalah is an esoteric philosophy combined with psychology.
2. Occult teachings of East and West meet and blend into the Tree of Life.
3. All religions stem from and return to the Tree.
4. Within the spheres of the Tree all the Gods have their dwellings.
5. Intellect, Spiritual Perception and Intuition—all three must be used to understand the Kabbalah.
6. The Kabbalah is a mathematically sound system.
7. Kabbalistic symbology is and can be a universal language.
8. The Tree can be a common meeting ground for the religious, philosophical and scientific; all are required for a full understanding of the Tree.
9. Thirty-two aspects of intelligence await an understanding.
10. Positive, Negative and Balance are the one Trinity underlying the whole of life which springs from the Ain.
11. This is the blue-print of all life, manifest and unmanifest.
12. A study of the Tree reveals the expansion of no-thing as it streams forth into the concretion of physical manifestation.
13. The unfolding is a repetitive plan covering all stages of consciousness.
14. The Ain expands to the Ain Soph and then projects itself to form the third aspect—Ain Soph Aur.
15. Three aspects of the Ain form the first Trinity, unmanifest, unknowable, without form and substance, but a vital force moving out from itself.

16. A point of light is formed—the first manifestation of the known unknowable.
17. The Tree is made up of ten spheres of Sephiroth (plural of Sephirah). These are connected by twenty-two paths.
18. There thirty-two points or intelligences in all. Ten objective and twenty-two subjective.
19. Kether is the first point of light which stands at the top point of the Tree and surmounts the middle pillar.
20. Pure existence, harmony, stability, androgynous, are the chief qualities of Kether.
21. Contained within the Sephirah Kether is the whole plan of life in nebulous form.
22. Each Sephirah contains all the elements and qualities of the other nine in varying proportions.
23. Chokmah, the second Sephirah, receives the life force from Kether and channels or directs it. This is called the sphere of the zodiac.
24. The positive pillar is ruled by Chokmah and here is the centre of abstract ideas.
25. Binah, the third Sephirah, accepts the life force from Chokmah and creates the first nebulous patterns or life forms, animate or inanimate.
26. The first form of restriction takes place in the sphere of Binah, it is appropriate that this Sephirah stands at the head of the negative pillar.
27. Kether, Chokmah and Binah form the first unmanifest, known, unknowable trinity and are known as the supernals.
28. The supernals stand above the abyss which separates force from force and matter combined.
29. Performing the function of a bridge across the abyss is the Sephirah Daath.
30. Daath is a Sephirah that is and yet is not. A concentrated yet nebulous point in the centre of the abyss.
31. Below the abyss the world of form opens out. This consists of the lower seven Sephiroth.

32. The first trinity in the world of form is that of the Moral World.
33. The Moral World is formed of Gedulah, Geburah and Tiphareth.
34. Mercy, Justice and the reasoning soul are the basic principles of the Moral World.
35. The second trinity is called the physical world and contains the Sephiroth Netzach, Hod and Yesod.
36. The principal qualities of the physical world are the Energetic principle, Glory, and the Generative principle.
37. The seventh Sephirah below the abyss is called Malkuth; it stands alone.
38. Malkuth has no principal quality; it contains all that has come down from Kether through the other Sephiroth.
39. The aphorisms 11 to 38 have outlined the basic tree. There are four trees.
40. Each of the four trees are described as a world at a different plane of existence.
41. Atziluth is at the highest level and is referred to as the Archetypal World.
42. In Atziluth is one Sephirah Kether, and in Kether is a complete tree.
43. Below Atziluth is the Briatic world. This is the Creative world.
44. In the world of Briah are two Sephiroth—Chokmah and Binah.
45. There are two trees in the Briatic world, one in each Sephirah.
46. Yetzirah, the third world, contains six Sephiroth: Gedulah, Geburah, Tiphareth, Netzach, Hod and Yesod.
47. The Yetziratic world is the Formative World and embraces six trees, one in each Sephirah.
48. Assiah is the fourth and lowest world. This is the physical world from an ant to a universe.
49. Malkuth is the only Sephirah in this world, but there is a tree in Malkuth.

50. The world of Assiah also contains the Qliphoth, which is a tree in reverse in the sense that manifest life places Malkuth where Kether should be and Kether at the point of Malkuth.

51. Qliphoth is the world of demons and also has ten grades.

52. The three supernals of Qliphoth are TOHU (the formless) the negative of Kether.

53. BOHU (the void) the opposite of Chokmah and CHASHEK (the darkness) the negative Binah.

54. The remaining seven Sephirah in the Qliphoth are seven hells

55. The Rules of Qliphoth are Satan and Lilith. This pair is known as the Beast.

56. In the four worlds there are ten trees plus one tree in which the four worlds exist.

57. One hundred and ten Sephiroth make up the four worlds plus one basic tree.

58. The four worlds contain ten trees and one hundred Sephiroth. In numerology both numbers revert to the one.

59. The one is the basic tree which originated from the Ain.

60. The tree contains three pillars. The outside pillars are the positive and negative, the middle pillar is balance.

61. Chokmah, Gedulah and Netzach are on the positive pillar.

62. Binah, Geburah and Hod are on the negative pillar.

63. Kether heads the middle pillar of balance with Tiphareth, Yesod and Malkuth following in that order.

64. The Kabbalistic tree is based on the two aspects of all life. Positive and Negative.

65. Chokmah heads the positive pillar and is a positive Sephirah but it is negative to Kether and positive to Gedulah.

66. Gedulah, positive in its position on the tree, is negative to Chokmah and positive to Netzach.

67. Netzach is the last Sephirah on the positive pillar and is positive to Yesod but negative to Gedulah.

68. Binah at the head of the negative pillar is still positive to Geburah.

69. Geburah is negative to Binah and positive to Hod.

70. Hod is the last Sephirah on the negative pillar and is negative to Geburah but positive to Yesod.

71. Gedulah is also called Chesed and Geburah has Pahad as an alternative.

72. Kether is the head of the pillar of balance and is the apex of the supernal trinity.

73. Tiphareth is the point of the first trinity below the abyss.

74. Yesod forms the point of the lowest trinity on the tree.

75. The Tiphareth and Yesodic trinities are reversed.

76. Malkuth, the last Sephirah on the middle pillar and on the tree, stands alone.

77. In standing alone Malkuth represents the fulfilment of Kether, whose likeness it reflects at the denser levels.

78. Malkuth in one world becomes Kether in the next world below.

79. On the return journey Kether of the lower world becomes Malkuth of the world immediately above.

80. Each Sephirah is the sphere of a God name.

81. There is an Archangel attached to each Sephirah.

82. Hosts of Angels combine with the forces or qualities of a specific Sephirah.

83. There is a mundane chakra to each Sephirah.

84. A mundane chakra is the sphere or point of the Sephirah through which the life force flows.

85. A mundane chakra denotes the particular aspect of the life plan that the Sephirah to which it belongs has to fulfil.

86. The Heavenly Man is Adam Kadmon, and the Sephiroth parts of his anatomy.

87. The tree is a man or a universe at all planes of consciousness and all stages of force, force and matter, form and formless.

88. Each Sephirah has three distinct qualities: its own functions, what it receives from the previous Sephirah and what it transmits to those below.

Section 2

THE AIN

1. The Ain is the illimitable source from which all emerges and the limitless ultimate to which all returns.
2. Even in its stillness, before expansion, it is a mass of pulsating life and force.
3. As the Ain is the ultimate and there is nothing outside of Ain expansion can only take place within itself.
4. There can be no expansion outwardly of an ultimate that has left no place in which to expand.
5. Outside of Ain is no-thing and no-thing is the ever-evolving Ain.
6. The inward expansion is at the same time one of contraction.
7. When the positive expands, the negative contracts and vice versa.
8. Each positive expansion is a forward movement in the evolution of a force that evolves in spite of itself.
9. All negative expansions are rest periods, or the night of sleep in the life of Ain.
10. Positive is white or light, negative dark or black, balance silver or grey.
11. Chaos is the dark, or negative in which no manifestation exists and the Ain slumbers.
12. Let there be light, and from the Chaos came ordered manifestation.
13. The first spark of light moves out and reflects back upon itself. This is the Ain Soph.
14. From the reactions of the Ain and Ain Soph emerges the Ain Soph Aur.

15. The eternal trinity of all life, one in three, but three in one in the negative existence of Chaos.
16. The Ain is negative existence—non manifestation.
17. Ain is the macroprosopus, and tetragrammaton the microprosopus.
18. The Ain Soph is the limitless.
19. This extension of the Ain becomes the duad of the invisible.
20. As the duad it is transcendent, infinite and exalted.
21. Here is pure mind and complete unity.
22. The Ain Soph Aur becomes the limitless light, the divisible, indivisible.
23. This is the motivating force which pushes out the first manifested light.
24. The trinity forms the limitless incomprehensible negative light.
25. The limitless incomprehensible creates a centre or point of negative light.
26. The point of reflected positive light which is concentrated into a sphere becomes the first sephirah.
27. At this point it is the trinity manifesting in the known unknowable.
28. All existence from Kether downwards forms the "Robe of Ain".
29. The Ain is demonstrated through the Tree or Robe in many aspects, formulating the attributes in conceptions of wisdom, understanding, beauty, power, mercy and matter.
30. The attributes are shown first in universality, inconceivable to spirits and men; this is the first world—Atziluth.
31. It is reflected from Atziluth to the plane of pure spirit beyond the conception of man; this is the second world—Briah.
32. Further condensed by another reflection down it becomes recognizable to those of humanity with the higher consciousness; this is the third world—Yetzirah.

33. The last projection, contracted to ultimate solidity is recognizable by the whole of manifested life. This is the fourth world—Assiah.
34. Briah is the world of the Archangels, and Yetzirah the world of Hosts of Angels.
35. The Host of Angels are the workers or officers of the Archangels.
36. The Archangels in the World of Briah have at their head Metatron.
37. Metatron means great teacher.

Section 3

KETHER

1. The first sephirah of the tree is called "The Admirable or Hidden Intelligence".
2. Kether is called the Crown, it is supreme at the centre top of the tree
3. It is equilibrium, androgenous, pure existence.
4. Kether contains all that has been, is and is to be.
5. In this sphere there is the Premium Mobile or the first swirlings of a nebulous force going out.
6. This is the macroprosopus, and the head of Adam Kadmon the heavenly man.
7. Kether is the focal point through which the creative life force flows to form all that follows.
8. The Archangel to Kether is Metatron.
9. The God name of Kether is Ahieh (I will be).
10. The Host of Angels to Kether are the four Holy Living Creatures.
11. The Host of Angels to any sephirah are the builders and with Kether they represent the four elements, Air, Earth, Fire and Water.
12. By the four Holy Living Creatures under the direction of Metatron all life is brought into being and sustained.
13. In the division of the soul Neschama corresponds to Kether, the higher aspirations.
14. Kether is the first principle of the manifesting life.
15. It is the light, giving the power of illumination of the first principle.
16. In the world of Atziluth exists the Archetype of all that is and is to be.

17. Kether could be described as Malkuth or number ten of the invisible sephiroth, hence Kether in Malkuth and Malkuth in Kether.
18. Kether is "I am What I am" and contains the other nine and issues them forth in order.
19. The crown of the greatest sephiratic trinity, of which Kether is the head, consists of The Crown, The King, The Queen.
20. Yod He Vau He is Tetragrammaton, the upper point of the Y is in Kether.
21. Kether is called the Ancient One and from here it reaches back into the Ain.
22. Kether in Briah is the focal point of the creative world.
23. The formative world of Yetzirah has Kether as the guiding principle.
24. Assiah has the physical perfection at the level of Kether consciousness.
25. From four stages can be gathered the full consciousness of Kether: The thought, The creative thought, The formation and The completed perfection.
26. Perfection is the key at each level of Kether.
27. Kether is the Alpha and Omega of the known unknowable.
28. The hilt of the flaming sword is in Kether.
29. The command "Let there be light"—Kether is that light.
30. No created life in any form can attain to Kether in Kether.
31. Beyond Kether in Gedulah in the world of Briah individuality ceases to exist.
32. Kabbalistic alchemy considers the three supernals as the three fountains of metallic things. Kether is the "Thick Water".
33. Kether is the root of metallic substance.
34. Each metal has ten orders or degrees. Chetham (that is pure fine gold) is applicable to Kether.

35. The colour attributable to Kether is brilliant white.
36. The point and point within a circle are the symbols of Kether.
37. Gods applicable to Kether are Cronus, Atum-Ra, Osiris and Zeus.
38. Ambergris and Diamond are the perfume and gem-stone attributed to Kether.
39. The Magical image aroused in this sephirah is a bearded King in profile.
40. A lamp is the magical weapon of Kether.
41. Symbolic in Kether is the Almond in Flower, the Swan and Hawk.
42. Here are the roots of the Elemental Powers, represented in the book of Thoth by the four aces.

Section 4

CHOKMAH

1. The second sphere or Sephirah is the Illuminating Intelligence.
2. Chokmah is wisdom. We see not as through a glass darkly but face to face.
3. This Sephirah directs forces and the influence of Chokmah is the sphere of the Zodiac.
4. Chokmah is the centre of abstract ideas. The crown of creation, and the second glory.
5. At the top of the positive pillar this Sephirah is the masculine aspect of the life force.
6. Positive to Gedulah but as the reflection from Kether it is negative to this Sephirah.
7. The wisdom of the ages is here stored and used, as the first abstract outline emerges.
8. The first abstract idea is the sphere of the zodiac.
9. Through the sphere of the zodiac the remainder of manifestation takes place.
10. Planetary symbols of the solar system are only symbolic of the quality supplied by the appropriate point in the sphere of the Zodiac.
11. The abstract idea is one of form, but form has not yet taken place.
12. Even the sphere of the Zodiac at this stage is not yet restricting in its nature.
13. All that is formed is done so by the power of Chokmah directing the life force of the Ain.
14. Pure dynamic energy and the stimulator of the Universe.
15. At this level of consciousness both vice and virtue or positive and negative are still abstract ideas.

16. A basic Chokmah principle is duality, it is the duad of Kether, it is the second phase of manifesting consciousness.
17. The Host of Angels attached to Chokmah are the Ophanim or Wheels.
18. It is through the Ophanim that Chokmah directs the Ain force.
19. The first swirlings of Kether are reflected into wheels of force in Chokmah.
20. Emerging from the wheels is the first abstract idea of the Universe, as yet force without form.
21. It is with this duad principle that we now see "not as through a glass darkly but face to face".
22. Here robed in glory is the great creative Father projecting out of the unknowable through Kether to Chokmah as the knowable unknowable.
23. Of unity Chokmah is the supernal Father and splendour.
24. The work of creative manifestation has begun and a third sphere is formed called Binah, into which the Chokmah force is directed.
25. Chokmah is the salt of Kabbalistic alchemy.
26. Batzar (gold in dust form), the second degree of gold, is related to Chokmah.
27. In the metallic doctrine Chokmah is the Sephirah of Lead —Lead is the Primordial Salt.
28. In the world of Atziluth Chokmah is pure alive wisdom.
29. At the Briatic level the wisdom of Chokmah is drawn upon in the work of creation.
30. The formation of wisdom takes place in Yetzirah.
31. Imperfect wisdom is to be found in the world of Assiah.
32. Chokmah in Kether, in the world of Assiah, is the highest form of wisdom in Malkuth.
33. Chokmah is the supreme sphere of magic and Thoth is connected to this Sephirah.
34. The Yang of Taoism corresponds to this Sephirah.

35. The Archangel for this sphere is Ratziel.
36. The first letter of the Tetragrammaton (Y.H.V.H.) Yod is attributed to this sphere.
37. The number two is associated to Chokmah.
38. God qualities in Chokmah are those of Thoth, Pallas, Athene, Minerva, Uranus and Hermes and the Scandinavian Odin.
39. Musk is the aromatic attributable to this sphere.
40. Chokmah is Mahat, Kwan Shin Yin, Vishnu and Ishvara.
41. The gems of this sphere are Turquoise and Ruby.
42. The flower corresponding to Chokmah is Amaranth.
43. The line and cross are symbols of Chokmah.
44. Chokmah has for magical weapons the wand and lingam.
45. Man is the animal associated to the Chokmah sphere of consciousness.
46. In the universal man Chokmah force enters through the Ajna centre.
47. This sphere represents the nostrils of Adam Kadmon.
48. The colour attributable to Chokmah is grey.

Section 5

BINAH

1. Binah is the Sephirah of form, the first of the three Sephiroth on the negative pillar.
2. This is the feminine aspect of Kether, which embraces the mother principle.
3. Binah completes the trinity known as the supernals.
4. There is now balance in the sphere of consciousness above the abyss.
5. The mundane chakra of Binah is Saturn, the symbol of restriction.
6. It is through restriction that Binah works.
7. Binah is mind and understanding, with a dimension of depth.
8. The pure force received from Chokmah, with the abstract ideas, are in Binah moulded into tenuous form.
9. This is the sphere of vital power which unites all forms.
10. The constructive power which carries out and puts into operation the Divine thought which comes from Kether through Chokmah.
11. Binah is objective, directive, abstraction, the objective reality that is behind all conscious existence.
12. Binah is behind all vehicles in every form of manifestation, physical, mental, emotional and spiritual.
13. From this Sephirah emanates the forces of construction and destruction.
14. Due to deviation there are unbalanced forces at high level.
15. Man must realize that there can only be construction if there is destruction.

16. As long as there is manifestation there must be deviation, and it is from the form side deviation springs.
17. Deviation must have been a thought in the Ain. There is nothing here that was not there first.
18. In Binah is mind and matter, that substance in which Kether can take form.
19. From mind and matter combined stems deviation; both are illusion.
20. Binah is the sphere from which illusion springs, although not illusion in itself.
21. This is the Sanctifying Intelligence and here lies the basis and foundation of primordial wisdom.
22. The understanding of life is at this level of consciousness.
23. Binah is also called a sphere of rest. This is the first pause of unrestricted force.
24. Resistance and receptivity are the two main qualities of this Sephirah.
25. Binah as the supernal mother expresses herself as Ama the dark sterile mother and Aima the bright fertile mother.
26. The four armed Goddess Kali of Hindu religions with both destructive and creative sides is appropriate to Binah.
27. In the world of Atziluth Binah composes the first Archetypal forms.
28. At the Briatic level Binah creates.
29. The formative world of yetzirah is the sphere where Binah brings form into being.
30. The world of Assiah is the sphere where Binah produces the solid form.
31. Binah is the third fountain of metallic things in Kabbalistic alchemy—sulphur.
32. The third degree of Gold, Charutz (the ore of Gold which is dug out) refers to Binah.
33. Tzaphkiel is the Archangel with a responsibility to Binah.
34. The Host of Angels to Binah are Thrones.

35. Three is the number associated with Binah, it is also associated with the God Sakti.
36. Here is the Kwan Yin of Chinese Buddhism and the Yin of Taoism.
37. Binah is the right side of the face of the Heavenly Man, Adam Kadmon.
38. The Dove, symbol of the Holy Spirit, is atrributable to this Sephirah.
39. The first He of the Tetragrammaton belongs to Binah.
40. A chalice or triangle and the Yoni are symbols of Binah.
41. Myrrh and Civet are the aromatics of Binah.
42. Pearl and sapphire have an affinity in this sphere of consciousness.
43. The magical weapon is a cup.
44. There is only one animal associated to Binah and that is woman.
45. Gods of Binah quality are Cybele, Rhea, Demeter, Isis, Frigg, Hera, Juno, Hecate and Saturn.
46. Binah flowers are Cypress and Poppy.
47. In universal man the Binah force enters through Visuddhi.
48. Black is the colour of Binah at the Briatic level.

Section 6

GEDULAH

1. The Sephirah Gedulah is also called Chesed and is the first Sephirah below the abyss.
2. It is the fourth Sephirah on the Tree and the second on the positive pillar.
3. The mundane chakra is Jupiter with all the expansion that it implies.
4. Gedulah is the sphere of love, emotions, sentiment, feeling and all that is part of an expansive nature.
5. This Sephirah is the symbol of life, and bears the qualities of grace and righteousness.
6. Negative to Chokmah and positive to Netzach and Tiphareth.
7. Through the nineteenth path Gedulah is connected to and forms the balance between itself and Geburah.
8. To temper justice with mercy is one of the functions and lessons to be learned in Gedulah.
9. This level of consciousness is the sphere of the Masters.
10. This is the Measuring and Receptacular Intelligence because it contains and emanates the Holy powers and spiritual virtues.
11. Wisdom and peace may here be understood.
12. Gedulah is the highest crown below the abyss receiving the Ain force in its first nebulous form direct from Binah through the lightning flash.
13. Chokmah emanates a certain amount of unrestricted force direct to Gedulah through the medium of the sixteenth path.
14. On the path of outgoing Gedulah has an influence on Tiphareth and Netzach and is itself influenced by Binah and Chokmah.

15. In the functions of the Tree Gedulah is connected to Chokmah, Geburah, Tiphareth and Netzach.
16. On the path of return it is the Sephirah that receives the crucified Gods from the sphere of Tiphareth.
17. The level of Gedulah in the world of Briah is beyond the wheel of re-birth.
18. The light of wisdom is received in this sphere direct from Chokmah and transmitted through to Tiphareth.
19. In the world of Atziluth it is pure compassion and universal mercy.
20. At the Briatic level it is the full unfoldment of the Christos love.
21. From the Yetziratic world Gedulah gives out the love and sentiment that stems directly from the emotional plane.
22. In the world of Assiah it is the love of physical attraction.
23. The quality of mercy which is an attribute of this sphere varies in a similar manner to the love aspect at the different levels of the four worlds.
24. The Archangel of Gedulah is Tzadkiel (righteousness of God).
25. The Host of Angels are the shining ones.
26. In this sphere of consciousness the quality of righteousness is prominent.
27. Although male and positive the element of water (usually classed as a feminine quality) is attributed to this Sephirah.
28. Silver and quicksilver are the metallic substances of Gedulah under the alchemical laws of Kabbalists.
29. Zahab Shachut (fine and drawn Gold) is the degree of this metal associated with Gedulah.
30. The blue, love and wisdom ray, is the colour of Gedulah.
31. Gedulah is in the sphere and forms an aspect of the higher mental plane of consciousness.
32. Here is predominant an aspect of that part of the tree known as individuality.
33. Its relationship to the Divine Man is the left arm.

34. Gods associated with Gedulah are Amoun, Poseidon, Wotan, Indra and Brahma.
35. The cross, pyramid and tetrahedron are symbols of Gedulah.
36. For magical weapons this sphere has the wand, sceptre and crook.
37. A shepherd's crook is the most appropriate symbol of Gedulah.
38. Amethyst and Lapis Lazuli are the Gems most closely attached to Gedulah.
39. Cedar is the aromatic of the fourth Sephirah.
40. The drug with affinity to Gedulah is Opium.
41. Olive and Shamrock are the plants of this sphere.
42. A mighty crowned enthroned King is the magical image of Gedulah.
43. The entry point in the Divine Man of the Gedulah force is the Anahata (heart) centre.
44. The unicorn is the animal sacred to Gedulah.
45. The Divine Name attached to Gedulah is AL (EL).

SECTION 7

GEBURAH

1. Geburah is the fifth Sephirah and the second on the negative pillar.
2. Pahad is the alternative name for Geburah.
3. The Archangel to Geburah is Khamael.
4. The Host of Angels are the Fiery Serpents.
5. The mundane chakra is Mars, with all the fire and turbulence associated with this planet.
6. Geburah is the sphere of punishment, rigour, fear, severity.
7. Vehement strength is associated with this sphere.
8. Geburah is the symbol of death, and the sphere of Justice.
9. Negative to Binah, but positive to Tiphareth and Hod.
10. This Sephirah is the negative to the positive of Gedulah.
11. From this sphere flows Justice in all its different aspects.
12. In the world of Atziluth the idea of Justice is born.
13. From the Briatic world perfect balanced Justice flows, created in the Universal law.
14. At the Yetziratic level Justice is formed into an operational system.
15. In the world of Assiah Justice is meted out into the physical with all its deviation, but the pure Justice of the higher levels still overshadows.
16. It is at this level in both the worlds of Yetzirah and Assiah where man thinks utopia can be established by fire and sword.
17. This sphere of consciousness in the world of Assiah can produce scientific, political or religious fanaticism.

18. Mars as the mundane chakra exercises the fiery influence that brings religious fanaticism into being.
19. Fanaticism can only be avoided if the sphere of Tiphareth has first been entered.
20. The foolish rise from Hod to Geburah only to fall back through fanatical cruelty.
21. Geburah is the centre of the dark night of the soul.
22. The sphere of cruelty and destruction is to be found at Geburah in the Yetziratic and Assiatic worlds.
23. It is the sphere of the scourge, the spear and the whip.
24. At this point the sacrificed God from Tiphareth destroys insincerities by the fire of Mars.
25. In Geburah can be experienced the vision of power.
26. Geburah is a reflection of Binah, and receives part of the life flow directly from this Sephirah.
27. This Sephirah is the Radical Intelligence, taking understanding from Binah and wisdom from Chokmah.
28. In Geburah is corrected rigidity, such as that of Binah.
29. Geburah is feminine in potency, but its attributes are masculine in nature.
30. All breaks in universal law are corrected in Geburah.
31. This is the centre of Karma.
32. Rising above Tiphareth to this sphere brings understanding that the goal is still out of reach.
33. Kabbalistic alchemy refers zahab (shining yellow) Gold to Geburah.
34. Iron is the metal associated with the red ray and both are attributable to Geburah.
35. The Divine name attached to this sphere is Elohim Gibor (Mighty Gods).
36. Nephthys is Goddess attached to Geburah.
37. The Gods of Geburah are Thor, Ares and Horus.
38. Magical weapons associated with this Sephirah are the sword, spear and scourge.

39. This is the right arm of the Divine Man.
40. A mighty warrior in his chariot is the magical image of Geburah.
41. The colour of this Sephirah is red.
42. The animal of Geburah is a Basilisk.
43. The point of entry for the Geburah force is the same as that for Gedulah (Anahata).
44. Drugs of the fifth sphere are Cocaine and Atropine.
45. Oak, Nettle and Hickory are all plants of Geburah.
46. Ruby is the gem most closely associated with this sphere.
47. The aromatic of Geburah is Tobacco.
48. An active red rose and passive white rose are the symbols of Geburah.

Section 8

TIPHARETH

1. Tiphareth is the middle point of the middle pillar.
2. This is the Intelligence of the mediating influence.
3. Tiphareth is the devotional centre, here is the point of spiritual marriage.
4. Here is the heart of Heaven and the end of esoteric religion.
5. The centre of the Tree, the Heart of the Universe.
6. In the world of Atziluth Tiphareth is the pivot of the Archetypal scheme.
7. Tiphareth is the balance of the creative world of Briah.
8. Yetzirah, the formative world, forms and feeds on the central sun Tiphareth.
9. At the physical level, the world of Assiah, Tiphareth is the centre of a universe or the heart of a man.
10. This is the sphere of paradoxes—death is life and life is death.
11. Here man understands how to be a child and a king at one and the same time.
12. Physical riches can make a spiritual pauper.
13. Tiphareth is the realm of Valhallah and the Phoenix.
14. From Tiphareth the sacrificed Gods rise to Gedulah, the sphere of the masters.
15. This is the level of the lesser or local Gods.
16. In this sphere spirit and matter are perfectly balanced.
17. Balance and Beauty are primary qualities of Tiphareth.
18. Tiphareth is the reasoning soul, harmony and ethical quality.

19. Kether is balance and Tiphareth receives an amount of Kether force direct down the middle pillar.
20. This is the uniting Sephirah, here Justice and Mercy blend in one.
21. Negative to the three supernals, also Geburah and Gedulah.
22. Positive to Yesod, Netzach and Hod.
23. The Archangel to Tiphareth is Raphael the Archangel of healing.
24. The Host of Angels are Kings. This is the sphere of Priest Kings and sacrificed Gods.
25. Tiphareth has for its mundane chakra the Sun, it is the centre of Solar Light.
26. It is the second division of the Soul (RVCH) Ruach the seat of Good and Evil.
27. Tiphareth is represented by the Divine name Eloah va Daath (ALVH V DOTH).
28. Vau the third letter of the Tetragrammaton is applied to Tiphareth.
29. The vice of Tiphareth in the two lower worlds is Pride.
30. Tiphareth completes the second trinity combined with Gedulah and Geburah.
31. This trinity projects itself into the third trinity, the first Sephirah being Netzach.
32. The sixth degree of the decade of Gold which is Paz and Zahab Muphaz is referred to Tiphareth.
33. Paz and Zahab Muphaz means pure gold.
34. In Kabbalistic alchemy the mineral Barzel (iron) corresponds to Tiphareth.
35. The Gods of Tiphareth are Ra, Adonis and Apollo.
36. The Acacia (symbol of resurrection) is the plant most closely related to Tiphareth.
37. Other plants associated to this Sephirah are Bay, Laurel and Vine.

38. Animals associated to this sphere are the Phoenix, Lion and Spider.
39. Tiphareth is the heart of the heavenly man, Adam Kadmon.
40. Symbols of Tiphareth are Calvary Cross, Cube and Truncated Pyramid.
41. The magical weapons are the Lamen and the Rosy Cross.
42. Olibanum is the aromatic of Tiphareth.
43. Drugs centred on this Sephirah are Stramonium, Digitalis, Coffee and Alcohol.
44. The chakra related to the heavenly man through which the Tiphareth force flows is Anahata (heart).
45. Topaz is the gem with the true affinity to Tiphareth.
46. The gorse flower and Tiphareth are in close harmony.
47. Golden Yellow is the colour of the Tiphareth centre.

Section 9

NETZACH

1. Netzach is the last Sephirah on the positive pillar.
2. Negative to Gedulah and Tiphareth, and positive to Yesod and Malkuth.
3. This is the Occult Intelligence, the refulgent splendour of all occult virtues.
4. Netzach is the Sephirah of triumph, victory, firmness and glittering splendour.
5. From the sphere of Gedulah, which is the level of inspiration, the quality flows down and becomes imagination in Netzach.
6. In Atziluth the imagination is only the archetype.
7. The world of Briah produces from abstract imagination, abstract ideas.
8. In the formative world of Yetzirah imagination produces concrete ideas.
9. Assiah is the world where the imaginative ideas are consolidated.
10. Exaggeration is in this sphere of consciousness, particularly at the level of Yetzirah and Assiah.
11. Embodied in Netzach is the energetic principle.
12. Netzach is the lower mental plane of consciousness.
13. It is at this level there is an appreciation of nature, and the ability to merge into the one life.
14. There is in this Sephirah the implication of sexual love, the lower aspect of Venus.
15. The first victory over the emotional level of Yesod is obtained in this sphere.
16. Netzach is the victory of God and the splendour of the rays.

17. At this point the anima emerges as the fully developed virgin.
18. The chakra through which flows the Netzach force is Manipura (solar plexus).
19. In this sphere can be found the vision of beauty triumphant.
20. Netzach is the sphere of lust and avarice but also of unselfishness.
21. In the Netzach state of consciousness the masculine finds the feminine within himself.
22. Here is the centre or sphere of the muse and the artist.
23. It is in Netzach where the feminine instinctive life can be found.
24. From Netzach flows the imaginative ideas that bring forth the growth of new life.
25. The anima is predominant on this plane of consciousness.
26. Zahab Sagur (Gold shut up) is referred to Netzach, this is the seventh degree of Gold.
27. Zahab Sagur is treasured or fine gold or gold shut up in the bowels of the earth or in a chemical close vessel.
28. In Kabbalistic alchemy tin is the mineral associated with Netzach.
29. The Divine name associated to this sphere is Jehovah Tzabaoth.
30. The Archangel of this sphere is Haniel.
31. The Host of Angels are Elohim or Gods.
32. Baal is the Arch-devil and the host of demons Harab-Serapel.
33. Venus is the mundane chakra of Netzach.
34. In the Divine Man Netzach relates to the left hip and left leg.
35. Attributable to this sphere are the Gods Nike, Hathor and Aphrodite.
36. The magical image is a beautiful naked woman.
37. Magical weapons are the lamp and the girdle.

38. The green ray portrays Netzach.
39. Animals connected to this Sephirah are the Lynx, Dove and Cat.
40. The perfumes of Netzach are Benzoin, Red Sandle and Rose.
41. The vegetable drug for this sphere of consciousness is Damiana.
42. The symbolic flower to this Sephirah is the Rose.
43. In the sparkling green of the Emerald lie some of the qualities of Netzach.

Section 10

HOD

1. Hod is the last Sephirah on the negative pillar and the eighth on the Tree.
2. This is the absolute or perfect intelligence because it is the mean of the primordial.
3. It has no root by which it can cleave, nor rest except in the hidden places of Gedulah.
4. Here is magnificence which emanates from its own proper essence.
5. This is the sphere of splendour and glory, and from it issues the stellar light.
6. Scintillating humour comes from the mental level of Hod.
7. Prudence can be discovered and developed at this level of consciousness.
8. In Kabbalistic alchemy Hod is of the class of Brass.
9. Nechuseth (Brass) is of the same root with Nachash, a serpent.
10. Hod is encompassed with a serpent.
11. In this sphere lies the belief in self-preservation and deceit.
12. It is the level of the diplomat and the sphere of intrigue.
13. From the root Nachash springs Nechashim, enchantments or illusion.
14. It is the sphere of illusion, and here religions are created and destroyed.
15. At this level of consciousness man worships the teacher and not the teachings.
16. In the world of Atziluth are the archetypes of Gods, religions, etc.

17. The world of Briah creates the abstract but pure forms.
18. At Yetzirah the formation with slight deviation takes place.
19. Hod in the world of Malkuth (Assiah) completes the Gods and religions with even more deviation, and here lies illusion.
20. From Hod the Masters and the Gods proceed through the sphere of Tiphareth to Gedulah.
21. To rise from this sphere to Geburah without going through Tiphareth can only bring disaster and a return to Hod.
22. Hod is negative to Geburah and Tiphareth, but positive to Yesod and Malkuth.
23. Here are the qualities of Chokmah at a lower level.
24. The ideas of Netzach brought down from the visualizations of Gedulah are clothed with form in Hod.
25. This sphere is the Glory of God where it is expressed through form and science.
26. The Archangel of Hod is Michael the Protector.
27. The Host of Angels are the sons of God.
28. The mundane chakra for Hod is Mercury.
29. Through its mundane chakra the Hod consciousness is quick moving and adaptable.
30. Hermaphrodite is the focal image of this sphere.
31. In Hod the individual can balance the harmony of the masculine and feminine within themselves.
32. The scepticism of Hod can destroy the spirit if not balanced with Netzach.
33. The God name of Hod is Elohim Tsabaoth.
34. Gods associated with this sphere are Hermes, Anubis, Hanuman, Odin and Loki.
35. Zahab Parvajim (red gold) is the eighth degree of Gold and related to Hod.
36. The animals with affinity to Hod are the Jackal and twin serpents.

37. Anubis is the jackal-headed God, and the twin serpents represent the double current.
38. Magical weapons used in the sphere of Hod are the Versicals and Apron.
39. The Apron conceals the splendour of the Magician.
40. Hod is placed in the west quarter.
41. Gems in affinity with this sphere are the Opal and in particular the Fire Opal.
42. The royal colour of violet/purple is closely associated with this Sephirah.
43. In the sphere of the Heavenly Man this is the right hip and leg.
44. The Chakra Centre is Svadistthana (Navel).
45. The Plants of Hod are Moly and Anhalonium Lewinii.
46. Anhalonium Lewinii is the drug of this Sephirah and produces colour visions.
47. Storax is the perfume of this sphere of consciousness.
48. In the Qliphotic realm the Archangel Samael rules this sphere. Samael is the false accuser.

Section 11

YESOD

1. This is the ninth Sephirah on the Tree and the third on the middle pillar.
2. Yesod is the path of Pure Intelligence, it purifies the numerations.
3. Malkuth is the only Sephirah to which Yesod is positive.
4. This is the foundation on which the physical world (Malkuth) is based.
5. Yesod also gives balance to the victory and splendour of Netzach and Hod.
6. At this point on the Tree the qualities of Chokmah and Binah meet.
7. Form and force make the ultimate union at this Sephirah.
8. Here the design and representation of all forms are corrected before their emergence into Malkuth.
9. Yesod is the desire world, and the link between the rest of the Tree and Malkuth.
10. The emotions of sex spring from this Sephirah.
11. This is the sphere of the generative principle.
12. In relation to the Heavenly Man this is the sphere of the reproductive organs.
13. Real understanding of sex, the surge of passion.
14. The magical image of Yesod is a strong naked man.
15. The spirit recognizes the Anima/Animus with the alternatives of the sex hunt or the conquest of physical sex.
16. At this sphere of consciousness man understands the nature of woman in both aspects.
17. In Yesod man understands the feminine in himself.

18. Yesod is the astral world, that subtle form of matter which permeates the whole of life.
19. Within this Sephirah the astral form has an endless ebb and flow of the life forces.
20. It provides a stability within the ever-fluctuating emotions.
21. The Archangel of Yesod is Gabriel, the ruler of the waters of wisdom.
22. The Host of Angels are The Strong.
23. The Mundane chakra of Yesod is the Moon and from here emanates the lunar flame.
24. Here are the waters of the Moon with all the feminine aspects attributed thereto.
25. The Moon is the centre of influence with its double nature.
26. Yesod through its mundane chakra is the transmuter of the solar force of Tiphareth.
27. It is the sphere of Zadik the law-giver, the just one who fulfils the Divine Law as the foundation.
28. Here is the sphere of hidden wisdom that calls to the intuition.
29. The machinery of the universe can be visualized at this level of consciousness.
30. Yesod is the sphere of the collective unconscious.
31. It is the Sephirah of independence and idleness.
32. The God name Shaddai-el-Chai means The Almighty Living God.
33. Diana the Goddess of Light and the God Shu, who is the God of space, belong to Yesod.
34. Yesod is represented by the Ashim, the flames.
35. It is the final Yod of the I.H.U.I. of the form of the Tetragrammaton.
36. I.H.U.I. which is referred to Yesod and not the initial which belongs to Chokmah the Father.
37. Symbols of Yesod are sandals and candlesticks.

38. The chakra corresponding to the Heavenly Man is Muladhara (Lingam and Anus).
39. Indigo, the ray of devotion, is the colour that flows through Yesod.
40. The gems associated to this Sephirah are Quartz and the Moonstone.
41. Plants that vibrate in harmony with Yesod are Banyan, Mandrake and Damiana.
42. The animals under the sway of, and symbolic with this sphere, are the Elephant, Tortoise and Toad.
43. Orchid root is the drug for the sphere of Yesod.
44. At this level of consciousness the perfumes in harmony are Jasmine and Jinsing.
45. Magical weapons of Yesod are perfumes and sandals.
46. Zahab Tob (which is good gold) is related to Yesod.
47. Mingle therefore iron and clay and thou shalt have the foundation of Gold.

Section 12

MALKUTH

1. This is the tenth and last Sephirah on the Tree.
2. Negative to all the Tree, but positive in itself.
3. This Sephirah represents the completion of the scheme formed in Kether.
4. Malkuth is the whole of physical manifestation.
5. It can be related to a man or a Universe.
6. Here evolution ends and involution commences.
7. From Malkuth it is possible to ascend to Heaven (Kether) or descend to the Qliphoth (Hell).
8. Malkuth is the end result of the life process, the fallen Sephirah and dense solidification.
9. This is the world of Assiah and the centre of experience.
10. In Malkuth high aspirations can develop and mature or be destroyed.
11. The world of temptations and corruptible riches.
12. Karma, good and bad, is accrued in this sphere of consciousness.
13. This is the path of Resplendent Intelligence because it is exalted above every head and sits upon the throne of Binah.
14. It illuminates the splendour of all the lights, and causes a supply of influence to emanate from the Prince of Countenances.
15. The Earth Mother, the anima of man's physical and spiritual function.
16. Here is found the female figure awaiting the awakening.
17. This Sephirah is the Microprosopus also called the Bride.

18. The sphere of Malkuth is the Kingdom and the door to the Kingdom.
19. As above so below, the symbol of the double cube.
20. Malkuth is the breaker of the foundation that releases spirit from matter.
21. This is the sphere of living ritual or the ritual of living.
22. Malkuth is the Sephirah in which all things live to die and die to live.
23. The Archangel Sandalphon holds sway over this sphere of activity.
24. In the Order of the Qliphoth the opposite force to Sandalphon is Lilith, the woman of the night.
25. The Host of Angels to Malkuth are Souls of Fire.
26. Malkuth's mundane chakra is formed of the elements, Air, Water, Fire and Earth.
27. The four Holy Living Creatures are the four elements.
28. Through the combined forces of the four elements is the task of Malkuth worked out.
29. Four rays make up the colour combination of Malkuth, Citrine, Olive, Russet and Black.
30. At this level of the Tree, the ten Sephirah become one.
31. In Kabbalistic alchemy the true medicine of metals is referred to Malkuth.
32. This Sephirah represents the rest of the natures under the metamorphosis of Gold and Silver, left and right.
33. Malkuth is the metallic woman and the Luna of the wise men.
34. Malkuth is the field which the seeds of secret minerals ought to be cast, that is the water of Gold.
35. The grade of Gold corresponding to Malkuth is Zahab Ophir (Gold of Ophir).
36. Symbols of Malkuth are the Calvary Cross and the Altar.
37. The Altar of Brass is referred to Malkuth, this altar may represent the notion of a woman.

38. In the anatomy of the Heavenly Man (Adam Kadmon), Malkuth is the feet.
39. The final He of Tetragrammaton is found in this sphere.
40. In Malkuth is found the scepticism of all things above Malkuth.
41. Here a vision of the Holy Guardian Angel can be seen.
42. Seb, the Egyptian God, and the Goddess Persephone, belong to Malkuth, and Ceres is also attributed to this sphere.
43. Magical weapons of this Sephirah are the Magical Circle and the Triangle.
44. The animal of Malkuth is the Sphinx, a combination of the four Holy Living Creatures.
45. Here is the seventh Heaven of the Arabs, the Garden of Eden or Everlasting Abode.
46. Rock Crystal is the gem of Malkuth.
47. Willow, Lily and Ivy are the plants of Malkuth.
48. Corn is the drug for this sphere of consciousness.
49. Dittany of Crete is the perfume of the Malkuth consciousness.
50. The situation of Malkuth in the Universe is placed at the North.
51. Kether is the concentrated point and Malkuth is The Points idea of itself fulfilled in its complement.

Section 13

THE DIVISIONS OF THE SOUL

1. The Soul has three aspects or divisions.
2. Neshamah, Nephesh and Ruach are the three divisions.
3. Neshamah lies within the regions of the Atziluthic and Briatic Worlds.
4. The Yetziratic plane of consciousness is ensouled with the Nephesh division.
5. Ruach, the third division, permeates the worlds of Assiah and Yetzirah.
6. Neshamah is subdivided into three parts, Yechidah, Chia and Neshamah.
7. The three subdivisions relate to the three Supernals.
8. Yechidah is in Kether the Crown, and is in all respects transcendental.
9. Chiah is the wisdom of the soul embracing Chokmah.
10. Neshamah the Minor is understanding the soul of the Supernal Mother, Binah.
11. These three in oneness embrace and are the higher aspirations of the soul.
12. Ruach is the spirit of the soul and is linked to the three Supernals.
13. Neshamah is the principle that forms the link between Ruach and the Supernals.
14. Ruach is the mind of the soul and in this respect has a close association with Binah.
15. Here lies the reasoning of the soul.
16. Tiphareth is not only the heart of the Universe, it is also the reasoning soul.
17. Tiphareth is at the centre of Nephesh.

18. Nephesh is the passions of the soul.
19. The power-house of the soul is Nephesh.
20. At birth man's soul is composed of Nephesh.
21. Ruach appears later as the spirit of intellect with man's spiritual progression.
22. Neshamah, which flows from the Atziluthic and Briatic worlds, now fills the soul with Celestial Understanding.
23. Represented in the divisions of the soul is: Body, Soul and Spirit.
24. What is Man without any one of these three divisions.
25. If Nephesh predominated Samael the evil angel of the soul would rule.
26. Where Neshamah is predominant Michael the angel of good reigns supreme.
27. Ruach with Neshamah would be cold reasoning.
28. Nephesh envelops the six Sephirah of the Yetziratic world, embedded in Malkuth the World of Assiah.
29. Assiah is the image of Atziluth.
30. It is a double image, reflecting positive and negative, Michael and Samael.
31. The image is the veil of the soul, hence it is endowed with the attributes of the veil—Malkuth.
32. From Malkuth being the veil, the Universe becomes the veil.
33. The divisions of the soul endow the Universe with three major aspects.
34. Nephesh in turn veils Ruach and Ruach veils Neshamah—Kether.
35. The true soul and spirit is veiled in Kether whence it came.
36. The Atziluthic qualities form the seed atom buried in Malkuth.
37. Kether in Malkuth—Atziluth in Assiah.
38. Soul and spirit are conceived in Kether and born in Malkuth.

39. As with a Universe so with **Man**.
40. A conception of nine Sephirah—a Universe, and a conception of nine months—a Man.
41. Man—Malkuth veiling spirit—**Kether**.

BOOK II

Section 1

GENERAL

1. The book of Thoth is commonly known as the Tarot.
2. Tarot means Royal Path.
3. It is also Rota, the cycle of life.
4. The cycle of life here means all the incarnations a divine spark passes through.
5. A Tarot card is called an arcanum.
6. Only the twenty-two major arcanum are used on the Tree of Life.
7. The book of Thoth covers twenty-two subjective paths on the Tree of Life.
8. These twenty-two subjective paths on the Tree are numbered from 11 to 32.
9. An arcanum number is not the same as the path number.
10. The first ten paths are the objective paths of the Sephirah detailed in Book I.
11. An individual may travel more than one path at any one time.
12. The paths are in all four worlds and each arcanum has its Archetypal, Creative, Formative and physical aspect.
13. Each path conquered is an inner initiation at the level it is conquered.
14. The paths are trodden by an individual, a Nation or a Planet.
15. There are influences of the elements or the astrological signs on each path.
16. Although a path has the influence of an astrological sign an element can still influence.

17. The element predominant is that associated with the sign.
18. Each path has assigned to it a Hebrew letter.
19. To each letter there is an interpretation, and a numerical value.
20. The rays and magical weapons give an indication to the lesson portrayed in the symbology of the arcanum.
21. An arcanum must be considered also in the light of the Sephiroth it joins together.
22. When the path of one arcanum crosses another path this must be taken into consideration.
23. Each path must be considered from two aspects, the journey down and the return.
24. The two-way aspect applies in all four worlds.
25. The Tree is the formation and continuation of life.
26. The book of Thoth is the journey of man through that Tree on all planes of consciousness.
27. Man is of the same elements as the spheres.
28. The initiates task is to harmonize with these elements.
29. Each path is a hurdle where the virtues must be cultivated and the vices controlled and conquered.
30. The Sephiroth are divided between positive, negative and balance.
31. The paths are not divided in clear-cut divisions.
32. Certain paths run from positive to negative and vice versa.
33. Other paths join either the positive or negative to the middle pillar of balance.
34. Twenty-two paths are twenty-two initiations in Assiah and Atziluth.
35. In Yetzirah there are twenty-two paths in each of six spheres.
36. In Briah there are twenty-two paths in each of two spheres.
37. There are in all two hundred and twenty paths through the four worlds.

38. In numerology this is the number 22.
39. The path down from Atziluth to Malkuth is one of taking.
40. The path from Malkuth is one of giving.
41. From Archetype to physical and back to Archetype.
42. The Minor arcanum consists of 56 symbols in the form of four suits.
43. In numerology 56 equals 11.
44. In Kabbalistic numerology 22 means—A master of superhuman personality—also Spirit, it is a number of the Sun.
45. Number 11 is the number of magic, revelation, martyrdom, this is the number of courage, will and force.
46. The complete book of seventy-eight arcanum becomes in numerology 6, the perfect number, $7 + 8 = 15 = 1 + 5 = 6$.
47. The four suits represent the four elements.
48. The Minor arcana gives supporting forces to the Major.

Section 2

THE FOOL

1. One man in his time plays many parts.
2. This is The Fool on The Tree, a man of many parts.
3. The eleventh path can be considered as the most important of the twenty-two.
4. This is the Alpha and Omega, the path is Aleph and the arcanum is O.
5. It is influenced by the element of air.
6. Air is symbolic of spirit, and this arcanum portrays the spirit at the commencement and the termination of its journey through time and space.
7. The Fool portrays innocence, ingenuity and foolishness.
8. This is the Court Jester, the Material Fool, the Blind Fool and the Fool that Fools.
9. On the downward path the Fool's bag is filled with the material and mental objects essential to his stay in Malkuth.
10. On the path of return the bag is emptied of the material and mental, and filled with the spiritual.
11. If the bag is not emptied in Malkuth, then he is the Material Fool.
12. Head in the air he walks towards the precipice without seeing it, this is the Blind Fool.
13. Conscience and subconscious are pulling at him in the shape of the dog.
14. Dog reversed is God. Microcosm and Macrocosm.
15. The dog also symbolizes the world that can tear the Fool to pieces.

16. The bag also on the path of return contains the Fool's Karma.
17. This is the scintillating Intelligence.
18. Aleph means ox. "For my yoke is easy and my burden is light."
19. The Fool hath said in his heart there is no God, which Fool?
20. This arcanum represents failure and success, the descent to hell (Qliphoth) or the flight to Heaven (Kether).
21. The staff carries the power of the hermits, or of the God Wotan.
22. The caduceus, Aaron's rod, the wand of Moses, all are embodied in The Fool's staff.
23. The universal law of compensation can be found in this arcanum.
24. Portrayed in this arcanum is the law of affinity.
25. "I will lift up mine eyes to the hills"—the hills are symbolic of Chokmah and Binah.
26. Here is the philosophy and doctrine of pure mind.
27. As all is embodied in Kether so all is embodied in The Fool.
28. All that is latent within can be drawn out and exploited in the journey through time and space.
29. Illustrated in this arcanum are the obstacles to be overcome.
30. The abyss is also to be seen, and crossed both on the downward path and the return.
31. The essence of Kether as represented in The Fool finds the reflection of itself in Chokmah.
32. Here is the commencement of mental activity in the designation of the path.
33. The arcanum is zero, the path is the eleventh, but the first in the journey of the spark.
34. This is the E.A. degree of Masonry, the commencement of a series of initiations.

35. An urge to go forward, but to the point of Chokmah and just beyond, without direction.

36. This is the pure spirit and mind awaiting the experience of transmutation from unconscious to conscious perfection.

37. The Fool has placed his first foot on Jacob's ladder and he will ascend and descend through all the four worlds.

38. On the journey he must conquer, folly, extravagance, negligence, apathy and vanity.

39. The Fool represents the spark within a man, a solar system or a galaxy.

40. This arcanum represents the final phase of creation.

41. The Fool is sense and nonsense, and eventually a realization that only The Fool can help the fool.

42. The head is in Kether and the feet are in Malkuth.

43. Having set your hand to the plough look not back, is well portrayed in this arcanum.

44. Le Mot, dead to understanding or dead to the material things of life.

45. This is the ultimate end that the fool can reach. He can also reach the point of complete annihilation.

46. Here is the Ain in manifestation fulfilling his own evolutionary progress.

47. The ever-evolving Ain, perfection at a given point, imperfection in transit.

48. Zero—no-thing, evolving in spite of itself.

49. Omnipresent, yes, omniscient in part.

50. The Fool, the Divine Alchemist. The Holy Ghost.

51. The path of The Fool responds to bright pale yellow.

52. Precious stones that correspond to this path are the **Topaz** and **Chalcedony**.

53. Aspen is the plant that vibrates in harmony with The Fool.

54. Animals of The Fool are the Eagle and the Man.

55. Magical power is divination and the magical weapons a dagger and a fan.
56. The perfume is Galbanum and the drug is Peppermint.
57. Gods of the path are Jupiter, Zeus and the Valkyries.

Section 3

THE MAGICIAN

1. This is the second arcanum but the twelfth path.
2. Connecting Kether and Binah there is direction of force into form.
3. It is the Intelligence of Transparency.
4. Here is the symbol of the ceaseless flow of life, the expression of eternity.
5. The four basic forces of life, the materials from which it is composed, are arrayed at this level.
6. The Magician's hands symbolize the drawing down of the Kether powers.
7. Here is the utilizing of the universal forces to bring light to Malkuth.
8. The powers can also be powers of darkness.
9. A Magician is just that, neither black nor white until he deploys the powers he controls.
10. The forces issuing down this path from Kether are just forces.
11. The Fool in the part of the Magician on the way down can use them wrongly.
12. At this level in the world of Atziluth exists the Archetypal Magician.
13. In the Briatic world on the path of return this is the perfected Magician.
14. At the Yetziratic level the Magician is inclined to let the emotions dictate the use of his powers.
15. On the return path in the Yetziratic world the mind will govern the use.

16. In the Assiatic world the Magician's powers are used at the dictates of the personality.
17. This arcanum represents the communications of the power of pure force from Kether to Malkuth.
18. In the arcanum is reflected the union of the four elements.
19. The union of the will to know, to dare, to do and to keep silent.
20. The Hebrew letter for this path is BETH—or house.
21. In my Father's house (The Tree) are many mansions or dimensions (The Sephiroth).
22. Mercury is the astrological sign for the twelfth path.
23. This brings in the element of Air which is symbolic of spirit.
24. Like the path of The Fool this path is above the abyss, the level of spirit.
25. The hands of the Magician also symbolize the two pillars before the temple.
26. The Magician therefore symbolizes the duality, positive and negative.
27. Reaching up to heaven (Ain) and reaching down to hell (Qliphoth).
28. In this arcanum there is depicted the Divine united to the Devil.
29. Seek and ye shall find, knock and it shall be opened, is fully expressed in this arcanum.
30. The wand, the cup, the sword and the pentacle are symbolic of the four major forces or elements, Air, Water, Fire and Earth.
31. It is the four elements that the Magician learns to handle.
32. Through the four elements the Magician can control nature, even the stars and planets will obey his commands.
33. At the level of Kether the power is dormant.
34. The Magician brings the power into action.
35. The Kether force being controlled at Binah (understanding).

36. Mercury is symbolic of the yellow ray which expresses creative activity.
37. Above the Magician's head, or contained within his hat, is the sign of eternity, a figure 8 on its side.
38. The Italian name for this arcanum is Pagad, the Master of Fortune.
39. He is the master of his fate, and the ruler of destiny.
40. At the highest level, the Divine motive in man.
41. Mercury symbolizes mental ability, the Magician is one whose mind has been highly developed.
42. In its duality it can be truth or deception.
43. The four great symbols of the Tarot, which the Magician has before him, symbolize Tetragrammaton.
44. Wands, the Yod. Cups, the He. Sword—Vau, and Pentacles—the second He.
45. The Magician is the transformer of the universe.
46. There are no limitations in the mind of the Magician.
47. The precious stones attached to this path are the Opal and Agate.
48. Plants that correspond to The Magician are vervain and herb mercury.
49. Animals of the Magician are the swallow and the ape.
50. Magical powers developed through this path are those of Healing, the Gift of Tongues and knowledge of Sciences.
51. Perfumes that combine with the Magician are Mastic, Mace and Storax.
52. Magical weapons, the wand or caduceus.
53. The Gods of the Magician are Mercury, Hermes, Thoth and Cynocephalus.

Section 4

THE HIGH PRIESTESS

1. This is the thirteenth path called the Uniting Intelligence because it is the consummation of the truth of individual spiritual things.
2. The High Priestess is the first path on the middle pillar and lies between Kether and Tiphareth.
3. With the High Priestess of the Kabbalistic Tree there is justifiable mystery as this path crosses the invisible Sephirah Daath.
4. On this path there is perfect balance and harmony as befits the middle pillar.
5. The arcanum shows the High Priestess seated between two pillars, Boaz and Joachin.
6. The two pillars are those of Solomon's temple, or the Tree of Life.
7. Here is represented the positive and negative being brought into balance by the High Priestess forming the middle pillar.
8. In this context the High Priestess represents the chelah on the lower levels and the high initiate on the higher planes.
9. The point between the two pillars is also known as "The Door of the Sanctuary".
10. In Masonic language the point between the two pillars is known as the "Middle Space".
11. To the Kabbalist this path should be the key to the mysteries.
12. Between these pillars is the path to infinity and to all understanding and wisdom.

13. Understanding and wisdom flank the top of the path in the form of Binah and Chokmah.
14. At the end of the path on the downward journey is the reasoning soul.
15. On the return journey the end of the path is the victor's crown.
16. In most packs the arcanum features the two binaries emphasizing the balance of positive and negative.
17. The perfect integration of active and passive spirit is here expressed.
18. The Moon is symbolic of the contemplative mood from which springs inspiration.
19. From the sun influence comes the vibrating activity that brings the inspiration of the moon to life.
20. The two binaries also emphasize that dark and light are both alike.
21. The evening and the morning are a day, day and night are two aspects of the same time period.
22. A day can be an Earth day, Galactic, Universal or Cosmic day.
23. In most packs the High Priestess is shown with an equal armed cross on her breast, this is symbolic of the control of the four quarters of the Universe.
24. The equal armed cross also signifies that there is perfect control of the four elements in each of the four worlds.
25. Here the Uniting Intelligence can be seen at work in the integration and balance of the four elements.
26. The moon is the astrological influence of this path and the element of water.
27. This is the moon at its highest aspect with Diana the celibate and Hecate the mistress of evil enchantments harmonized.
28. At this level on the return the qualities and experiences of the two Goddesses have been absorbed and balanced.
29. On the downward path of outgoing they are absorbed only to express the predominance of one or the other at the lower levels of the Tree.

30. There is a great affinity between this path and the twenty-ninth path, that of "The Moon".
31. Held within the hands of the High Priestess is a book or scroll. The last wisdom to be absorbed by the Initiate.
32. Part of that wisdom is for the Chelah or Initiate to realize they are the middle pillar and it is the opposites within them that have to be neutralized.
33. The other part of the wisdom is to be read and deciphered by the higher faculties, the last to be awakened.
34. This is the Buddhic level of consciousness in Briah just before the annihilation of personality.
35. Here is the awakening of true understanding that "The Fool" is unconsciously seeking.
36. Through this path flows the last great initiation by water, the element of the path.
37. The waters of wisdom that wash away the ashes of burnt-out wasted thoughts.
38. Gimel is the Hebrew letter for this path, it means Camel.
39. The Camel in its wisdom stores water, and the waters of wisdom are stored in this path.
40. "It is easier for a Camel to get through the eye of a needle."
41. The path of the High Priestess leads to the eye of the needle.
42. Blue is the colour of this path, blue is also the ray of love and wisdom.
43. Precious stones that vibrate to the path of the High Priestess are moonstone, pearl and crystal.
44. The dog is the animal associated with the thirteenth path.
45. Plants belonging to the path of the High Priestess are almond, hazel, moonwort and ranunculus.
46. Magical powers of the path are clairvoyance, and divination by dreams.
47. The magical weapon is a bow and arrow.
48. In working with the path the following perfumes should be used: camphor and aloes.

49. Drugs of the thirteenth path are juniper and pennyroyal.
50. Some Gods connected to the High Priestess are—Chomse, Artemis, Hecate and Diana.
51. The mystic number of the path is 91.

Section 5

THE EMPRESS

1. This is the fourteenth path and the third arcanum.
2. Illuminating Intelligence is the Yetziratic title for this path.
3. The illumination on this path comes from the two sephiroth which it joins.
4. Chokmah-wisdom and Binah-understanding are the sephiroth concerned.
5. The path runs horizontal across The Tree and is the first barrier on the way down and the last on the return.
6. Daleth is the Hebrew name for this path, and means door.
7. The door is the eye of the needle the Camel (High Priestess) must pass through.
8. It is the barrier that crosses the path of the High Priestess.
9. Venus has influence on this path and brings in the element of Earth.
10. Through this Earth element The Empress rules nature.
11. This is the path of true compassion, the quality essential to cross the last barrier.
12. Within this path is the mother quality from Binah and father quality from Chokmah.
13. On this path force and matter are combined.
14. Here is the dividing line between the waters above the firmament and the waters below the firmament.
15. The Empress is the path just above the great abyss.
16. From "The Empress" the vitality of the life force flows out.
17. This is a path of union and creation as befits the influence of Chokmah and Binah.

18. Here the dual principle becomes one on the return path.
19. The anima and the animus recognize each other.
20. On the outward journey the two principles split on this path and flow down as separate entities.
21. Male and female created he them, at this point.
22. On leaving the path of The Empress the major portion of life is influenced by Chokmah or Binah.
23. Only a small section retain the perfect balance that flows down the middle pillar.
24. This arcanum is the perfect symbol of Hermaphrodite.
25. The Egyptian arcanum shows The Empress seated within a sun of thirty rays.
26. Other packs show an Empress crowned with a crown of twelve stars.
27. Different symbology for the same basic teaching.
28. The thirty rays symbolize the twelve signs of the zodiac as do the twelve stars.
29. The astrological aspects symbolize that embodied within The Empress are all the qualities of the twelve types.
30. The symbol of Venus is found on this arcanum in most Tarot packs.
31. Venus is the planet of love and also of healing, it is the love aspect of the Love/Wisdom ray.
32. Nature comes under the sway of Venus which is a planet of the element Earth.
33. Progress and evolution of the plant world comes under the guiding hand of The Empress.
34. In her hand is a sceptre which has the globe of the world on the top.
35. Dominion over the Kingdom of Nature is here symbolized.
36. The Empress is the Mother of all Nature, the womb of life.
37. This arcanum is symbolic of the subconscious mind with all its conflicts and turbulence.

38. The colour for this path is emerald green, green is the ray of harmony through struggle and conflict.
39. One of the precious stones of this path is Emerald and the other Turquoise.
40. Myrtle, Rose and Clover are the plants of The Empress.
41. The animals that vibrate in harmony to this path are Sparrow, Dove and Swan.
42. Love philtres are the magical powers of the path and the magical weapon a girdle.
43. Perfumes that work on this path are Sandalwood and Myrtle.
44. Gods in harmony with the path of The Empress include Venus, Lalita, Freya and Aphrodite.
45. The mystic number of the path is 105.

Section 6

THE STAR

1. This is the fifteenth path but the seventeenth arcanum.
2. The star connects Chokmah to Tiphareth running down through the abyss.
3. Commencing on the positive pillar the path crosses over to the middle pillar on the outward journey.
4. This would imply wisdom and the pure Chokmah force being brought into balance.
5. "He" is the Hebrew letter for this path and interpreted means window.
6. The clear light of the star shines through bringing illumination.
7. On the return journey the path commences at Tiphareth, sphere of the crucified Gods.
8. Even at this level there is not all wisdom, but the top of the path is wisdom (Chokmah).
9. Chokmah, the perfect reflection of Kether, its projected image.
10. At Tiphareth "we now see as through a glass (window) darkly but then face to face" at Chokmah.
11. The large star depicted on this arcanum in all packs can symbolize the Monad.
12. It is the guilding light, the star of Bethlehem.
13. The watcher on the threshold is also an apt description for the star.
14. Represented in this arcanum is "The dweller between the waters".
15. The two water jugs with the outflow of water symbolize the waters of life.

16. "Let the firmament (abyss) divide the waters from the waters, the waters above the firmament and those below the firmament" (Genesis).
17. This path is the link between the "waters above the firmament" and the "waters below the firmament".
18. In many packs the woman is shown with one foot in water and one on dry land, bridging the abyss.
19. In some packs the arcanum depicts water from one jug being poured into water and the other on to the Earth. Water to water, negative, water to earth, positive.
20. This path is called "The Constituting Intelligence".
21. It constitutes the substance of creation in pure darkness. Men have spoken of these contemplations.
22. The Ibis perched on the tree behind the woman represents the wisdom of silence.
23. Silence is an aid to meditation through which the ancient wisdom can be found.
24. An eight-point star symbolizes the balance of universal forces within matter.
25. The large star can be the akashic records and the small stars the seals.
26. Seven seals, seven bodies, to break each seal, purify each body.
27. Through this path flow all the differing cosmic forces coming from Chokmah that are not channelled through Binah.
28. The Star is the spirit, the small stars "they are but broken lights of Thee".
29. Seven alchemical minerals, seven stars, implies this is the path of alchemy.
30. The woman is nude, symbolic of the purity of spirit.
31. Spirit unclothed at this point on the outward path and stripped of matter on the return.
32. Aries influences the path of The Star and the element is fire.

33. This is one of the major initiatory paths, in all four worlds.
34. In the world of Assiah this is the stage of material wisdom that leads upwards to the Yetziratic world.
35. At the Yetziratic level this path leads to the spiritual wisdom that can take the initiate on to the Briatic world.
36. The Star in Briah is one of the last initiations before The Fool makes complete union in Atziluth.
37. In Atziluth the initiatory fire burns away the last dross before the spark returns to the Ain (The One) or No-Thing.
38. In Atziluth The Fool and The Path of The Star are archetypal with all potentials positive and negative.
39. On the return the archetype is dismantled as it proceeds back to the Ain.
40. Archetypal integration, archetypal disintegration.
41. The colour ray for this arcanum is scarlet.
42. Ruby is the precious stone that vibrates in harmony with this path.
43. Plants associated with the fifteenth path are Tiger Lily and Geranium.
44. The Ram and The Owl belong to this path.
45. Magical power connected with this arcanum is that of consecrating things.
46. Magical weapons associated to the path are The Horns, Energy, The Burin.
47. Dragons Blood is the perfume in harmony with the fifteenth path.
48. Gods associated with the fifteenth path are Mars, Minerva, Shiva and Athena.
49. All cerebral excitants are the drugs for this path.

Section 7

THE HIEROPHANT

1. This is the sixteenth path and the fifth arcanum.
2. The Hierophant joins Chokmah with Gedulah (Chesed).
3. A combination of wisdom (Chokmah) and Love and Mercy (Gedulah).
4. Both sephiroth are on the positive pillar and this is the first path completely positive.
5. It is the path of Triumphal or Eternal Intelligence.
6. The Paradise prepared for the righteous is another name for this arcanum.
7. It is the pleasure of the Glory beyond which no other Glory is like unto it.
8. The Hierophant is depicted on the arcanum, in most packs, seated between two pillars.
9. The pillars of the Sanctuary, the positive and negative, the pillars before the Temple.
10. The pillars represent the entrance to high initiation.
11. Once through the pillars of initiation aided by the Hierophant the initiate himself becomes an Hierophant.
12. At this level the mysteries of universal forces are known and mastered.
13. In one hand the Hierophant holds a sceptre of a triple cross.
14. The triple cross is a symbol that he has mastered the physical, emotional and mental worlds.
15. Conquest of the spiritual world is not yet completed.
16. The two pillars representing positive and negative indicate that even at this stage the negative path can be taken.

17. An initiate can successfully pass his initiation and become an Hierophant but not a God.
18. At this level he is a God in the making.
19. The subtle temptations of power can lure him from the positive to the negative path.
20. It can be seen and it is important to understand this is a dangerous path.
21. The path of the Hierophant is one of the major initiations.
22. In the world of Assiah this could be the advanced occultist.
23. At the Yetziratic level an high initiate.
24. On the Briatic level The Hierophant is a master of universal forces.
25. The astrological influence on this path is Taurus and the element Earth.
26. This is the last but one of the Earth initiations, second only to "The Empress".
27. On this path the intuitive powers are developed in preparation for the next path on the return.
28. Intuition is becoming dim at this level on the outward journey.
29. On the arcanum in some packs The Hierophant is depicted with an equal armed cross on his glove.
30. The equal armed cross is symbolic of power over the four elements in the universe.
31. This path is an injunction to "Be still and know that I am God".
32. "I am God"—The Hierophant or the Ain Force?
33. In Atziluth the archetype of spiritual self-mastery.
34. At the Briatic level self-mastery at the buddhic level.
35. The Yetziratic level is self-mastery of the emotional body.
36. Self-mastery of the physical body takes place on this path in the world of Assiah.

37. The Hierophant can take the form of a high religious dignitary in Malkuth in Assiah.
38. Taurus indicates the firm basis of this path.
39. The Hebrew letter connected to this arcanum is VAU.
40. Translated VAU means nail. "Give us a nail in his holy place that our God may lighten our eyes" (Ezra 9, v. 8).
41. Red orange is the colour in affinity with the path of the Hierophant.
42. The Topaz is the precious stone in harmony with the sixteenth path.
43. Mallow is the plant of this arcanum and the Bull the animal related to it.
44. The secret of physical strength is its magical power.
45. The magical weapon of the Hierophant is the labour of preparation.
46. Storax is the perfume with which the path is endowed.
47. The drug of the Hierophant is sugar cane.
48. Gods attached to the sixteenth path are Venus, Apis, Osiris and Herè.

Section 8

THE LOVERS

1. This is the sixth arcanum but the seventeenth path.
2. The path joins Binah and Tiphareth running from the negative pillar to the pillar of balance.
3. It is the path of the Disposing Intelligence, which provides faith to the righteous.
4. It is also called The Foundation of Excellence in the state of higher things.
5. The majority of arcanums depict a young man standing between two feminine figures being drawn in two different directions.
6. Here is a path of choice, the crossroads of life meet here.
7. No longer can the student or initiate hesitate and delay, this is the point of decision.
8. Binah, sephirah of restriction and form, demands one of two paths.
9. At the level of Assiah the paths are broad but at Briah narrow is the way.
10. The Tiphareth influence flows along this path demanding sacrifice.
11. Whatever decision the young man comes to means sacrifice.
12. The path of The Lovers is the parting of the ways.
13. Sacrifice of material treasures for those of the spirit, or a renunciation of the spiritual for the material.
14. There is no compromise on this path of decision.
15. The right choice can take the student or initiate up to the level of Binah consciousness.

16. A wrong choice on this path can mean a plunge down through Tiphareth to the path of probation.
17. Gemini is the astrological influence on this path with the element of Air being predominant.
18. The Geminian twins have to be reconciled and integrated.
19. The twins of Gemini can represent rivalry and opposition.
20. Balance and harmony (Tiphareth qualities) can also be found on this path.
21. In the Briatic world this is the ultimate Air initiation.
22. At the Yetziratic and Assiatic levels it is the final major initiation by air.
23. The arrow being fired by the angel, depicted on the arcanum, is a symbol of air.
24. Air is the element symbolic of spirit.
25. An arrow also conveys the meaning of direction, here is the direction of the spirit.
26. The bow is a symbol of promise, and eternal truth.
27. On this path discrimination is an essential quality if the right choice is to be made.
28. In the world of Assiah the decision is between the material life with spiritual overtones or pure materialization.
29. The choice of the Yetziratic level is between emotional religion and logical belief of universal forces.
30. The world of Briah brings the choice to a selective use of the universal forces through the powers developed.
31. "So shall thy judgement be, thou thyself has decided it" (1 Kings).
32. Zayin is the Hebrew letter for the path of the Lovers.
33. The meaning attributed to Zayin is sword.
34. The Lovers is truly a path over which the sword of Damocles hangs.
35. On this level of consciousness the choice to "live by the sword and die by the sword" or "Turn the swords into ploughshares" is made.

36. The path, like the sword, is double-edged.
37. The right choice and successful conquest of the path leads to full understanding (Binah).
38. The sword is a symbol of the will and power of the Ain force.
39. It can be protector and destroyer, again the double edge.
40. This is the sword of Arthur and of Siegfried.
41. How to use the sword is one of the lessons of this path.
42. Some packs show cupid with a bow, others show a winged figure hovering over The Lovers, they both represent the Guardian Angel.
43. The rays of the Sun represent the sphere of the universe and the paths of The Tree.
44. They are rays of promise that if the initiate or student makes the effort the Guardian Angel is there to help.
45. When the pupil is ready the master is there, this is a path to help the student make ready.
46. On the seventeenth path the free will of the student can be exercised more than on some of the lower paths.
47. The colour for this path is the orange ray of the concrete mind which on a higher level can be the higher reaches of the mind.
48. Precious stones associated to this path are the Tourmaline, Alexandrite.
49. Orchids are the plants and magpie the bird in harmony with the seventeenth path.
50. Magical powers of the path are those of prophecy and being in two places at the same time.
51. The vegetable drug is the Ergot and the perfume Wormwood.
52. The magical weapon is the tripod.
53. Gods attached to the seventeenth path are Castor and Pollux and other twin Deities also Apollo the Diviner.

Section 9

THE CHARIOT

1. This is the eighteenth path and the seventh arcanum.
2. Binah and Geburah (Pahad) are joined by the Chariot.
3. The first path entirely on the negative pillar.
4. It is a path of severity and rigour, strict and unbending.
5. The restriction of saturnian influence comes from Binah.
6. Severity and rigour stem from Geburah and influence the path of "The Chariot".
7. This is the Intelligence of the House of Influence.
8. From the midst of the investigation of the arcanum the hidden senses are drawn forth.
9. The hidden senses dwell in the shade of the arcanum and cling to it from the cause of all causes.
10. This arcanum depicts and symbolizes the conqueror crowned and victorious.
11. The cube-shaped chariot with the four columns supporting a canopy symbolize the quaternary in all its aspects.
12. To know, to be silent, to dare and to do.
13. The four holy living creatures, the Bull, the Lion, the Eagle and the Man.
14. The four corners of the universe suspended over the cube of matter.
15. Here man is symbolized in the centre of the quaternaries.
16. Conqueror of the elements and controller of universal forces.
17. At the Briatic level this is symbolizing spirit over matter.
18. In the Yetziratic world it is Logic over Emotion.
19. Lust for power is the attribute in the world of Assiah.

20. One great lesson to be learned from this path is the right use of power.
21. This is the path of two faces as indicated by the faces on the shoulders of the Charioteer.
22. The faces are nestled in crescent moons which symbolizes positive and negative.
23. Cancer is the astrological sign of the path, the moon is the ruling planet of Cancer.
24. Truly a path governed by the element of water.
25. Cancer is the sign of occultism as also is the moon, here lies the influences of the senses.
26. Understanding of universal law is a quality of the path.
27. The two faces of the moon can portray both shadow and substance.
28. Initiate or student must be careful to differentiate between the two.
29. The two faces of the moon can also represent the Urim and Thummim, which glow brightly or become dull.
30. A guide and signal to the Charioteer along this path.
31. Seven is the number of the moon, this is the seventh arcanum.
32. Seven is a sacred number associated with the ancient mysteries and occult influences.
33. Man has seven bodies. Has he conquered them all?
34. Here is The Fool as the warrior king with his chariot as the vehicle that carries the spirit on the path of conquest over matter.
35. The square Chariot below, the square canopy above form a double cube.
36. As above so below is the meaning of the double cube.
37. The Chariot is the vehicle which links spirit with matter.
38. Cheth is the Hebrew letter assigned to this path, it means fence.
39. And he fenced it and gathered out the stones thereof and planted it with the choicest vine, that it should bring forth grapes, and it brought forth wild grapes.

40. How true the path of the Chariot can bring forth the extremes.
41. "Thou hast clothed me with skin and flesh and has fenced me with bones and sinews" (Job 10, v.11).
42. The colour associated with this path is amber, and the precious stone of the same name.
43. Lotus is the plant and flower of the eighteenth path.
44. Animals on the path of The Chariot are the Crab and the Turtle.
45. The magical power is that of casting enchantments.
46. On the eighteenth path the magical weapon is The Furnace.
47. Its perfume is Onycha and vegetable drug watercress.
48. Gods of the path are Mercury, Apollo the Charioteer and Khephra.

Section 10

STRENGTH

1. The nineteenth path and the eighth arcanum.
2. Strength is the path that joins Geburah (Pahad) and Gedulah (Chesed).
3. This is the middle barrier, the second on the path of outgoing and on the path of return.
4. On the path of outgoing it is the veil before the abyss of Parakeeth.
5. It is the Intelligence of all the activities of the spiritual beings.
6. Here is symbolized strength and vitality with a purposeful calm.
7. Depicted on the arcanum is a girl calmly closing a lion's mouth. Powers of persuasion not force.
8. Over the girl's head is the figure 8 on its side, the symbol of vitality.
9. It is also the symbol of eternity, the Divine Life.
10. The symbol of a Lion is strength and courage.
11. Uncontrolled, this arcanum would be symbolic of animal passion.
12. Through a calm loving nature with spiritual strength, the initiate or student controls the animal world.
13. Moral and spiritual strength must be developed through the negative aspects of his nature.
14. The negative aspect is symbolized and emphasized by the girl.
15. One lesson to be learned from this path is to control the beast within.
16. Geburah and Gedulah at either end of the path are the extremes.

17. In extreme either of them become unbalanced forces which must be brought into balance and harmony.
18. Justice and Mercy is the keynote of this arcanum.
19. Expressed in this arcanum is the ascendancy of spirit over matter.
20. The Hebrew letter for this path is Teth which means snake.
21. The snake in all occult teachings is the symbol of Serpent Power.
22. This symbol is one of the oldest known and has always been endowed with a positive and negative aspect.
23. The serpent of evil, the tempter, but at the same time the adviser of wisdom.
24. Had man not obtained the knowledge of Good and Evil or Positive and Negative, he would have been an automaton.
25. Without knowledge of the negative, the positive could not be recognized and vice versa.
26. There is subtlety with the snake and the old saying "snake in the grass" must be more closely looked at.
27. The saying purely means it is hidden, man is not aware of it.
28. Also hidden is the ancient wisdom, many are not aware of it.
29. Beware of illusion, this is an aspect of the serpent.
30. Illusion overcome can lead to the eternal wisdom and the gift of healing.
31. The snake curled round the caduceus was in ancient times a symbol of the wandering physician.
32. "Be ye therefore wise as serpents and harmless as doves" (Mat. 10, v.16).
33. The astrological affinity to this path is Leo and the predominant element fire.
34. This is the fire that gives the driving force.
35. It is the fire of passion and the purifying fire at one and the same time.

36. The inner beast must be conquered before the outer beast can be mastered.
37. To those who know the secret this is the path of Divine Mercy (Gedulah).
38. It is also the path of Divine justice for those possessed of the serpent wisdom.
39. In the Archetypal World it is the perfect balance of Justice and Mercy.
40. At the Briatic level it is a biased justice or mercy.
41. On the Yetziratic level it is the emotional applied to either.
42. In the world of Assiah it is strength of convictions, right or wrong.
43. The colour of this path is yellow with a greenish shading.
44. A cat's eye is the precious stone that vibrates in harmony to strength.
45. The plant in harmony is the sunflower and the animal a lion.
46. Training of wild beasts is the magical power bestowed on the path of strength.
47. Discipline is the magical weapon for those who conquer the nineteenth path.
48. Olibanum is the perfume to use in working the path.
49. Vegetable drugs of use on the path are carminatives.
50. Gods attached to the path are Venus, Vishnu, Demeter and Man.
51. The path has many nature affinities with The Empress.

Section 11

THE HERMIT

1. This is the twentieth path and the ninth arcanum.
2. Gedulah and Tiphareth are joined by the path of The Hermit.
3. From the positive pillar to the middle pillar on the outward journey and vice versa on the path of return.
4. One end of this path touches the heart of The Tree.
5. This is the path of the crucified Gods from the sphere of crucifixion (Tiphareth) to the sphere of the Masters (Gedulah).
6. The Hermit as the title signifies is one of the paths where the initiate or student walks alone.
7. The esoteric interpretation of the 23rd Psalm includes this path, "Thy rod and Thy staff do comfort me."
8. Arcanum 9 depicts The Hermit walking with staff and lantern, a lonely cowled and robed figure.
9. Here is symbolized physical, mental and spiritual loneliness.
10. The only aid in the darkness of the path is the lantern (spiritual light) he carries.
11. He is cloaked in wisdom, his mental body shielded from the ideas of the world.
12. The test of this path is that of living with the self.
13. Mercy, love and grace are the qualities on the path from the influence of Gedulah.
14. Even at this level qualities can be perverted.
15. In the world of Assiah this can be mercy of emotion, selfish love and grace of the confidence trickster.

16. At the Yetziratic level, mercy from logical reasoning, emotional love, the grace of education.
17. On the plane of Briah mercy is balanced with justice, love becomes compassion and the true grace born of a gentle spiritual nature.
18. In Atziluth it is the perfected man who like Enoch "walks and talks with God".
19. This is the Intelligence of Will because it is the means and preparation of all created being.
20. By this Intelligence the existence of the primordial wisdom becomes known.
21. Although named The Hermit, this is not the path of a recluse but of stepping out into the world.
22. The path of being alone in the madding crowd, with a calm peace and quiet within in spite of the noise without.
23. His staff is for protection and to defend those who suffer under injustice.
24. It is the shepherd's crook as well as a staff of power.
25. In some Tarot packs this arcanum is called The Protector.
26. The Hebrew letter for the path is Yod, which means hand.
27. The first stage of Yod He Vau He (Jehovah).
28. "Mine own hand hath saved me" (Judges 7, v.2).
29. Virgo is the astrological sign of the path bringing the influence of the element Earth.
30. This is the sign of the Virgin, a path of purity or unsullied by temptations of earthly things.
31. Straight is the road and narrow, this is the path of The Hermit.
32. Sacrifice and compassion are the keynotes of this path.
33. The path is one of obstacles that have to be tackled with caution.
34. In most packs the arcanum shows The Hermit standing on a mountain peak, the point of achievement.
35. The initiate who follows this path must also light the way for others.

36. A follower and a leader, to follow the path of true wisdom and lead others to and along the path.
37. The colour for this path is green with a yellowish tinge running through it.
38. Green is harmony through struggle and conflict, yellow is creative activity.
39. A peridot is the precious stone that vibrates to the path of The Hermit.
40. Plants that are in affinity to this path are the snowdrop and the lily.
41. Any solitary animal belongs to the path of The Hermit.
42. The magical powers of this path are invisibility and initiation.
43. Virile or viril force (the wand) and the lamp are the magical weapons of The Hermit.
44. Narcissus is the perfume to be used in working this path.
45. Vegetable drugs concerned with The Hermit are the anaphrodisiacs.
46. Gods associated with the path are Ceres, The Lord of Yoga, Attis and Isis.
47. The mystic number is 210, this equals 3, the trinity, or the staff, the lamp and the cloak.

Section 12

THE WHEEL OF FORTUNE

1. This is the twenty-first path and the tenth arcanum and is called The Intelligence of conciliation and reward.
2. On this path conciliation or integration of the four elements can take place.
3. In all Tarot packs the Four Holy Living Creatures are depicted at the four corners of the arcanum.
4. These creatures not only represent the four basic elements but also the four fixed astrological signs.
5. The influence of these four creatures on the whole of life commenced at Kether, the first point.
6. To reconcile the wisdom obtained up to this point on The Tree is one of the major aims of this path.
7. Reward, the second aspect of the Intelligence, is received on this path.
8. The reward can be good or bad according to how we have lived in this incarnation up to any given point in the life of the initiate or student.
9. Previous incarnations are also rewarded on this path according to our deeds.
10. The Wheel of Fortune is also the wheel of life and rebirth.
11. On this path karma, good or ill, is put into action.
12. Universal law inexorably working out the sentence passed on the twenty-second path "Justice".
13. It is on this path that the initiate or student prepares for the next part of his journey.
14. The arcanum in most Tarot packs depicts the letters T.A.R.O. on the wheel, as the Wheel of Fortune turns it spells out a different lesson.

15. T.A.R.O. means Royal Path, the way of truth and knowledge.

16. A.T.O.R. is the same as Hathor the Egyptian God, it is therefore The Wheel of the Law of Hathor. The way of a God or Gods.

17. R.O.T.A. implies the cyclic effect, a repetition of the paths round four worlds, and many incarnations.

18. T.O.R.A. the scroll of universal law and ancient wisdom, first glimpsed, but not understood, in the hand of The High Priestess, on the outward journey.

19. The serpent is depicted descending on the left side of the wheel and the jackal-headed God ascending on the right.

20. Wisdom and knowledge with power is the symbol of the serpent.

21. The Jackal-headed God represents the judgement that is meted out.

22. As the wheel turns the serpent and the jackal-headed Gods change their positions, implying that their qualities are there on both the downward and upward journeys.

23. The sphinx on top of the wheel is a composite of The Four Holy Living Creatures.

24. As a perfect integration of the Four the sphinx has perfect balance and always remains at the top of the wheel.

25. This is a level of consciousness that has reached the stage of being beyond rebirth in the physical.

26. On this path lies all the strife, quarrels and contentions of the daily round.

27. It is the joy and ecstasy of the mountain-top and the misery and suffering of Hell.

28. Both the mountain-top and valley of Hell are essential to the experience of man.

29. Until the student has grovelled in the abyss of suffering and drunk the purified air of the mountain-top he has not lived.

30. Both must be experienced on the wheel of life.
31. The path joins Gedulah and Netzach and has the influence of Jupiter (Gedulah) and Venus (Netzach).
32. Jupiter also governs the path of The Wheel of Fortune.
33. The expansion of Jupiter, which at the lower levels is material expansion.
34. In the Yetziratic world it is the expansion of emotions, lower aspects of the Gedulah love.
35. At the level of Briah the expansion takes the form of wisdom and understanding.
36. In Atziluth it is the perfect archetype of the expansion of consciousness in all its aspects.
37. The element of water belongs to the twenty-first path.
38. The whole of this path is on the positive pillar, and the action is always of a positive nature.
39. Kaph is the Hebrew letter for the path and means Palm of the Hand.
40. "Who hath measured the waters in the hollow of his hand, and meted out heaven with the span" (Isaiah 40, v.12).
41. Violet is the colour ray for this path and this is one of the royal rays.
42. Amethyst and Lapis Lazuli are the precious stones connected to the Wheel of Fortune.
43. Amethyst is a spiritual stone, and the law was given to Moses on tablets of Lapis Lazuli, known in those days as the Emerald.
44. Plants in harmony with the twenty-first path are Hyssop, Oak, Poplar and Fig Tree.
45. The Eagle, symbol of spirit and air, belongs to this path.
46. Magical powers are those of acquiring ascendancy in all fields.
47. Saffron is the perfume and cocaine the drug of the twenty-first path.

48. The magical weapon of this path is the sceptre.
49. Gods belonging to The Wheel of Fortune are Jupiter. Pluto, Brahma, Zeus and Amoun-Ra.

Section 13

JUSTICE

1. Justice is the twenty-second path and the eleventh arcanum, it is the Faithful Intelligence.
2. At one end of the path is Geburah (Pahad) the sphere of severity and the symbol of death.
3. Tiphareth lies at the other end of the path with its quality of balance and harmony.
4. The path runs from the negative pillar to the middle pillar.
5. Here is embodied the qualities of balanced justice differing from the nineteenth path of justice with mercy.
6. Balanced justice is pure justice, the justice of universal law.
7. It is on this path that the Lords of Karma pronounce sentence.
8. The Martian influence of Geburah sends forth the red ray of will and power, sometimes called the destroyer ray.
9. On the downward or path of outgoing the lesson learned is one of sacrifice which is met with at Tiphareth.
10. On the path of return the sacrifice having been made at Tiphareth to a major or minor degree the initiate or student proceeds to Geburah.
11. Karma, good or bad, is judged on this path in accord with pure justice.
12. The Hebrew letter for his path is Lamed, which means Ox Goad.
13. It is at this stage of his journey "The Fool" gives an account of his actions.
14. Here "The Fool" looks back on the road he has travelled and could be complacent.

15. Lamed goads him on, destroys the complacency and whips him to life.
16. The ox goad is the spur to even greater striving.
17. Which direction the striving takes is of prime importance.
18. In the world of Assiah it can be a driving force for power, material wealth.
19. It can be a striving to leave the material things and gain the spiritual.
20. Yetzirah, the world of emotions, is probably the most difficult plane of consciousness for this path.
21. In this world it is so easy to drive forward to the wrong goal, vision can be so easily distorted by emotion.
22. On the Yetziratic level religions can be followed blindly, including the religion of the left-hand path.
23. The world of Briah with archangelic forces is the sphere of universal power, it is to control this "The Fool" is driven.
24. At one and the same time the initiate is spurred on and judged by his reaction to the spur.
25. The path of justice is governed by the element of Air.
26. If the student or initiate has not learned the lesson of The Hermit (Intelligence of Will) he can be blown from the right hand to the left hand.
27. The path is ruled by the astrological sign of Libra, the scales of balance.
28. On the path with strength of will balance can be found.
29. With the balance of Tiphareth and the driving force of Mars, the path can be successfully overcome.
30. All the time the student or initiate is on this path the scales are poised and he is weighed in the balance.
31. On this path the lesson of cause and effect can be learned.
32. The sword held with point upwards is a symbol of the double-edged justice.
33. Pitiless to those on the black path, but just to the true initiate of the right-hand path.

34. Spiritual virtues can be developed by the right attitude towards this path.
35. All men come under the shadow of justice, knowingly or otherwise.
36. It is a path of cold reason, methodical, logical and immune to all emotions.
37. The Hierophant is closely connected with the path of justice.
38. Use of the knowledge and wisdom gained on the path of the Hierophant is judged on the path of justice.
39. "The words of the wise are as Goads (Justice) and as Nails (Hierophant) fastened by the masters of assemblies, which are given from one shepherd" (Ecc. 12, v.11).
40. The colour of this path is emerald green, the green ray of harmony through struggle and conflict.
41. Emerald is the precious stone of path twenty-two and Aloe the plant.
42. The Elephant is the animal that is connected with the path of Justice.
43. Magical powers of the path are works of Justice and Equilibrium.
44. An equal armed cross is the magical weapon of path twenty-two.
45. The perfume to work with on this path is Galbanum.
46. Tobacco is the vegetable drug of the path of Justice.
47. Gods attached to this path are: Vulcan, Yama, Minos, Ma and Maat.

Section 14

THE HANGED MAN

1. This is the twenty-third path and the twelfth arcanum.
2. Geburah is at one end of the path and the sphere of Hod at the other end.
3. In the Yetziratic text it is the Stable Intelligence.
4. It has the virtue of consistency among all numerations.
5. In all Tarot packs the arcanum depicts a man hanging upside down by one foot.
6. This is a double symbol, seeing things from the wrong angle and an act of sacrifice.
7. Wisdom is only obtained by sacrifice of service and rejection of worldly things.
8. From the Hanged Man's pockets fall coins, a rejection of material wealth.
9. He who makes the ultimate sacrifice conquers the world.
10. The sacrifice of life gives life.
11. To prize the preservation of life is the upside-down view.
12. One leg of the Hanged Man is crossed behind the other and so forms a cross.
13. He is hanging between two posts, the pillars before the temple or the positive and negative pillars of the Tree.
14. The two pillars can symbolize the choice of two ways.
15. Hod, at one end of this path, is also the sphere from which runs the path of the sacrificed Gods.
16. With head down his eyes are gazing heavenward, fixed on higher things.
17. The path is ruled by the element of water.
18. Water of wisdom, water of life from which all things spring.

19. Changeless in itself, this is the stability of The Hanged Man.

20. It is the element of water that gives this path an affinity with that of the High Priestess.

21. Both are paths of initiation at different levels of consciousness.

22. A water initiation is the commencement of an entirely new circle of life. Other elements commence a new cycle or phase within the circle.

23. The importance of initiation by water is expressed in Wagner's Ring Cycle, here in music is expressed the journey of The Fool.

24. Commencing with the waters of Rhinegold, terminating with the waters surging over Valhalla at the end of Gotterdammerung.

25. The Hanged Man can be found in the shape of Woton, who made a great sacrifice.

26. Mem is the Hebrew word for this path and means waters or seas.

27. Binah at the head of this pillar is the great sea from which all form springs.

28. The whole of this path is on the negative pillar and receives an amount of Binah influence in a direct line.

29. Justice (Geburah) and Glory (Hod) are the two basic qualities of this path.

30. The student or initiate should beware of the wrong forms of Justice and Glory, this is the danger of the path.

31. The eyes of the Hanged Man could turn down just as easily as they look up.

32. In the world of Atziluth it is perfected sacrifice at this stage of development.

33. At the Briatic level it can be the final renunciation of the lower worlds.

34. On the Yetziratic level it is an act performed through the mental and emotional planes as the martyrs.

35. The world of Assiah is the sphere of the first sacrifice of either the spiritual or material things.
36. "The depths of the sea, a way for the ransomed to pass over" (Isaiah 51, v.10).
37. Mem also means atom or spot.
38. "For then shalt thou lift up thy face without a spot" (Job 11, v.15).
39. Phoenix rising from the ashes is a perfect expression of this arcanum.
40. The colour attributable to this path is deep blue.
41. Beryl is the gem-stone to be taken in conjunction with this path.
42. All water plants belong to this path, in particular the Lotus.
43. Animals of the arcanum are Eagle and Scorpio.
44. The magical powers belonging to The Hanged Man—talismans.
45. The magical weapons are the cup and the cross.
46. Perfume to be used in working this path is Myrrh.
47. Mineral drugs of this twenty-third path are sulphates and the vegetable drug is cascara.
48. Gods of the path are Neptune and Poseidon.

Section 15

DEATH

1. This is the twenty-fourth path and the thirteenth arcanum.
2. Tiphareth and Netzach are the sephiroth joined by the twenty-fourth path.
3. The path crosses between the middle pillar of balance and the positive pillar.
4. Imaginative Intelligence is the designation for the twenty-fourth path.
5. It gives a likeness to all the similitudes which are created in like manner similar to its harmonious elegancies.
6. The Hebrew letter assigned to this path is Nun, which has two meanings, (*a*) propagation, by budding or division, (*b*) fish.
7. Death does not destroy but propagates and the arcanum symbolizes life.
8. Netzach is a common meeting place for this path of the Wheel of Fortune.
9. From Tiphareth (sphere of the sacrificed Gods) the initiate or student is propelled along the path of Death to the foot of the Wheel of Fortune.
10. According to the sacrifice made the wheel will turn and the initiate's transition is made.
11. A new life or cycle is commenced and will again be terminated by Death the propagator.
12. Netzach is the sphere of victory and the energetic principle.
13. Through the influence of Netzach victory over Death is obtained.

14. The energetic principle carries the initiate from the end of one phase to the commencement of the next.
15. A second name for this arcanum is The Reaper.
16. The whole essence of the arcanum is symbolizing Life through Death.
17. In the world of Assiah it is Death to a way of life.
18. From atheism to orthodox religion and from there to philosophy or to the metaphysical and occult sphere.
19. A change from material riches to spiritual or vice versa.
20. At the Yetziratic level death to emotions and birth to logic, from blind faith to faith born of reason and knowledge.
21. In the world of Yetzirah it could be the death of reason and the birth of emotion.
22. The transpositions of death and birth depend on whether the path of outgoing or the path of return is being followed.
23. Even on the path of return it could be a fall and retrogression.
24. At the Briatic level a complete transition takes place, from being to force on the return, and force to being on the outward journey.
25. In the Archetypal world (Atziluth) this is the perfect blue-print of the ever-recurring and indestructible life.
26. When the Fool reaches Death on the return path he begins to see wisdom.
27. On the outward journey Death brings new experiences of the different form of senses as the Fool traverses the four worlds from force to form and matter.
28. The Reaper is an appropriate second title for this arcanum. It is at Death man reaps what he has sown.
29. St. Paul expressed this path when he said, "That which thou sowest is not quickened except it die."
30. Here is destruction for the purpose of reconstruction.
31. Death is the covered way which leadeth into light, the passage from one world to the next.

32. Form is always changing, generation by generation, and this change is made through the action of Death.

33. The Imaginative Intelligence operates in all men and all change.

34. According to the world the student or initiate is in so is the imaginative function.

35. This Intelligence is always there in varying degrees.

36. If not correctly controlled the Imaginative Intelligence can turn to illusion.

37. On this path the student or initiate is in the sphere of the "dark night of the soul" commenced in "Temperance" the sixteenth path.

38. The letter Nun means also generation besides propagation.

39. "For riches are not for ever, and doth the Crown endure to every generation" (Prov. 27, v. 24).

40. Kether (the Crown) doth endure to every generation from Malkuth to Atziluth.

41. Green blue is the colour in harmony with this path.

42. Snakestone is the gem that vibrates to this path.

43. The cactus is the plant and the animals are the Scorpion and the Wolf.

44. Necromancy is the magical power of the path.

45. The magical weapon is the pain of obligation.

46. In working the path the perfume to be used is Opopanax.

47. Gods of this path are Mars, Ares and Kephra.

Section 16

TEMPERANCE

1. The fourteenth arcanum and the twenty-fifth path.
2. Temperance joins together Tiphareth and Yesod on the middle pillar.
3. This is the path of balancing after leaving the emotional sphere of Yesod.
4. Yesod, however, still sends the emotional influence down the path, just as the harmonious influence flows from Tiphareth.
5. This is the path of Probationary Intelligence, because it is the primary temptation.
6. On this path the courage and sincerity of the initiate or student is tried and tested.
7. The first steps on the path of the dark night of the soul commence on the path of Temperance.
8. Here is the first inclination that each individual who treads the path of the ancient wisdom must one day walk alone.
9. It is in the aspect of walking alone that this path has a link with "The Hermit".
10. On the path of outgoing it is leaving the solitary for the many, which is easy.
11. The path of return is difficult unless "The Fool" realizes he has been living in a fool's paradise.
12. All the experiences the Fool has been through from the time he travelled the first path does not make it any easier to walk alone.
13. In the world of Assiah to walk alone means sacrifice of rank, power and material pleasure.

14. Following in the wake of the sacrifices in Assiah comes those of Yetzirah, control of emotions.
15. To break with family and friends who are not on this path.
16. The world of Briah is the culminating point in walking alone through the dark night of the soul.
17. At the Briatic level it is the first step towards the destruction of personality.
18. In the world of Atziluth towards the destruction of the archetypal individuality.
19. The student or initiate is not yet, however, alone, at this early stage there is a Guardian to help.
20. All arcanums in the various Tarot packs depict this Guardian in the form of an archangel.
21. There is always the overshadowing figure with the waters of wisdom.
22. In due course and much further up the Tree, in the Briatic world, the Guardian becomes the higher self.
23. This must be, because Briah is the world of the Archangels.
24. At this level the initiate will of his own accord control the Archangelic force.
25. On some arcanums the Archangel is depicted astride a river, symbolizing the flow of wisdom.
26. Most packs depict the Archangel with one foot in water and one on dry land, bridging the gap between physical and spiritual.
27. Temperance is a bridge crossing from one way of life to another.
28. Two cups are held by the Archangel and water flows from one to the other, symbolic of the life force pouring down.
29. The Hebrew letter for this path is Samech, which means "a tree or support".
30. "The Tree of the field is man's life" (Deut. 20, v. 19). The field is the Universe and The Tree is just that.

31. The arcanum is also called "The Angel of Time".
32. Water flowing from one vase to the other represents the flowing of the past to the present and into the future.
33. "There are vessels of Gold and Silver, but also of Wood and Earth, and some to honour and some to dishonour" (St. Paul).
34. Following "Death" the water in this arcanum can symbolize the cleansing, as with baptismal water.
35. Valhalla died and the waters washed away the ashes.
36. Sagittarius rules this path and brings with it the element of fire.
37. In symbolism and influence there is both fire and water on this path.
38. Yesod sends out the influence of the moon (water) and Tiphareth the sun (fire).
39. On this path of probation we have the lunar flame and the solar light.
40. Here fire and water mix in perfect harmony.
41. The fire of desire and the waters of wisdom are there for those who can take and keep them in balance.
42. To balance these elements brings success to the probationer.
43. Blue is the colour in harmonious vibration with the path.
44. Jacinth is the precious stone that harmonizes with this path.
45. Plant of the path is rush and the animals a dog and a horse.
46. Magical power of the path is for the transmutations.
47. The magical weapon is the arrow.
48. Perfume to be used on this path is aloes.
49. Gods of the path are Diana and Artemis.

Section 17

THE DEVIL

1. This is the fifteenth arcanum and the twenty-sixth path.
2. Tiphareth is at one end of the path with Hod at the other end.
3. On the outward journey the path runs from the middle pillar of balance to the negative pillar.
4. The return journey takes the student or initiate from the negative to balance.
5. It is the path taken by the sacrificed Gods.
6. Here is a connection with Gedulah which is the sphere of the masters.
7. From Tiphareth where the path of The Devil terminates the path of The Hermit commences.
8. Illusion can be a feature of this path with its double-edged interpretation.
9. The arcanum depicts The Devil holding two humans in captivity, in one hand a whip, in the other a torch.
10. The first interpretation of this arcanum is that man is following a path of lust and things of the Devil.
11. Here is the path of temptation with the problem of whether man can resist it.
12. The second interpretation is that the student is being driven (whip) along the path.
13. It is a path of illumination (torch) which the student or initiate can use to his advantage.
14. The Devil is also known as Lucifer who is the Light Bringer.
15. From the Devil or Lucifer man receives his first light of knowledge and sees good and evil.

16. Without the knowledge of evil good could not be recognized and vice versa.
17. The Devil is essential to the progress of student or initiate and to the whole human race.
18. Embodied in this arcanum is the Devil and Divine.
19. This path is the Renovating Intelligence because by it all changing things are renewed.
20. Ayin is the Hebrew letter for this path and means eye and foundation.
21. "Whence then cometh wisdom and where is the place of understanding? seeing it is hid from the eyes of all living" (Job 28, vv. 20 and 21).
22. In the duality lies the foundation of all truth and wisdom.
23. Capricorn is the astrological sign of the path and the influence of the element of earth.
24. The two humans chained together symbolize the positive and negative of life.
25. The Devil as the two in one balances the two opposites.
26. There is no division between good and evil, life is one.
27. A main lesson to be learned from this card is to understand all things.
28. Know evil to enable good to be carried out.
29. Be chained neither to Earth or Heaven, dwell in Earth at the physical level and in Heaven at the Spiritual level.
30. Ayin also means a cloud, and it is for the student or initiate to see through.
31. This arcanum is or can be a cloud of unknowing containing the truth of knowing.
32. The cube the Devil sits upon is symbolic of the cube of space.
33. It is in reality a double cube, the humans chained to the lower and the devil sits on the upper.
34. The double cube is symbolic of as above—so below.
35. The negative forces can always be made to serve the positive.

36. Indigo is the ray of this path, the colour that is cleansing.
37. Black diamond is the gem-stone of this path.
38. Plants of the path are Hemp and Thistle.
39. The goat and the ass are the two animals associated with this path.
40. Magical power of The Devil is the witches sabbath.
41. The magical weapon is the Lamp and the secret force.
42. Musk is the perfume to use on this path.
43. Gods of the path are Pan and Set.

SECTION 18

THE LIGHTNING-STRUCK TOWER

1. This is the sixteenth arcanum and the twenty-seventh path.
2. The third barrier or veil is formed by this path, the last on the path of outgoing and the first on the way back.
3. Netzach and Hod are joined by this path to give a balance of Victory and Glory.
4. Imagination, Illusion and the energetic principle are brought together on the twenty-seventh path.
5. In all packs the arcanum is depicted as a tower struck by lightning, two figures are falling from the tower, one crowned and one uncrowned.
6. Here indeed is the Tower of Babel being brought to ruin.
7. Hod is the sphere where religions are built up and destroyed because imagination runs riot.
8. Man builds in imagination and with illusion and this is the path that brings it to nothing.
9. This path shows that in universal law all men are equal.
10. Destruction for reconstruction is also an aspect of this path.
11. Here is the point where a way of life is broken down by choice.
12. With a true knowledge and understanding of the sephiroth Netzach and Hod, the student or initiate can use the twenty-seventh path to his advantage.
13. Rigid thoughts can be broken down and a new outlook or thought process commenced.
14. On the path of outgoing these changes are made involuntarily.

15. On the path of return the change must be made voluntarily if this barrier is to be passed.
16. If the student or initiate is on the path of return and an involuntary change is brought about the barrier will not be passed.
17. On the path of return only negative actions are involuntarily brought to destruction.
18. Heaven, God, The source of life, will never be discovered by building a physical tower.
19. This is the path of active or exciting intelligence.
20. By this path is created the intellect of all created beings.
21. It is the purpose of this path to destroy all thoughts not in accord with the Universal Law.
22. Thought within Universal Law differs in degree with the world in which the student or initiate is operating.
23. In the world of Assiah the trend of thought should be towards helping humanity, a conquest of the I.
24. At the Yetziratic level the power of thought should extend beyond the personality and individuality level.
25. On the Briatic level this barrier of the twenty-seventh path can only be passed when the thought process is joined more to the Universal Mind.
26. In the world of Atziluth it is the archetypal potential of Universal Mind.
27. The Lightning-struck Tower is a minor punitive path.
28. There is a link with Geburah (Justice) as both have the astrological influence of Mars.
29. Fire is the element of the path with all its burnishing and purification.
30. The Hebrew letter for this path is Peh, meaning assent or agreement.
31. It also means to come into harmony, and this is also a lesson of the Lightning-struck Tower.
32. Harmony with life, with Universal Law and within the individual.

33. Only perfect agreement and harmony with the life consciousness at his level of being will take the student or initiate across the barrier.
34. It is the path where the individual has to say, and mean, "not my will but thine be done".
35. An alternative name for this arcanum is "The House of God".
36. The colour for this path is scarlet, the fire of divine justice which strikes the Tower.
37. 378 is the mystic number which in numerology becomes 9.
38. 9 is the ultimate number, and by it the student or initiate will rise or fall.
39. Ruby is the precious stone that vibrates to this path.
40. Absinth and Rue are the plants that belong to the twenty-seventh path.
41. The Bear and the Wolf are the animals of the Lightning-struck Tower.
42. Its magical powers are wrath and vengeance.
43. The magical weapon is a two-edged sword.
44. Pepper is the perfume to be used in working this path.
45. Gods predominant on this path are Mars and Ares.

Section 19

THE EMPEROR

1. This is the seventeenth arcanum and the twenty-eighth path.
2. Netzach and Yesod are joined by this path which is part on the positive and part on the middle pillar.
3. The twenty-eigth path is the path of "Natural Intelligence" because through it is consummated and perfected the nature of every existing being under the orb of the sun.
4. Natural Intelligence is the quality of one who rules and the arcanum depicts this with the symbol of The Emperor.
5. Rulership at both physical and spiritual levels.
6. On the outward journey this is the first test of rulership or control of the material aspects of life.
7. Rule over the material and spiritual is the test on the path of return.
8. Imperfect rule on this path will bring the student or initiate tumbling down at the barrier of the Lightning-struck Tower.
9. It is not just the rulership of Kings and Presidents, it is rulership enjoyed by every individual, low or high estate.
10. The Kingdom he has to rule is composed of his own bodies, physical, mental and spiritual.
11. It is the principles of Netzach (firmness, energy) that rightly used can bring triumph and victory.
12. Still linked to Yesod the physical/emotional plane still has a strong hold, rulership will be difficult to establish.
13. On this path commences the first struggle of the mental body for spiritual freedom.

14. In the world of Assiah it is the object to rule over the material.
15. Domination of material and emotional planes is the task in Yetzirah.
16. At the Briatic level it is the spirit's struggle to rule and command the buddhic plane.
17. In the world of Atziluth it is the archetype of the perfect ruling spirit.
18. The Emperor is not the consort of The Empress as so often expressed and is wrongly placed on the fifteenth path.
19. The Emperor is gaining rulership over himself, The Empress over self and the whole of nature.
20. The astrological sign of the path is Aquarius and the element air.
21. Air is symbolic of spirit and its freedom, it is equally symbolic of indecision.
22. The Hebrew letter for this path is Tzaddi, which means to lie in wait, to hunt, to hide preparatory to springing out.
23. Here is the spirit of enterprise, it can give the power to spring forth new-born.
24. To hunt for experience, and gain the crown of rulership.
25. The Emperor is seated on a cubic stone in the form of a Throne. On the arms of the throne are rams' heads.
26. A ram's head is symbolic of Aries, the first astrological sign, the commencement of a new era.
27. This is also a symbol of will and power, qualities of the Red Ray, which is the ray of Aries.
28. Courage is also a quality expressed by the Ram's head, a quality much needed on this path.
29. Held in the hand of The Emperor is a sceptre in the form of the Egyptian ankh, spirit ruling matter.
30. The ankh also symbolizes spiritual rulership over earthly rulership.

31. A christian cross stands erect on top of his crown, the symbol of supreme sacrifice.
32. Tzaddi the Hebrew letter also means fish hook.
33. "I will put my hook in thy nose" (2 Kings).
34. The colour ray for this path is violet, a royal earthly colour, and a high spiritual ray.
35. 406 is the mystic number; in numerology it comes back to 1.
36. 406 is also 10, this is the number of the beginning and the end.
37. The Crystal with its fragmentary rays is the precious stone in harmony with the path.
38. Olive is the plant for the twenty-eighth path, the olive branch of peace.
39. The proud peacock is the animal of The Emperor.
40. Astrology is the magical power of The Emperor.
41. The magical weapon is a censor.
42. Galbanum is the perfume to be used in working the path.
43. Gods of the path are Juno and Athena.

Section 20

THE MOON

1. This is the eighteenth arcanum and the twenty-ninth path.
2. The Corporeal Intelligence, so called because it forms every body which is formed beneath the whole set of worlds.
3. Commencing at Netzach the path runs straight down to Malkuth by passing Yesod.
4. The avoidance of Yesod equally applies on the return journey.
5. It is on this path the traveller can be deluded by missing a plane of consciousness (Yesod).
6. Yesod is the emotional, astral sphere, but these are also characteristics of The Moon.
7. As Yesod is a sphere of illusion so is the Moon.
8. On this path the student does well to heed the Hebrew letter corresponding to this path—QOPH.
9. QOPH has two meanings—"back of the head" and "ear".
10. "He that hath ears to hear let him hear" is very appropriate for the path of the Moon.
11. This path is essentially a path controlled by the element of water.
12. The Moon—a water planet, rules Cancer a water sign.
13. The Waters of Wisdom or The Waters of the Moon, which is it to be?
14. Both aspects of water are embodied in this arcanum.
15. The waters of wisdom stem from Chokmah, which is at the head of the pillar this path commences on.
16. Malkuth at the bottom of the middle pillar is where the path terminates.

17. The middle pillar implies balance and this can be obtained from the Path of the Moon.
18. Pisces is the governing sign of the path, again water, and the two-way pull of the fishes.
19. The Crayfish pictured on the arcanum climbing out of the water symbolizes the spirit rising from the material world having partaken of the waters of wisdom.
20. Dog in reverse is God. The two dogs represent two Gods, the opposites, the Divine and the Devil.
21. These are the two tools for the student and initiate to use on his journey through the four worlds.
22. Positive and negative—Good and Evil—Active and Passive.
23. The arcanum further emphasizes this idea of opposition, duality and struggle of the two poles by the two towers.
24. The path between the towers is the middle way of balance.
25. Here is also the pathway into the unknown, a future that is only theory until the issue is resolved.
26. The two dogs, or dog and wolf in this context, are symbolic of the fears of the mind when there is only reflected light to guide it.
27. The light of mind or intellect is but a dim flicker on the path of the unknown.
28. This is indeed part of the larger path of the dark night of the soul.
29. On some arcanum the moon has thirty-two rays penetrating, although cradled in the sun.
30. The thirty-two rays represent the ten sephiroth and twenty-two paths.
31. Reflected light and the light of full illumination can be found on this path, symbolized by the moon in the sun.
32. This also is symbolic of the need for the two binaries.
33. This can be a path of deception and also of imagination.
34. Netzach, the sphere from which the path commences, is the plane of imaginative ideas.

35. It is the sephirah of victory and triumph.
36. The energetic principle is in Netzach, also the glittering splendour.
37. Down the path of the moon flow these qualities.
38. The glittering splendour of the moonlight can bring the inspiration required to obtain victory through the waters of wisdom.
39. Appropriate to this path are the words of Shakespeare, "There comes a time in the affairs of man if taken at the flood."
40. This path is a minor initiation in the element of water.
41. There is a resemblance of the thirteenth path "The High Priestess" on this path.
42. It is a path where the exploration of the secret of life may be commenced.
43. The wisdom here is not at the level of the thirteenth path, but more dangers attend it.
44. Astral projection and psychic experiences, such as trance and materialization, is also part of this arcanum.
45. Here the aroused curiosity must be controlled and not allowed to run free on this fascinating aspect of the path.
46. So much illusion and deception comes from this realm of psychic belief.
47. The guiding light for this path is stop, look, listen and be silent.
48. A lesson to be learned from this path is that of discrimination.
49. The colour ray on this path is violet, ultra-violet in the Atziluthic world.
50. Poppy, Hibiscus and Nettle are the plants corresponding to the path of the moon.
51. Chrysolight is the precious stone that spreads its influence down the path.
52. Some of the Gods that correspond to "The Moon" are Neptune, Vishnu and Poseidon.

53. The animal sacred to the path is the Dolphin, and Ambergris its perfume.
54. Magical powers are those of creating illusions and the magical weapon is the magic mirror.
55. Drugs in vibratory harmony with the path are all narcotics.

Section 21

THE SUN

1. This is the nineteenth arcanum and the thirtieth path.
2. The path of the Collecting Intelligence, from it is deduced the judgement of the stars.
3. Hod is at one end of the path and Yesod at the other end.
4. It is a path of splendour and along it flows the stellar light of Mercury and the lunar flame.
5. Embodied in this path are all four elements, Mercury—Air, Moon—Water, Sun—Fire and the child depicted on it—Earth.
6. The ruling element of the path is fire through the influence of the sun, the planet of the path.
7. On the arcanum is a naked child riding a horse, behind him is a wall and above the sun sending down its rays of light.
8. Above the wall rises the heads of sunflowers, as always with faces turned towards the sun.
9. Here is the indication of what the student or initiate must do, turn his face towards the spiritual sun.
10. The spirit is confined within the material as symbolized by the wall.
11. Freedom is to be obtained by turning towards the sun.
12. The naked child indicates that the student or initiate must strip himself of everything material.
13. Innocence is also expressed by the child, "except ye become as a little child".
14. The white horse is a symbol of purity, the child on its back—victory of spiritual purity.
15. Collecting Intelligence means just that, on the outward journey denser matter is collected.

16. On the return journey, to conquer this path, the student or initiate must collect the spiritual intelligence.
17. In the world of Assiah both material and spiritual are collected.
18. At the Yetziratic level spiritual emotions are collected.
19. On the Briatic level of being purity is collected.
20. Atziluth is the archetypal world and shows on this path perfect purity and innocence can be obtained.
21. Pride is a quality associated with the sun and the student or initiate must be careful not to develop spiritual pride.
22. Stubbornness can also be developed on this path, if care is not taken, through the influence of Hod.
23. Mercury the mundane chakra of Hod can influence in quick decisions which are stubbornly held although wrong.
24. With the combination of Hod and the Moon from Yesod imagination can run riot.
25. Typical of this path are those who believe they have been sent for a Divine purpose.
26. This is the path of the puritan and rigid orthodox.
27. It is here that true spiritual light can dawn and the waters of wisdom be absorbed.
28. The spirit can take the first step towards complete freedom.
29. The Hebrew letter for this path is Resh, which means head or face.
30. "He shall drink of the brook (waters of wisdom) in the way therefore shall he lift up the head."
31. "A man's wisdom maketh his face to shine" (Ecclesiastes 8).
32. From this path the student or initiate can rise to the heights or fall to the depths.
33. The spirit of air, the purifying forces of fire and water, if used as such, are there to help in the conquest.
34. Victory over this path on the return journey leads to the Glory of Hod.

35. It also leads us to the sphere of the host of angels known as the sons of God.
36. The ray of this path is orange, the ray of concrete mind.
37. 465 is the mystic number of the thirtieth path.
38. Heliotrope is the precious stone in harmony with the sun.
39. Sunflowers are the plants associated with the path.
40. The sparrowhawk is the animal of the sun.
41. Symbolized in the sparrowhawk is the lesser spirit imprisoned in mass material, and the spirit expanded in its conquest.
42. Acquiring wealth, spiritual or material, is the magical power of the path of the sun.
43. The magical weapon is the bow and arrow.
44. The bow of promise and the arrow of destruction.
45. The arrow is also symbolic of direction—straight as a die.
46. Cinnamon is the perfume to use in working this path.
47. Alcohol is the danger drug on the path of the sun.
48. Gods prominent on the thirtieth path are Apollo, Surya, Helios and Ra.

Section 22

JUDGEMENT

1. This is the thirty-first path and the twentieth arcanum.
2. Judgement commences on the negative pillar and joins Hod direct with Malkuth.
3. Perpetual Intelligence is the name for the arcanum in the Yetziratic text.
4. The sun and moon are regulated in their orbits by the Perpetual Intelligence.
5. As the luminaries are regulated in their cycles so is man, either as an individual or a community.
6. An alternative title for this arcanum used in some Tarot packs is "The Last Judgement".
7. This title applies only in part, it is the last judgement on the outward journey but not on the path of return.
8. No astrological sign governs this path, it is influenced solely by the element of fire.
9. Depicted on the arcanum is an archangel awakening the dead; a woman, a man and a child are standing up in their coffins.
10. In symbolism the woman represents the negative, the man positive and the child balance.
11. The child also represents rebirth, a new cycle or beginning, in the round of Perpetual Intelligence or perpetual motion.
12. On this path the final burnishing by fire takes place before the next cycle in Malkuth commences.
13. At this point it is the Last Judgement on previous cycles.
14. The sole influence of Fire could make this path the Hell of the Christian beliefs.

15. To achieve balance in the next cycle or incarnation is the message of the path of Judgement.
16. The child between the two adults is indicative of balancing the opposites.
17. This arcanum is also a path of hope as well as fear.
18. A new beginning is promised with the opportunity of clearing past debts.
19. An individual's environment in Malkuth is the Judgement passed upon him on the thirty-first path.
20. If the environment is overcome spiritual progress has been made and debts paid.
21. At this point on The Tree the student or initiate can look back and forward.
22. Here can be seen and understood the sum total of the past and the full potential of tomorrow.
23. The Archangel depicted in most Tarot packs is Michael, Archangel of the element of Fire.
24. Michael is protector and destroyer at one and the same time.
25. The sun behind him holds out the rays of hope.
26. Where this path joins Hod it meets the paths of The Sun, Lightning-struck Tower, the Devil and the Hanged Man.
27. Two qualities are common to all these paths, including "Judgement", they are sacrifice and illumination.
28. Three of these six paths are under the influence of the element of Fire.
29. This corner of The Tree is one of restriction, curbing and correcting.
30. The equal armed cross on the flag of the archangel is expressive of the four worlds and the four corners of the Universe.
31. All the figures are naked, and prior to reaching Malkuth this is the state of each individual.
32. Only in Malkuth does the individual have possessions other than wisdom.

33. Judgement is no fixed era as expressed in some religions when all shall rise again from the dead.
34. The end of any incarnation with the beginning of the next is the path of Judgement.
35. Shin is the Hebrew letter for this path and means "fang" or "tooth".
36. This arcanum is well expressed in the words "An eye for an eye".
37. No other path on The Tree expresses Universal Law with Divine justice as does the thirty-first path.
38. In Atziluth this is the archetype of perfected judgement.
39. In the world of Briah it is judgement expressed in the creation of Universal Law.
40. The Yetziratic world has the type of judgement that is tinged by the emotional plane.
41. At the Assiatic level it is the judgement that prepares the individual for a new incarnation.
42. On this last plane it can also be the judgement of going down to try again or rising up to the next plane of consciousness.
43. The colour of the path is scarlet red tinged with a fiery orange.
44. Opal is the precious stone that vibrates to the path of Judgement, particularly the fire opal.
45. The Lion is the animal associated with Judgement.
46. Plants of the path are Nettle and Hibiscus.
47. The magical power is that of evocation.
48. Magical weapons are the Wand and Lamp.
49. To work this path the perfume of Olibanum should be used.
50. Gods attached to the path are Pluto, the God of breaking up, Hades and Horus.

Section 23

THE UNIVERSE

1. This is the twenty-first arcanum and the thirty-second path, also the last path.
2. Joining Malkuth to Yesod it is the base and support of The Tree.
3. In the Yetziratic text it is known as the Administrative Intelligence.
4. It directs and administers the planets in their operations and due courses.
5. In some Tarot packs this arcanum is known as the world, a misleading title.
6. The Tree of Life refers to *all* life in every sphere of consciousness in and out of manifestation wherever it may be.
7. This arcanum must then be The Universe and administers the planets in every system.
8. All Tarot packs have the same hieroglyph on the arcanum, that of a young woman with a single drape encircled by a laurel wreath.
9. At the four corners are the four Holy Living Creatures, first encountered at Kether.
10. The Holy Living Creatures (Host of Angels to Kether) commence at the top of The Tree and run all the way through it.
11. This is the last point on The Tree where they are the unseen builders.
12. At Malkuth they are the four elements known by the physical senses.

13. They represent on the arcanum the four elements and Yod He Vau He.

14. The four corners of the Universe are also symbolized.

15. This is the arcanum of victory as symbolized by the laurel wreath.

16. It is also symbolic of the Ain force which encloses all within itself.

17. Humanity stands at the centre of the four forces, to balance and to administer.

18. Here can be obtained the final freedom from matter if the elements are controlled.

19. To control them the student or initiate must absorb their qualities.

20. The Lion—strength and courage. The Bull or Ox—patience. The Eagle—ability to soar to the heights. The Man—spiritual wisdom.

21. Expressed here is also the axiom To Dare—To do—To know—To Be Silent.

22. The Lion—Fire. The Bull—Earth. The Eagle—Air. The Man—Water.

23. Here is represented macrocosm and microcosm, man being a universe in himself.

24. The ellipse which surrounds the figure is symbolic of the never-ending cycles of life.

25. There is no beginning and there is no end, just a ceaseless life flow.

26. To physical matter there is an end at any given time, the student or initiate decides that time himself.

27. The decision made and matter conquered, the spirit returns through the four worlds to the Ain.

28. This is the last path on the outward journey and the first on the return.

29. At this point all has been taken and it is at this point all must be discarded.

30. Saturn rules the path with its restriction, this is the link with Binah.
31. The surrounding laurel wreath is the ultimate ring-pass-not, the sphere of the zodiac which is the link with Chokmah.
32. Four Holy Living Creatures are the connection with Kether.
33. As above so below is clearly portrayed by the Universe.
34. On the conquest of this path depends the future of the student or initiate.
35. Here victory can be obtained and the whole edifice of the Tree supported and administered.
36. Student and initiate alike will find this the most difficult path on the whole Tree.
37. Here dense matter has to be broken through to let the spirit soar free.
38. On no other path is the spirit so restricted by dense elements, this is the Saturn influence.
39. On no other path is there such opportunity to reach the ultimate goal.
40. Tau is the Hebrew letter for this path and means a Tau Cross or a boundary.
41. The Boundary is the Universe, the Universe is my parish.
42. A Christian cross is the symbol of spirit crucified on matter, the Tau Cross symbolizes spirit over matter.
43. The colour ray for this path is Indigo, the devotional ray at the physical level and the synthesizing ray on the higher octaves.
44. Onyx is the precious stone for the thirty-second path, it is the stone of Saturn.
45. The animal associated with the Universe is the crocodile.
46. Ash and Cypress are the plants of path thirty-two.
47. Alchemy is the magical power of The Universe.
48. The magical weapon is a sickle.

49. Frankincense is the perfume to use when working on this path.
50. Gods associated with the path of The Universe are Saturn, Brahma, Nephthys and Athene.

Section 24

GENERAL

1. The Kabbalah is not just part of the Judaic religion, it is more.
2. Chaldeans, Babylonians and Egyptians were aware of and studied it.
3. The Tree, including the paths of the twenty-two major arcana, is the ultimate in occult and ancient wisdom.
4. Iamblichus quotes the major arcana in his description of an "Egyptian Initiation" of which it was an integral part.
5. On the wheel of life which includes many incarnations, an individual goes through many initiations, major and minor.
6. Although an individual can be taken through a form of initiation, the real initiation is within.
7. However many ceremonies an individual goes through it is to no avail unless an inner change takes place.
8. Many organizations of an occult and spiritual nature break up or harbour in their midst discontent through the folly of initiation and with the consequent grades or ranks.
9. No individual can be made a master or a magus by a physical initiation.
10. All are students or initiates at various levels of progress.
11. A student is one who has commenced on the path but is still very much with Malkuth.
12. An initiate is one who in consciousness has gone beyond Malkuth.
13. All titles are false and temporary within occultism as expressed in "Judgement"—we come into and go out of a cycle stripped of the material.

14. What an individual brings in and takes out is wisdom obtained through experiences on The Tree of Life.
15. The Kabbalah should be studied without hopes of rank or gain, other than the gain of inner wisdom.
16. The journey of life commences with the blind "Fool" and ends with the wise "Fool".
17. What does rank and possessions avail when in the final reckoning the personality and individuality is merged in the all-embracing consciousness of the whole.
18. In the vast cosmos of the Ain Man is less than a grain of sand and yet he is a God in the making.
19. Student, Initiate, Master, God—this is the future in store for Man.

Streams in the Desert —
The Brother #38
   Fort Worth Texas

With special thanks to Betty Pershing and the faithful staff people of Hansi Ministries for all the time-consuming help and the unselfish dedication to God's cause and service.

CONTENTS

Beginnings 9
A Gift for Babes 13
Introduction 15

ABOUT OURSELVES
1. How Are We Born Again? 17
2. Born in the Spirit 20
3. The Human Soul 22
4. The Human Body 24

FUNCTIONS OF THE SPIRIT
5. Communion 27
6. Conscience 29
7. Intuition 32

ABOUT GOD
8. The Godhead 35
9. God the Father 37
10. God the Son 40
11. God the Holy Spirit 42

ABOUT SATAN AND THE BEGINNING OF SIN
12. Origin of Evil 47
13. Why God Permitted Evil 49
14. Sin and Death 52

ABOUT PRAYER
15. We Talk to God 57
16. God Talks to Us 60
17. We Talk to God About Others 63

ABOUT WITNESSING, JOINING AND GROWING
18. Confessing Christ 69
19. About Doctrines 72
20. Day by Day Growing Pains 74

ABOUT OUR SOUL
21. The Will 79
22. Our Emotions and Feelings 82
23. Our Minds 85

CONTENTS (Continued)

ABOUT OUR BODY
24. Our Defense 89
25. Our Body's Intakes 92
26. Nutrition and Diet 95
27. Sex and Reproduction 98

GOD'S APPAREL FOR US
28. God's Best Robe 103
29. The Armor of God 106
30. Getting Dressed 109
31. A Shield, A Helmet and a Sword 112

ABOUT GOD'S SCHOOL
32. God's Three R's 117
33. Relationship to Ourselves 120
34. Our Relationship to Others 123
35. Our Relationship to God 126

CHILDHOOD PROBLEMS
36. Loneliness 130
37. Depression 134
38. Anxiety and Fears 137

COMMUNICATION SKILLS
39. Talking 143
40. Listening 146
41. Sharing and Receiving 149

ABOUT GOD'S FRUIT
42. Abiding in the Vine 155
43. Love 158
44. Joy 161
45. Peace 164
46. Longsuffering 167
47. Gentleness 169
48. Goodness 172
49. Faith 175
50. Meekness 178
51. Temperance 181

GRADUATION
52. Finals 185

BEGINNINGS

I shall never forget the first time my foster mother read a Bible story about Solomon to me. I was seven or eight years old, and able to read quite well in my native German tongue. Mother's Bible was an old Martin Luther translation, however, and I often had a hard time understanding the archaic words in that big black book. One evening, though, while sitting at my mother's knee and listening to her gentle, tired voice as she read about Solomon, something happened. My imagination began to grasp that Bible story, and history came alive.

"And Solomon loved the Lord, walking in the statutes of David his father: only he sacrificed and burnt incense in high places. And the king went to Gibeon to sacrifice there; for that was the great high place: a thousand burnt offerings did Solomon offer upon that altar. In Gibeon the Lord appeared to Solomon in a dream by night: and God said, Ask what I shall give thee. And Solomon said, Thou hast shewed unto thy servant David my father great mercy, according as he walked before thee in truth, and righteousness, and in uprightness of heart with thee; and thou hast kept for him this great kindness, that thou hast given him a son to sit on his throne, as it is this day. And now, O Lord my God, thou hast made thy servant king instead of David my father: and I AM BUT A LITTLE CHILD: *I know not how to go out or come in. And thy servant is in the midst of thy people which thou hast chosen, a great people, that cannot be numbered nor counted for multitude. Give therefore thy servant an understanding heart to judge thy people, that I may discern between good and bad:*

for who is able to judge this thy so great a people? And the speech pleased the Lord, that Solomon had asked this thing. And God said unto him, Because thou hast asked this thing, and hast not asked for thyself long life; neither hast asked riches for thyself, nor hast asked the life of thine enemies; but hast asked for thyself understanding to discern judgment; behold, I have done according to thy words: lo, I have given thee a wise and an understanding heart; so that there was none like thee before thee, neither after thee shall any arise like unto thee. And I have also given thee that which thou hast not asked, both riches and honour: so that there shall not be any among the kings like unto thee all thy days. And if thou wilt walk in my ways, to keep my statutes and my commandments, as thy father David did walk, then I will lengthen thy days. And Solomon awoke . . ."
(I Kings 3:3-15a King James Version).

In my mind's eye, I could see exactly how King Solomon looked! My favorite school library book of *Marchen* (fairy tales) contained a picture of a handsome storybook king who had a long beard, wore a golden crown and a long purple velvet train with white fur trim and held a golden sceptre in his leather-gloved hand. To me, that was King Solomon.

I also knew about magical dreams in which a person was granted a free wish. The fairy tales I read told of such things happening all the time, and I often wondered what I would wish for if such luck were ever to strike me. Not that I expected it; I was big enough to know that *Marchen* were not real. But when mother read such a story from God's Bible, I knew that everything I heard was absolutely true.

To think that such a thing *really* happened! And it wasn't a fairy godmother but God Himself who gave Solomon that free wish! And what a wish Solomon made!

What would I have asked for if I had been in his place?

I thought about that as I crawled under my featherbed in the hayloft that night. I thought about it the next day, too, when I picked up mother's old Bible and re-read the story myself. And I thought about it some more the next evening, as I lay on my straw bed.

Why were wisdom, understanding and an obedient heart so good that God would add riches and honor and a long life on top of them? And why did Solomon say that he was *ein junger knabe* (but a little child) when he was really a big, grownup king with a long beard and a fancy crown?

After much thought, I eventually came to understand the story as well as my young years would allow, and decided that I would give the same answer as Solomon did if God ever granted me a free wish.

Of course, I didn't think He would ever do so! I wasn't a noble king or queen; I was only a naughty little orphan girl who nobody really wanted or needed. But if God *should* ever ask, I thought (after all, I was still "but a little child" and therefore might qualify for such a wish), I knew my answer.

But the little girl grew up! I forgot my Bible stories, fairy tales and all my answers and wandered far away from my mother and her God.

Brainwashed by the Nazis, hurt and emotionally crippled by a cruel world and a horrible war, I grew older fast, but not very wise!

Then one night the miracle happened! Jesus came to me, not in a dream but in reality. He knocked on the door of my heart and I opened. He stepped in and we became friends.

"Do you have a wish?" He asked one day.

"Jesus," I said, "I am not a king like Solomon, so why might I be worthy enough to be granted a wish?"

"You are the daughter of a King," Jesus said, "and you

have more than one wish free; I'll give you the desires of your heart!"

"But I am no longer a little child!" I exclaimed. "I am old, gray-haired, and not able to do the youthful things I once did!"

"When you believed in Me," said the Lord Jesus, "and invited Me into your heart, you were born again — not in the body, but in the Spirit. Anyone who is born into the family of God begins as a babe in Christ. One can be ten or eighty years old; it does not matter. You all must become like children to enter My heavenly kingdom. Remember, you *are* but a little child!"

"I understand, my Lord," I replied. "May I now tell You my wish?"

"You don't need to," Jesus said. "I know it already. Ever since you first desired it as a lonely little girl, I have been trying to give you what you wanted. All the hunger, the hardships and agonies of war, all the disappointments, the ups and downs of your turbulent life have become blessings in My hand to give you insight, understanding, wisdom, and an obedient heart. Are you ready to receive these gifts more fully now?"

"Yes, my Lord," I said humbly. "But can I have one other wish, please?"

"As many as you want, My child," Jesus answered.

"May I someday share what You are teaching me right now with other babes in Christ? They need some insight and understanding in spiritual matters, too — and the wisdom that comes from God!"

"Someday you may," my Jesus said with tender love, "after you have matured a bit in Me. And when the time comes, we'll write the book together. I know you can't do it alone. After all, you are still but a little child!"

"Thank You, Jesus," I cried. "I love You!"

A Gift To Babes

This book has been written as a devotional study for anyone who is "but a little child" — a babe in Christ — and for those who are trying to guide and help new Christians.

Sometimes, those who have already matured in the Lord forget their early growing pains and demand too much of beginners. They answer in cliches when basic questions are asked. They make things too complicated and argue in theological terms when in reality all the essentials to the Christian life are clear and easy to understand. God's truth is simple, and very great. It is God's will that everyone understand His wisdom, no matter whether you are a seeking teenager, a housewife, or a highly educated scholar. You need only be humble enough to start where God begins with *all* His children: at the moment of spiritual rebirth.

So, my young fellow Christian, may you mature from day to day as you read this book and study and digest what God has provided — the milk of His Word!

INTRODUCTION

How To Use This Book

Welcome to the family of God! As a brand-new babe in Christ, you are undoubtedly wondering what your new life is all about, and feeling a bit overwhelmed. There are many things you can't understand yet. Your fellow Christians use words that are new to you, and act as though you're supposed to know everything they do!

Well, don't worry. Don't feel embarrassed because you have so many "dumb" questions in your heart. You see, those questions are not "dumb" at all. Everyone has them at the beginning; it's just that many mature Christians forget once they've found the answers.

I, for one, have never forgotten my confusion as a beginner, and pray I never will. I hope you won't either, so that you can better understand and help other babes in Christ once you do outgrow your "baby shoes"... and that *will* happen!

You must, however, decide for yourself just how fast you shall grow and mature. Even though you are a spiritual babe, you are not as helpless as a real infant. When you were born physically, you depended wholly on your mother or another person to provide for your basic needs. All babies must breathe, eat, get exercise and feel loved.

As a spiritual infant you have the same needs, but you yourself must determine when and how often to breathe, eat, and walk. Prayer is the breath of your soul, God's

Word is the food; your exercise comes by sharing the Good News with others. And God always makes you feel loved and wanted.

Remember too that this devotional book is not meant to be read in one sitting. If you drink too much milk at once, you get a tummy ache. If you try to digest too much spiritual truth in too short a time, you will end up discouraged. So take just one lesson at a time; but please, do more than simple reading. You must study this book, and to do so properly you will also need (a) your Bible, (b) pencil and paper and (c) sufficient time. It is best if you can set aside a regular hour and study at the same time each day. For more intensive study secure the study guide prepared for this book.

Each section in this volume contains several Bible references. When you come to one, look the passage up in your Bible and read every word carefully. Then, when you've completed a lesson, write down in your own words what you've learned that day. Don't be embarrassed; your notes are for your eyes only. Careful study and rewriting are very important to your spiritual growth. It is a well-known fact that students don't truly learn until they're able to restate material themselves that they've read or heard. So always write down what you think you've learned at the end of every lesson. You must digest the milk of the Word!

You will also find at the end of each section some short, simple prayers. These are samples of the kind of prayers you should learn to use during the day. It isn't wise to breathe just *once* daily, so learn to talk to Jesus often, as your best friend. You don't need to kneel down; you can speak to Him at any given moment — while you ride, work, play, or rest.

Most important of all, learn to be patient with yourself! It takes time to grow up! God is in no hurry — so why should you be?

ABOUT OURSELVES

1. How Are We Born Again?

I had just finished a message to three thousand young people at a youth congress and watched nearly all of them stand in special dedication to the Lord at the end of the meeting. Afterwards, a sweet teenage girl came to me and said: "Hansi, I didn't stand up with the others; I couldn't!" Then she burst into tears. We went to a quiet spot and I said, "Honey, don't you want to follow Jesus?"

"Yes," she said, "but I just don't know how!"

"Are you born again?" I asked.

"I'm not sure," she replied. "I've tried hard, but I'm still not sure!"

"What did you try hard?" I asked, puzzled.

"Well, I did what you said in your speech," she explained. "I invited Jesus into my heart several times, but it never seems to work. I go to school the next day and do wrong things again!" She cried some more.

I looked at her and my heart ached. "God, forgive us teachers and parents for what we do to our children," I thought, and shed a few tears myself. Then I said to her, "Open your Bible and read John 1, verses 12 and 13 to me." She read, and when she had finished I asked, "What does that passage say?"

She said, "To all who received Him, who believed in His name, He gave power to become children of God . . . who were born . . . of God."

"Alright," I said, "but what does it mean to 'receive' Him?"

"That's what I don't know!" she replied, with a forlorn look on her face.

"Well, let's read Revelation 3:20," I suggested gently. Again the girl read, and again, when she had finished, I asked "What does that passage say?"

"It says that Jesus stands at the door and knocks, and if anyone opens, He comes in," she answered.

"Notice that Jesus knocks and waits," I pointed out. "He doesn't push the door open, and He never forces His way in. Jesus' love is too gentle for that. So we must open the door ourselves, by our own choice and will, and invite Him in. Have you done that?" I asked quietly.

"Yes, several times," she said, looking miserable, "but I can't tell if He came in!"

"Why can't you tell?" I said

"Because I can't feel Him!" she exclaimed. "I've had no special experience or real conversion like some of my friends. I've grown up in a Christian home and read the Bible all my life. My mother says I should be a shining example to the kids in school but I can't; I just run along with the crowd. I'm hopeless!" She sobbed.

"Honey," I asked, "does the Bible say anywhere that you must feel what Jesus is doing? All it says is that you must believe in Him and open the door yourself, doesn't it? Now let's see what it means to believe in His name. What does His name mean?"

We read Matthew 1:21 together. "His name means that He will save His people from their sins," I said. "And that means He will rescue you from temptations you are not able to resist by yourself. Do you need Him for that?"

"I surely do!" she replied.

"Then I have news for you," I said, smiling. "You are already born again! You just don't dare believe it because it sounds too simple. You want to experience something out of the ordinary and, because it hasn't happened, you wonder if your rebirth is real. You see, some natural births are very dramatic and complicated, but others are born simply and normally. Spiritual births come in various forms, too. Yours was a very normal rebirth. You might have a hard time putting your finger on a certain experience or date when you were born into the family of God, but — nevertheless — it happened at the moment you did your part. You believed in Christ and invited Him into your life as the One who would save you from your sins. Okay?"

"But what if I go back to school tomorrow and do something wrong again?" she asked, still not completely convinced.

"My dear," I said, "go home and ask your parents a question. After you were born and learned to walk, did you fall down ever so often? Did you have fits of screaming and yelling; did you throw temper tantrums when someone didn't pick you up from your crib?"

"Yes, I did," the girl said, smiling under her tears. "My mom told me that I was always getting tummy aches and crying when I was a baby."

"Did your mother ever tell you that every time something went wrong with you, every time you fell and bumped your nose, she disowned you, and put you back into her womb to be born again?"

"No, of course not," she said; and new light came into her tear-stained eyes. "No, my parents would never disown me! They love me!"

"Do you think that God would ever do less than your parents," I asked, "when He loves you so much more than your parents ever could? He even died for you, He cares so deeply. When you are born into God's household, it is because God said He would receive you, you believe it, and *that* settled it! Now, is it settled for you?"

LET'S PRAY: Dear Jesus, thank You that I can trust Your words and not my own feelings. I did my part and now I believe that I am born again. Hold me tight for I cannot yet walk. Save me from wrongdoing, for I cannot stop by myself. I am so glad I found You and I want to love You, Jesus! Amen.

2. *Born in the Spirit*

What happens when we are born into God's family? Jesus taught us that rebirth takes place in the spirit (John 3:6-8). But where *is* the spirit in human beings?

The Bible tells us that we are put together in three parts: spirit, soul and body (I Thessalonians 5:23). Notice the order: In God's thinking the spirit comes first, then the soul, and last the body.

The earthly man, however, tends to think just the opposite. The body comes first, the soul next, and he doesn't even worry about his spirit; he doesn't know what it is. Nevertheless, if we didn't have our spirits we wouldn't live.

We read in Genesis 2:7 that God formed man's body from the dust of the ground and then breathed the breath of life into his nostrils and man became a living soul. God's breath of life became man's spirit and only as the spirit made contact with man's body was the soul produced, and man lived. So it is the spirit that gives us life (Numbers 16:22, John 6:63).

Everyone receives the spark of life from God when he is born into the world (Job 33:4). We begin to react to our environment with our first cry only when the breath of God comes into our little bodies and activates our souls. So it's important to understand, first, that God created not only our bodies but also the human spirit that made us come alive. Every living being has *that* spirit, for whenever it leaves, a person is dead and becomes a lifeless form again which returns to dust.

But what happens when we are reborn in God's *Holy Spirit?*

In Romans 8:16 God shows how His Spirit and ours connect to bear witness together that we are children of God. It is this connection that brings a new dimension to us. God's Spirit is eternal; He never dies. He creates something new in us.

In order to picture that, look at an ordinary light bulb. Our body is the outside glass, our soul is the wire. There is no connection to electrical power. As long as we live in our sins and are controlled by Satan, we are in darkness; there is no light. The glass and wire only exist until the bulb is eventually smashed and thrown away.

Say, though, that one day you decide to use the switch that God has provided. Your will says "yes" to God's power. His Holy Spirit has been available and waiting all along, and can now connect and unite with your spirit to make it a new spirit: the kind that is eternal, that can shed light.

When you are born again, a light turns on in you that you never had before. You also have a new life in you that natural death cannot turn off, for God's children, even the newborn spiritual babes, have eternal life (John 3:15). You don't earn it, you don't have to work for it. Some babes in Christ never had a chance to "mature" into it; they just received it. If that were not true, the thief on the cross could never have gone to Heaven (Luke 23:39-43).

LET'S PRAY: Dear Jesus, I am glad I don't have to earn my way to Heaven. I can't; I've tried, but it doesn't work. Will You help me understand how Your Holy Spirit and my spirit work together? Will You remind me that I don't need to be afraid of anything anymore, not even myself? I have eternal life; even if I must die now, I'll be with You. Thank You, Jesus! Amen.

3. The Human Soul

As we've just learned in the previous lesson, God clearly sees His children in three parts: the spirit, soul, and body. So let's compare ourselves to a sphere with three layers. The soul is the middle part and links the spirit and body together.

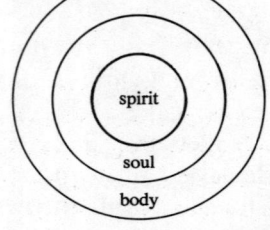

The spirit, of course, is the innermost part of a human being; in fact, it is sometimes called "the heart" in the Bible. Our spirit can either communicate with God's Holy Spirit or be controlled by Satan (John 4:24, Luke 11:24).

The body, on the other hand, is the outer shell that brings us in contact with the world through our senses.

The soul, however, is our own individual self, and makes us a conscious being. In our soul we carry our intellect, our emotions and our will power. And that particular combination makes us different from angels, which are spirits and on a somewhat higher level than humans (Psalm 8:5), and animals, which, although they have a body and the breath of life — as well as a certain degree of intelligence and even some emotions — do not have a free power of choice as do humans. Man was given dominion over the animal world (Genesis 1:26).

So, it is our special combination of intellect, emotion, and volition (the exercise of the will) that makes us distinctly individual selves and humans. It is our soul that stands between the body and the spirit, belonging to both.

It is extremely important for you, as a babe in Christ, to understand from the very beginning the differences between the spirit, soul, and body, and the effects one can have on the other. If you don't, Satan can confuse you constantly.

Before Adam sinned (Genesis 3) the spirit controlled his soul, and the body obeyed. When sin came, however, the "flesh" (body) began to rule the soul, which then lost its ability to conceive spiritual things (I Corinthians 2:14).

Unfortunately, many Christians rely totally on their souls; they approach everything with either their intellect or their emotions. All their decisions of free will are based only on reasoning power or on how they "feel" at any given moment. Worse yet, some Christians give the lusts and desires of their bodies first priority. Either way, they are not understanding God's plan for their lives. God wants you to be ruled by your spirit, not by your soul (self) or your body.

Your soul's importance lies in the fact that it is the essence of your personality, and the middle point of your entire being on which everything else turns. It decides if you sin or obey God's Spirit, and also determines if your spirit, your body, or the soul itself rules. No wonder the Bible calls man "a living soul"! No wonder, too, that God is trying so hard to make us all understand the difference between spirit, soul and body that He calls the Word of God a two-edged sword that divides soul and spirit (Hebrews 4:12)!

LET'S PRAY: Dear Lord, I don't really understand the three parts of me very clearly yet, but I *do* want to obey Your will. I want to be ruled by Your Spirit and do it Your way, but my body and soul are putting up a fight. I am so glad You understand. Just hold me very close, please! Amen.

4. The Human Body

The body is the last in God's order of spirit, soul and body. It is the part that is furthest away from the spirit — and the one that most often leads the soul into sin. That's why God often refers to the "flesh" when He speaks of sin, corruption and the unconverted person (Ephesians 2:3, Romans 9:8).

Nevertheless, the body is still important and in the reborn person becomes the temple of the Holy Spirit (I Corinthians 3:16). Let's compare, then, the temple of Old Testament times with your body.

We know that the temple was divided into three parts. The outer court could be seen and visited by anyone; all external worship and sacrifices were offered there. The inner court was the holy place where only the priests were permitted to enter in order to present oil, incense and bread to God. The center of the temple was the holy of holies — no man was allowed there, for God dwelled within. The high priest did enter once every year, but he had to go behind a veil, and for the people of Israel it was a very solemn time of atonement and trembling before God.

Man is God's temple also, and he too has three parts: The inner court is the soul, the holy of holies is our spirit where God's Spirit dwells, and our body is the outer court.

Let's think about the outer court and its functions.

People look at each other and see the body and conclude from there what's inside, just as men in Biblical times visited, viewed and worshiped in the outer court of the temple. So it is our body that reflects either God, self or Satan; it is the protective outer shell around our inner life.

In fact, our body has three main functions: (1) It is responsible for the existence of the whole person; after sin came into the world that responsibility became a survival or *defense* instinct. (2) It is the part that receives *nourishment* from day to day. And (3) it carries forward the *reproduction* of the human race.

It is in those three functions that the "fleshly" (unconverted) person sins the most.

For instance, let's remember that the first sin came into the world because Eve's appetite for a forbidden fruit was aroused. She was tempted by her bodily senses. She didn't need *nourishment,* for the garden had plenty of wholesome food to eat; she just lusted after something that appealed to her eye — which was one of her senses.

When we become God's children we understand that when we eat or drink or do anything else, we do it all to the glory of God (I Corinthians 10:31).

Reproduction was turned into human lust after Eve sinned through her appetite. In fact, the two seem to go together quite often. In I Corinthians 6:13, 15, Paul tells his babes in Christ in Corinth to watch out for both. In his day, the sins of feasting, drinking and lust were such a problem with some of the churches that Paul gave clear orders to his beloved Timothy not to install elders or deacons unless they had overcome in those points (I Timothy 3:3).

How does our body sin in *defense?* When tempers flare, anger kindles, and fists strike. And we do it all in self-defense because something or someone interferes with our own comfort or pleasure.

No wonder the Bible calls sin the "work of the flesh" (Galatians 5:19-21)! Even the sins of the soul and spirit are mostly initiated by the cravings of the body. Therefore, we must expect our hardest struggle to be that of overcoming sin in the body. We will often be very discouraged about it; Paul was (Romans 7:18-21) but he knew the answer to that bitter conflict: "There is therefore now *no* condemnation to them which are in Christ Jesus" (Romans 8:1).

LET'S PRAY: Dear Jesus, I already know about the struggle with my sinful body. I know what I should do, and I try; but I fail most of the time. I feel as helpless as a baby, and that's what I am! Help me to have patience with myself and to not condemn myself, for You are not condemning me. You pick me up when I fall, and love me. Thank You for such undeserved love! I want to love You, too! Amen.

FUNCTIONS OF THE SPIRIT

5. Communion

Man is divided into three parts, each of which serves three main functions. We have already learned that the body operates defense, nourishment and reproduction, and that the soul contains our will power, emotions, and our mind. Now let's examine the third dimension — the spirit — and its functions: communion, intuition, and conscience.

Let's look at communion first. Our spirit is able to commune with God. It is the only way that God can be approached and worshiped (John 4:23, Romans 1:9, Romans 7:6).

Because spirit can only be touched by spirit, the unconverted person is also open to communication with the devil. Some people's spirits, in fact, are totally inhabited by evil spirits. Jesus had to drive such evils out when He was on earth (Luke 7:21).

When the Holy Spirit comes to dwell in *our* spirit, however, all evil spirits must leave for we cannot worship God and Satan at the same time. Sometimes a person is so possessed by bad spirits that it takes special fasting and prayer to drive them out. Often, in fact, the possessed person is not able to do it by himself; he needs the prayers and power of other Christians to help (Matthew 10:1 and Matthew 17:14-21).

Unfortunately, many Christians just don't understand how to worship God in the spirit. They do it by intellect, emotion, or with their bodies only and carry on a "form of godliness" (II Timothy 3:5). This is what most babes in Christ do at first because to worship and walk in the spirit is new to them. It has to be learned just as an infant must learn to walk: one step at a time.

The trouble is that many Christians never outgrow their first spiritual baby shoes and remain "old" babes who still cannot walk in the spirit. That was a problem in the church of Corinth. Paul called the believers "babes" and "carnal Christians" (I Corinthians 3:1-3) because — although they had plenty of time to mature, and a lot of knowledge and grace and enrichment (I Corinthians 1:5) — they were not spiritual; they lacked the third dimension.

The believers of Paul's time had their heads stuffed full of learning, and when they preached they simply transmitted religious knowledge from one mind (soul or self) to others. They knew everything, they had clever and wonderful thoughts, they carried on intellectual discussions and most likely had much religious pride. That's why they argued so much; everyone was sure that his knowledge was better, smarter, and more profound than anyone else's. In other words, they *knew* better but didn't *act* differently than any ordinary uncoverted man (I Corinthians 3:3 RSV).

Sadly, we still have many Corinthians in the Christian churches of today. They either boast about all their head knowledge or go on and on about the special emotional experiences they've had from time to time. Others point to all their "works" of perfect attendance, paying of the tithe, the handing out of tracts, the works of charity and the keeping of laws as proof that they have arrived. Well, they haven't! Such things are good in themselves, but they don't make a person grow spiritually.

You and I and all Christians must learn to walk in the Spirit from the moment of our rebirth (Galatians 5:16, 25). If we do, we save ourselves years of frustration and fruitless livng. We also grow and learn to know God as a reality, even as our Father (Romans 8:15). We shall walk with Him and talk with Him and listen to Him as He speaks to us; we shall know what it means to be led by the Holy Spirit. It takes time — you will not know and understand it all instantly — but you can begin with the first step: Ask God to show you and teach you how to discern (distinguish) spiritual things (I Corinthians 2:10-14).

LET'S PRAY: Dear Jesus, please show me what it means to communicate with You in the spirit. I have a hard time grasping it now, but a baby doesn't need to understand how to walk before it takes its first step. So I am trying to wobble with my first few shaky steps, and I trust that You stand there with hands reaching out to catch me into Your arms. Thank You, Jesus, I am Your helpless, ignorant child. Teach me how to walk! Amen.

6. *Conscience*

Conscience is another function of the spirit. That function actually came into play before your rebirth, for it is the spirit that convinces us of sin (John 16:8). You and I were reborn and became a part of God's family because we finally realized that we were sinners in need of help. Yes, maybe we did try various ways in our life to get rid of sin and "be good." Young people who are brought up in Christian homes often try for years to reform themselves, to discipline the flesh, to control the lusts and passions and evil thoughts; but they eventually give up. They get so discouraged with themselves that they swing to the other extreme, rebel, and go wild.

Other youngsters manage to put up a good front and get "brownie points" from adults for good behavior. They're held up as shining examples to others who have gone "bad," and become very self-righteous and judgmental in the process.

Both types are described by Jesus in the story of the prodigal (spendthrift) son (Luke 15:11-32). In that parable, both sons needed to be convinced of their sins, and needed to understand that they couldn't change themselves. Nobody can change himself, neither of deepest wickedness nor of religious conceit and self-righteous superiority. One is as much a sin as the other and the Holy Spirit works on our spirits until we can face it.

When we confess our sins (I John 1:9) and confess Jesus Christ as our Savior and Lord (Romans 10:9, 10, 13) we are forgiven and Christ's blood washes away our *entire* past (I John 1:7). Notice that the Bible says we are cleansed from *all* sins, so that we are born into the kingdom without past sins. We start clean — and very helpless, for we are babes in the Spirit.

Now, our new spirit has caught a glimpse of that newness in Christ, but our soul and especially our body have a much harder time catching on because the body and soul cannot go back to babyhood and start over. The two outer parts of us are well set in their "fleshly" ways. We have habits that have formed over long years of natural living.

Our souls also carry pseudo-consciences which have been instilled in us by ourselves and our environment. "Pseudo" means counterfeit, and that is exactly the kind of conscience our self puts up as long as the spirit isn't led by God's Spirit so that we can see in a new way.

Satan uses a person's pseudo-conscience to confuse and torture him. As long as a person is not born again, he uses the pseudo-conscience mostly to rationalize wrong behavior.

"So what if I cheated (or lied or gossiped or did this or that)! I had a right to do so — the other people had it coming! They provoked me, my parents taught me so, etc., etc...."

We have a hundred excuses coming out of our minds and emotions to justify our behavior.

When we come to Christ, however, our spirit's conscience comes out of the dark coma and begins to whisper to us. I say "whisper" because our pseudo-conscience is shouting so loud that it is often very hard to hear the real conscience.

Satan will try anything to drown out that still small voice that comes from our new spirit. He will try to activate our self-conscience anytime the real conscience speaks up, and even when it doesn't. Satan will either tempt us to rationalize or torture us with guilt. It is the devil's favorite pastime to torture Christians with remorse and guilt. How tragic that so many Christians believe that guilt and the fear to which it is connected come from God! It *never* does, for God is love.

The conscience of our spirit comes to us as a still small voice that convinces us that we did something wrong. It comes from our very innermost part, past our self, our thinking and our feeling. It's the uneasiness and our troubled spirit that we sense regardless of whether or not we rationalize or try to atone by feeling guilty and punishing ourselves to no end. Both approaches are *wrong*. The only way to bring peace to your real conscience is to say: "*I am sorry*, God. Please forgive me. Jesus, will You wash me clean with Your blood?"

The moment we ask, Jesus does what He promised. Our sin is gone at that instant. He has forgotten it (Jeremiah 31:34, Psalm 85:2) but Satan hasn't. He comes back and tries to convince us that we must crucify ourselves over and over again because we are yet babes! Jesus was crucified for our sins and paid the price ahead of time; why not just thank Him and accept it? Tell Satan to get lost!

LET'S PRAY: Dear Jesus, I am still too ignorant to know when it is Your Spirit or the devil who troubles me. Help me to remember that You never use fear or guilt to punish me. You love me and when I say that I am sorry, it is all over. Help me to walk better very soon; so far I'm falling constantly, so I am constantly sorry, and You have to wash me clean all the time. I am so glad I am Your baby. Amen.

7. Intuition

Intuition, the third part of the spirit, is often the hardest of all for a babe in Christ to grasp. But you eventually *will,* of course, as you come to mature in Christ. So let us look now at the function of intuition.

With your intuition, you very directly sense the Holy Spirit. Through it, you know the revelations of God and the moving of the Spirit. It comes to you without the help or influence of your mind, your feelings or your will power; in fact, it is totally independent of any kind of outside influence. Your mind can help you to *understand* your intuition, but it is your spirit from which "knowing" actually comes.

The Bible, gives us many examples of the function of intuition in the human spirit:

Jesus, while He was here on earth as a human, perceived in His Spirit (Mark 2:8).

Paul was pressed in the spirit (Acts 18:5). He was also bound in the spirit, though his mind and emotions could not know what would befall him at a future time (Acts 20:22, 23). By intuition (in other words, direct revelation of God), he knew that the believers would see his face no more (Acts 20:25). And we see in I Corinthians 16:18, II Corinthians 7:13, and John 11:33 that intuition also often refreshes or moves our human spirit.

Unfortunately, our soul (self) frequently produces a counterfeit intuition that is really only our feelings. Many casual Christians mistake that "fake" intuition — their various emotions — for real intuition, and, as a result, waver between ecstasy and black despair. They go up and down like the waves of the sea and claim that it is the moving of the Holy Spirit. But it is *not!* We cannot receive true intuition as long as our own feelings reign (James 1:6,7). As a babe in Christ, you can expect to be tossed about in your early Christian experience by feelings and by your mind — particularly when other well-meaning Christians throw foolish doctrines at you — but you must never mistake such happenings for intuition (Ephesians 4:14, 15).

Perhaps I can give you a better idea of the difference between feelings, convictions, reasoning power and intuition by telling you about an experience I had while working in an office in Western Germany.

At the time, I was still a babe in Christ and was at the stage where I preached to anyone, no matter whether he wanted to listen or not. None of the other workers in the office were Christians, however, and I often served as the brunt of their teasing and ridicule. One of my superiors in particular seemed to enjoy being especially verbal about his unbelief, and would deliberately use the name of God in vain in my presence.

Well, one evening I decided I would teach that heathen fellow a lesson! I put together a whole list of Bible verses that would show him, once and for all, that he would *burn* for all his blasphemy and unbelief! Fortunately though, I remembered to pray first to ask the Lord for His blessing on my "missionary work."

When I stopped talking to God in order to listen to Him, my spirit's still, small voice said, "Don't do it! Throw that paper away! Don't preach to him at all; just be kind and sweet." I didn't know what to do!

I argued with God for a while, and pointed out (through my mind's reasoning power) that I was going to leave for America soon and wouldn't be able to serve witness — that is, preach! — to my fellow German workers. My feelings surfaced too, and complained loudly. How else, I thought, would I ever be able to make those unbelievers see the light?

Nevertheless, a certain deep "knowing" was within me, and I decided to obey it. For months afterward, I refrained from preaching, and went out of my way to be sweet and helpful to my fellow workers. And when the time came for me to leave for America, they gave me a farewell party.

Do you know who organized that party? The same cantankerous fellow I'd been so determined to "show up!" He made such an effort, in fact, that he nearly overdid it; I was touched, and we all cried a bit. And then, when it was all over and I thanked him for everything, he said quietly, "Mrs. H., I will never forget you. You know that I don't want to be religious but I can't help but admire *you* for it. We all need what you have. Who knows, I might even find it myself someday!"

Well, I never heard from that man again, but I don't need to be concerned about what has happened to him. I obeyed God's orders, and He in His wisdom can take care of the rest.

On that occasion, I learned to be quiet when my mind told me to speak; at other times, my intuition has prompted me to speak even though my mind said to be silent. In other words, I came to trust what God told me and learned not to lean on my own understanding (Proverbs 3:5). Undoubtedly, you too will experience such lessons; believe me, they're all part of a great adventure!

LET'S PRAY: Dear Jesus, I know that I have feelings (sometimes too many), but I don't know too much about my spirit's intuition yet. Please show me the difference, and don't let Satan confuse me. I want to learn such things but I know that it will take time. Help me to have patience with others and — most important — with myself. Please, refresh my spirit today. Amen.

ABOUT GOD

8. The Godhead

To define or describe God has been one of the greatest challenges to humans since the beginning of our time on earth. Nevertheless, the existence of God is proven universally simply by the existence of mankind (Romans 1:19, 20). Because we exist, God *has* to exist; someone had to start the human race. Truly, those who frown on believers in God by saying that such a conviction is "blind faith" can only be fooling themselves. It would take a lot more "blind faith" to believe that the earth, the people on it, and the millions of heavenly galaxies around us have come from "nothing," or have "just happened" without intelligent planning or a designed purpose!

God has revealed Himself to us in His creation (nature) and in the nature of man, in the Bible, and — most completely — in the person of Jesus Christ (John 1:18).

Of course, God has not revealed *everything* about Himself to us — rather, He has revealed only as much as we need to know. The reason for that is that our spirit, soul and body aren't able to grasp it all. So God in His wisdom has told us only as much as we are able to comprehend (Deuteronomy 29:29). Man has tried, through philosophy and speculation, to go beyond the revelation that God gave to us of Himself, but such efforts are futile — yes, even dangerous — because in the end mankind has to face his own limitations (Job 11:7, 38:1-4). Therefore we must go to the Scriptures, especially to the Gospel narratives and the teachings of the Apostles, to find true information about God.

The Bible tells us that God is One, but that He is three persons: the Father, the Son, and the Holy Spirit. The King James version of the Bible calls that concept the Godhead (Acts 17:29, Romans 1:20, Colossians 2:9). Jesus told His followers to go and teach all nations what He had taught them and to baptize them in the threefold name of the Godhead (Matthew 28:19).

Now, I must admit that — like all babes in Christ — I had a hard time grasping the idea of the deity and form of God. Jesus said that He and the Father were one (John 10:30, 38; John 17:21, 22). But how could they be one and yet be three distinct persons at the same time?

To clear up my confusion, someone once told me to look at water, ice and steam as an example. All three forms are different, but are of the same substance. Admittedly, such an earthly example can give only a limited picture of the real idea, but it helped me to understand how God is One and also a Trinity, and I hope it helps you too.

We know that God is a Spirit (John 4:24). We also know that God became flesh in Jesus (John 1:1, 14). Jesus told us that one who has seen Him has seen the Father (John 14:8-11). We might never understand *all* of it, but we can know that the Father, the Son, and the Holy Spirit *are* one in character, purpose and love. There is no bickering or jealousy between them — only divine harmony and order.

The Father is above everything and everybody and Christ is His beloved Son who was with the Father always (Hebrews 1:8). The Son came to this earth in the flesh to reveal the Father to us (John 1:14, 18). Ever since sin came to this planet, man has not been able to stand in the unveiled presence of the eternal God (in Spirit form) and live (Exodus 20:19-21). Sinful beings are consumed when they come near the power and might of the Father Himself (Psalm 76:7, Malachi 3:2, Nahum 1:6). Therefore

Jesus lowered Himself and became like us that we might be able to be in the veiled presence of God and live (John 14:19, Philippians 2:6, 7). Christ loves the Father above everything, and He wants to honor His Father above everybody. Christ submits Himself to the Father, though He is like Him and one with Him (I Corinthians 15:24-28). The Father loves the Son just as much and appoints Him to be heir of all things, and has set Him at the right hand of God's throne in heaven (Colossians 1:19, Ephesians 1:22, Hebrews 1:1-4).

The Holy Spirit was sent by Jesus to be our Comforter and Teacher (John 14:16-26). As Christ came to reveal the Father, so the Holy Spirit came to reveal the Son (John 16:14, John 15:26). The Holy Spirit dwells in us after rebirth (Romans 8:9).

LET'S PRAY: Dear Father, I don't know too much about You yet, but I am eager to meet You. As I learn more about Jesus, I will see You better. Holy Spirit, help me to learn quickly, for I want to know all three of You better than I could ever know any earthly thing or person. In the name of the Father, and the Son and the Holy Spirit. Amen.

9. God the Father

Why was it that Jesus had to come to earth to reveal His God-Father to the human race? Let me try to explain.

In the beginning, Adam and Eve knew God: the Father and the Son and the Holy Spirit. They communicated face to face with God and were not afraid (Genesis 3:8, 9).

When the couple disobeyed God, however, they both began to be afraid and to "die" (Genesis 2:17, 3:10). It's important to remember that the original meaning of that word "die" is "dying thou shalt die." Thus, men began to die in stages.

The part that died immediately at the first act of sinning was the part of the human spirit which had so far communicated (communed) with God face to face. At the time, conscience and intuition were most likely not activated as functions of the human spirit, because man lived in total harmony with God, and God spoke to him directly. Sin caused the light and life of the spirit to die first, and when the life of the spirit began to die, the soul and body started to fall apart and die too.

As men's enlightened spirits died, they lost more than just their ability to commune with God — they also were no longer born in the image of God. Now they were born in the image of Adam instead (Genesis 5:1-3). They didn't know God and His character anymore. Rather, they began to worship the god of this world: Satan. (John 12:31, John 14:30, II Corinthians 4:4). Since both God and Satan are spirits, men decided to re-establish "the face to face" communication in their own sinful way: In rebellion to God, they made themselves gods of metal, stone and earthly substances that could be seen and touched. Satan encouraged such practices in his followers, and still does today, because he knows that God does not want us humans to do such things (Isaiah 2, Psalm 115:1-9).

Eventually, things got so badly out of hand that God had to destroy all the wickedness on earth by a flood and start over with just one family that still knew the true God (Genesis 7). That one family not only carried the story of the true God with them but also His promise that someday — through that family — God would send "the seed of the woman" (Genesis 3:15) who would destroy the god of this earth.

Until Jesus came, the image and nature of God was constantly distorted by Satan, even to those who held steadfast to the worship of the true God. Satan always tries to make us picture God as a hard, cruel, destructive and revengeful tyrant.

After the flood, from the line of Shem (Genesis 11:10, 26), God found Himself a very special man: Abraham. God chose Abraham to be the earthly father of a special nation (Genesis 12:1-3). Through the people of that nation, God would bless every family on earth. But the same sad story continued!

By God's promise, Abraham became the forefather of the people of Israel, and the Israelites became the Jewish nation into which Jesus was born. The Israelites were God's chosen people and had been called to show the heathen nations the true God (Deuteronomy 7:6-14).

Later, as you study the Old Testament in detail, you will find that Israel and the Jews failed to represent the true Father-God to the world. They forgot the love and friendship of God toward their forefather Abraham. They forgot what Moses, David, Daniel and all the prophets said about God. Of course, it is true that God is "merciful and gracious, longsuffering and abundant in goodness and truth, keeping mercy for thousands, forgiving iniquity and transgression and sin" (Exodus 34:6, 7). But He is also a God of justice who will "by no means clear the guilty."

By the time Christ was born in a manger, the Jews had buried the loving Father image of God under a mountain of burdensome worship requirements and senseless rituals and a cold form of ceremonies. They saw Him *only* as a God of justice and revenge. People who wanted to serve the true God by trying to obey their religious leaders (rabbis) toiled under an extremely heavy burden. They could find no rest for their souls, nor peace for their troubled consciences. And because people had a very wrong and low picture of God, Satan triumphed.

So Jesus came at the fullness of time, to make "sons" out of "people under the law" (Galatians 4:4, 5). Jesus came to restore the "Father" image of God by *being* like His Father (John 17:26, 1:18). He also came to make us children of the Heavenly Father (I John 3:1, 2). And He taught us to pray to God as our Father without fear and in perfect trust (Matthew 6:8, 9; Luke 11:2, 13).

Let's Pray: Dear Father in Heaven, help me not to be afraid of You and to trust You. Don't let Satan tell me that You are going to do bad things to me because I make so many mistakes every day. You love me, Father; I know because Jesus said so. I love You, too, and I am so thankful that I have a right to call on You — through Jesus, Your Son. Amen.

10. God the Son

We know that the second person of the Godhead is God's only Son, who became the "only begotten Son" when He came to this earth (John 1:14, 18). He was with the Father always (Hebrews 1:8). Christ is the Creator God (Colossians 1:16, 17; John 1:3, 4).

It was Christ who laid the foundations of the earth and hung the worlds in space. He designed the tiniest flower and the most majestic landscapes. His strength set the mountains (Psalm 65:6). He made the sea and His hands formed the dry land (Psalm 95:5). He is our Maker (Psalm 95:6, 7). He designed the form of Adam and blew the breath of God into his nostrils.

Because the Godhead is *One*, it is fair to assume that God the Father and the Holy Spirit were involved in the creation act too. In Genesis 1:26 we learn that the Godhead planned together; Genesis 1:2 tells us that the Spirit of God moved upon the waters. But, Christ was the active agent, appointed by the Father to be "in charge" and do it (John 1:3). Whatever Christ did and designed, He did to glorify His Father and to proclaim the love of God and His glory (Hebrews 1:1-3).

When Christ created the earth He knew that someday He Himself would walk the earth and suffer and die. He created the tree that would later become His cross. He knew that He would become the Lamb of God that was slain long before the foundation of the earth was laid (Revelation 13:8, Romans 16:25, II Timothy 1:9). He Himself had given Eve the promise of a Redeemer at the time of the first sin. He had been foretold by the prophets and was promised to Abraham. He was the "Messiah" (the Anointed One) for whom Abraham's people — the Jews — looked from generation to generation.

So, when the time was right, the Son of God laid His honored position down and came to this earth (Galatians 4:4).

The Bible does not reveal in what form Christ existed before He became a human being. We only know that He lowered Himself to become like us (Philippians 2:6-8). Christ came and the Father *gave*: He gave His only Son *forever* to the human race!

When Christ left heaven to come to this earth He knew that He would never return in the same form to His Father. The Father knew it, too. But the Father loved us, His created children, so much that He gave His only Son to us (John 3:16).

God said: "Lo, I come to do Thy will, O God" (Hebrews 10:7) "...a body hast Thou prepared Me" (Hebrews 10:5). The Father prepared the body of a little human baby for His beloved Son (Luke 2:7). And that act was such a lowering of position that our human minds cannot even comprehend it until we enter heaven and see for ourselves what Christ left to come to our earth! He *had* to become human for us — if He had come in the glory that He had before the world existed (John 17:5), sinful men would have died in His presence.

Christ in human form became the visible expression of God's invisible glory (II Corinthians 4:6). He became the audible "Word" (John 1:14) of His Father's thoughts toward us; He became the image of His Father to us human beings (Colossians 1:15). And He did even more that that.

Christ not only humbled Himself and became human, He became a servant (Philippians 2:7, 8) and He died the death that was used to punish slaves. A curse rested upon those who were crucified (Deuteronomy 21:23, Galatians 3:13).

In His life and in His death, the Son had just one desire: to show us that God was love, that He had not forsaken the sinner, that God Himself paid the price for sin. The Son of God, the second person of the Godhead, became by His life and death on earth our "Big Brother" (Romans 8:29). Through Him we are adopted into the heavenly family of God.

Significantly, we know that He did not carry the name "Jesus" (Matthew 1:21, Luke 2:21) until He came to *us* (Isaiah 9:6). We know too what that name means: "He will save His people from their sins." It was a common name given to Jewish baby boys by their parents, who loved God and believed that God would send One to bring salvation to Israel. And Christ was the One!

When Christ had finished His work on earth He returned to heaven to be part of the Godhead again. He took with Him His human body and His human name. We know that He is coming again someday in the same name and form to take us home to heaven (Acts 1:11).

LET'S PRAY: Dear Jesus, I can't even comprehend what You did. I am afraid that because I can't understand it fully I might take Your love and the cross for granted. Teach me through the Holy Spirit to gain deep insights and to learn to appreciate Your great sacrifice. Thank You, Jesus, that You became human. I know that You can understand me because of it. Help me to understand You, too. Amen.

11. God the Holy Spirit

The third member of the Godhead is the Holy Spirit, or

Holy Ghost. The Bible does not reveal too much about the nature of the Holy Spirit, but many Bible scholars have speculated about it. Some believe that the Holy Spirit was only a "power" sent by the Father. Others imagine Him as Christ's "influence" on this earth. Most Christians in the various denominations, however, believe and accept the Holy Spirit as a person and part of the Godhead.

We see in the New Testament that the Holy Spirit has personal characteristics: He has knowledge (I Corinthians 2:11), a will (I Corinthians 12:11), a mind (Romans 8:27), love (Romans 15:30), communion (II Corinthians 13:14) and grief (Ephesians 4:30). People can insult Him (Hebrews 10:29) and lie to Him (Acts 5:3, 4).

The Holy Spirit was present at the creation (Genesis 1:2). He also took a part, mysterious to our limited minds, in the conception of Jesus (Matthew 1:18, 20). In fact, the Holy Spirit worked among men long before Christ was born. It was in Old Testament history, when people got so very wicked and God had to destroy them, that God said, "My Spirit shall not always strive with man" (Genesis 6:3).

The Spirit of the Lord came upon such men as Saul (I Samuel 11:6), David (Psalm 51:11), and Joel, who prophesied about God's Spirit (Joel 2:28, 29). At the time of Christ's birth, people such as Elizabeth (Luke 1:41), Zacharias (Luke 1:67) and Simeon (Luke 2:25, 26) acted under the influence of the Holy Spirit.

Truly, the Holy Spirit had a special part in Christ's ministry on this earth!

The Spirit descended in the form of a dove on the occasion of Jesus' water baptism (Mark 1:10) and the same Spirit led our Lord into the wilderness of temptation (Mark 1:12).

Luke tells us that Christ was "full of the Holy Ghost" (Luke 4:1), and John the Baptist foretold that Jesus would baptize with the Holy Ghost (Matthew 3:11).

Christ told His disciples that after He had gone back to heaven the Holy Spirit would teach them. He would also help them remember things that had been taught by Christ (John 14:26).

On the last night before His crucifixion, Christ gave His disciples a special promise: "I'll send you another Comforter," Jesus said, "and He will stay with you forever" (John 14:16). This has special meaning to all Christians, because the original definition of the word "Comforter" is "one called alongside." The Holy Spirit, then, was to carry on the work of Jesus in all the world, throughout all ages.

The disciples, however, did not understand, and were sad when Christ spoke about His departure (John 16:6). Christ even told them, "It is very expedient (in other words, 'to your advantage') that I go away. If I don't leave, the Comforter will not come. If I go, I will send Him to you" (John 16:7).

Nevertheless, the disciples grieved — and I can sympathize with them. I wondered for a long time what could possibly be better than having Jesus here on earth, in person, right in our midst.

The comparison of water, ice and steam to the Godhead, however, helped me to understand the special role of the Holy Spirit on earth. I look at it this way:

God the Father is represented by the water. If water were to cover the entire earth, we would not live. The might and power of water is overwhelming, just as is the might and power of God the Father.

Christ, when He became man, tied Himself to a single form. Ice does that, too. Christ isn't cold, of course; He is beautifully warm. But He is one form which cannot be at every place at the same time — except through the Holy Spirit!

The Holy Spirit, however, like steam (or fog), *can* spread over the whole globe and be everywhere at once.

He can spread thin or thick, as people let Him, and when He concentrates in one place there is power! He can even go into people — and that's where He has been ever since you were born again: in *you*!

LET'S PRAY: Dear Father, I am so glad You arranged everything so wonderfully for me. First, You sent Your Son. Even though You are God, it must have been hard for You to watch Him live and die on earth. But You and Jesus together did it for me. Then, You sent the Holy Spirit to stay with me always! I shall never be alone again, even to the time when Jesus Himself returns to earth, so that I might see Him. It is all overwhelming to me, but I love it! Thank You, Father, Son and Holy Spirit! Amen.

ABOUT SATAN AND THE BEGINNING OF SIN

12. Origin of Evil

In the beginning there was God (Genesis 1:1). God is love (I John 4:8). God is perfect and doesn't change (Matthew 5:48, Malachi 3:6). God created the heavens and the earth and everything He made was "good" and perfect (Genesis 1:31). It was so good that the sons of God shouted together for joy and the morning stars sang (Job 38:7).

That last passage from Job is essential to understanding the origin of evil, because it tells us that other created beings of God already existed when the earth came into existence. It's true that at the end of creation week God had only one human son and one human daughter, but it's apparent from the text — and from other passages that you will come across as you get deeper into the study of the Bible — that He also had many angels (sons and morning stars) in different classes or ranks (Genesis 3:24, Isaiah 6:2).

The story of the origin of evil begins with an angel called Lucifer (Isaiah 14:12-14). He occupied a very high and exalted position as a covering cherub (Ezekiel 28:14, 15). Lucifer was created perfect "till iniquity was found in him." Like all beings of God, he was given complete freedom of choice (we shall study that subject more completely in a later lesson). But Lucifer misused that freedom and turned against God. His first sin was pride.

Lucifer was so proud of his beauty and wisdom — both of which were gifts that God had created and given to him — that he fell from his special position (Ezekiel 28:12-19). And he started a war in heaven.

The beautiful angel became a hateful dragon who fought against God; he didn't fight alone, either. Lucifer managed to seduce one third of the angelic host (Revelation 12:4). As a result, he was cast out of heaven and received another name: devil, Satan (Revelation 12:7-9). The rebellious angels were cast out, too (Revelation 12:9, II Peter 2:4, Jude 6). Thus, his war was lost.

The reason for Satan's rebellion and war was jealousy. Satan decided to sit above the stars (angels) of God and on the throne of God (Isaiah 14:13). The Father-God, however, had put Christ, His Son, on the throne forever and exalted Him above everything (Hebrews 1:1-13). Satan wanted to be like God — part of the Godhead — (Isaiah 14:12-14), and coveted a God-like position.

Because he wasn't permitted to reign in heaven, however, he decided to find another kingdom where be could become "god." And the earth looked like a fine place to do just that. So while the good angels sang and rejoiced over that beautiful new creation called earth, and over those two special beings created in the image of God, Satan and his angels (demons or evil spirits) laid their plans.

The devil had watched and listened carefully to what the Creator said and did. He knew that God had planted a garden, and had put two special trees in it. One was the Tree of Life, the other the Tree of Knowledge of Good and Evil. He knew too that the newly created couple — Adam and Eve — was permitted to eat freely everything available, *except* fruit from the tree of knowledge (Genesis 2:16, 17). He also knew that Adam was "in charge" of the earth and was God's "keeper" of the garden, and had dominion over everything (Genesis 1:26). By observing that one restriction from God, Adam and Eve acknowledged God's sovereignty and showed their loyalty to Him.

So, Satan used the guise of a serpent and seduced man into disobedience (Genesis 3:1-6). As a result, he brought sin and death upon the entire human race that was yet to come (Romans 5:12).

Adam sold out to Satan, and the devil became the ruler, prince or "god" of this earth (John 14:30). The situation looked hopeless, but God — as always — was still in control. At the moment of deepest agony for Adam and Eve, God's love gave them a promise and a new hope (Genesis 3:15, Titus 1:2).

How typical of God! He wasn't angry and revengeful; He was Love even at a time when His creatures had disobeyed Him for no good reason. He cursed the serpent (Genesis 3:14) for deceiving His two children, and He reassured Eve. He also gave them some animal skins to cover their nakedness — and I suspect that He even slew the first little lamb for those skins (Genesis 3:21). If so, it was a symbol of the Lamb of God that would someday be slain to take away the sins of the world. Yes, the *Lamb* would be victorious over Satan! (Revelation 17:14).

LET'S PRAY: Dear Jesus, it doesn't seem fair that all of us suffer trouble and sin because Adam sinned. Neither is it fair that You had to pay the price of death for our first parents and all of us who followed them. It all happened because someone decided to turn against You in the beginning. As I see evil in the light of Your love, I want no part of it. Deliver me from *all* evil. Amen.

13. Why God Permitted Evil

As we have just learned, in the beginning there was no evil. In the beginning was God. God is love (John 3:16, I John 4:7, 8). He is also a God of justice who cannot ignore and overlook wrong things (Romans 11:22). Religious scholars describe God as "omnipotent," "omniscient" and "omnipresent," and — as you become better acquainted with the teachings of the Bible — you will learn that they are right. We also know that God is uncreated or self-existing, and that He created everything in the universe.

However, since the Bible is God's Word to humans alone, it concerns itself mainly about things here on earth. When it comes to things or beings not related to earth life, we have only fragmented reports; and even they are somehow related to human history. The Bible does not give us a detailed description about the self-existence of God and His creation of angels or other beings in the universe. It only tells us that God created everybody and everything.

By studying God's character and His unchanging ways of doing things, though, we *can* learn some things without having a specific Biblical reference to them. We can rely on the Holy Spirit to open our understanding of the characteristics and attributes of God, for God doesn't change (Malachi 3:6). He is the great and only "I Am" (Exodus 3:14). He is also love.

God's love is called agape in the New Testament. The classic definition of that kind of love is given to us in I Corinthians 13. It is also the term used in the texts that show Christ's love for man (Romans 5:8, Ephesians 2:4, I John 3:1 and many more). Agape is the relation between God and Christ (John 15:10, 17:26). And it is also used in certain cases to refer to human love (Romans 12:9, II Corinthians 6:6). Galatians 5:22 lists agape as the first fruit of the Spirit that we shall grow.

Agape love has certain unchangeable traits: it never "seeketh its own," it cannot be exercised by force, it cannot be commanded or demanded. Love does everything out of love, not because it has to.

When God contemplated the creation of creatures, He had to make a decision. Would He create beings who would worship and obey Him like robots — like machines that He turned on or wound up like a music box? Or would He create beings who had a free will, a freedom of choice to worship God because they loved Him enough to *want* to worship Him?

Well, as we have learned, God is love. So He created sons and daughters who were free to worship and love Him by choice — or to turn against Him if they so willed.

God's gift of freedom of choice was His greatest gift of love to the beings He created. Why? Because with it, God opened the door to the possibility of evil, which in turn was the first step toward Calvary's hill and God's own supreme sacrifice.

But God gave the gift anyway and chose at the same time to die on a cross rather than force anyone to serve Him. Force, of course, is absolutely contrary to the nature of God, and He cannot be untrue to Himself and His love (II Timothy 2:13).

When God's children received the gift of free will, they had to have more than one side to choose from. In the beginning, when God created angels and mankind, there was only one reality to choose: God, the good side. So He permitted the possibility of evil. And that possibility became reality (the second reality) when Lucifer turned into Satan by his own free will. Satan misused the gift of freedom of choice, and now hates it; he never gives his subjects that freedom. Instead, he forces, deceives, traps and enslaves anyone under his power.

Adam and Eve also misused God's gift, and sinned against Him. They subjected themselves by their own choice to the evil power of Satan.

Did God design and formulate His plan to rescue us humans from the bondage of evil and the slavery of sin simply as an afterthought, once Adam had sinned?

No, He didn't. God did not ordain that sin should exist. He didn't create sin, but He did permit its possible existence and He, being Love, planned to meet the terrible conflict on His own terms. Long before the foundation of the earth was laid, at the moment when God gave freedom of choice to His beings (Revelation 13:8), Christ agreed to be the Lamb that would set men free. For centuries, God kept silent about the mystery of the Lamb (Romans 16:25). But when the horrible moment came, He revealed His plan, and acted. And love, of course, acts just opposite to the way evil does. Whereas Satan exalted himself (Isaiah 14:13, 14), God *lowered* Himself into the form of a servant or slave (Philippians 2:6, 7). What more can God do?

LET'S PRAY: Dear Jesus, You — who gave us all a freedom of choice — gave up that freedom for Yourself when You died on a cross. You suffered the death of a servant, a slave. I confess that such love boggles my mind; I cannot grasp it. I am so glad that I don't have to depend on my own understanding, that all I need to do is accept Your love. Thank You for setting me free! Amen.

14. Sin and Death

For a long time, I wondered about two things: (1) Why didn't God destroy Satan and his angels when they rebelled? If He had taken care of evil immediately, we humans wouldn't have to be in such a mess. And (2) why did Christ have to die on a cross? If He had simply come to earth and lived among us and died of old age before He went back to heaven, wouldn't that have been enough?

The answer to both questions lies in the nature of God. He is perfect Love, and perfect (absolutely fair and righteous) justice. He is also unlimited wisdom!

When the first rebellion occurred, God didn't "rescue" Satan and the evil angels. Instead, according to Jude 6, they were held or permitted to exist until final destruction. Some people believe that Satan and everyone will finally be saved, but the Bible doesn't teach that. Jesus says that all evil will burn, and that the ones on God's side will be with God (Matthew 13:30, 3:12).

God has not brought the final destruction of Satan for several reasons. First, He is love and completely fair. Satan obviously believed that he had a plan worthwhile enough to risk losing heaven and to burn in hell. So God permitted him to demonstrate his plan.

Satan tricked Adam out of his dominion and found himself a "demon"-stration ground for his demons. The earth is the great "showplace" of the conflict between good and evil.

Who is observing the battle? The entire universe, the angels and men. Paul calls our earth a *theater* for everyone under heaven and on earth (I Corinthians 4:9 LB). The earth is the stage where God's creatures (including human beings) can see or "experience" the two sides of our freedom of choice.

Evil has demonstrated since the fall of Adam its sinister program. And God has demonstrated His kingdom of love ever since He made His creatures.

If God had destroyed the rebels immediately when they sinned, the nature of evil would never have been revealed to us (Ephesians 2:3, II Thessalonians 2:7-10). God's loyal angels — and perhaps we humans, too — would have wondered if God were keeping something special from His creatures. Fear would have entered into the freedom of choice. "If we don't obey," we might have thought, "God will annihilate us — so we'd better be good!" God, however, did not want to be served in fear. His love desires that His creatures want to love and worship Him. It seems that in order to make that choice, men and angels needed to see the contrast between God's regime and Satan's. So God did not destroy Satan and his evil demons, for only as the years unfolded would all created beings have the chance to see the rebellion in its true light and to observe the justice and mercy of God.

The Bible does not tell us why God had no plan of salvation for Satan and the angels. Was it because Satan sinned in the clear, unveiled presence of God's love? What *more* could God have done but *be* HIMSELF — if that isn't enough, what more can even Love do?

In the case of Adam and Eve, however, it wasn't pure, undiluted evil rebellion; Eve was tricked. Could the serpent be right when he said she would not surely die? What was this knowledge of good and evil? She then took the fruit to Adam, who in turn was seduced by Eve. But he did make a clear choice when he took the fruit and ate it (Genesis 3:4-6).

I've often wondered why Adam chose to do so. Did he love his helpmate so much that he wanted to die with her? The Bible doesn't say, but we do know from Romans 5:19 and I Corinthians 15:22 that in Adam everyone sinned. Sin is a deliberate choice of disobedience toward God (I John 3:4, James 4:7). Adam chose to disobey God, but he didn't do it out of pride, envy or jealousy, and God knew it. His two earth children were deceived by a murderer, a "father of lies" (John 8:44), so God's love took over and showed mercy on them.

God could not change His verdict toward sin, however. Anyone who sins must die (Ezekiel 18:4). God's nature is like the sun in the sky. The same sun that gives warmth, growth and life to our planet when its beams reach the *right* kind of soil also dries and hardens clay to bricks and destroys life when conditions are not favorable to growth. The sun stays the same — it's the condition of the soil that determines whether there will be life or burning and total destruction. Likewise, God never changes, nor does His Word. Justice demanded the payment for sin, and God — perfect Love — designed a plan where both could meet — on Golgotha!

In other words, the Creator Himself took the responsibility for the creatures He had made. He met the demands of justice while, at the same time, He demonstrated on the stage of this earth His program of perfect love. It was for justice and love's sake that Christ had to die on the cross. Perfect justice cannot condemn an innocent man, and Jesus was sinless, innocent and not born under the curse of sin (Hebrews 4:15, Matthew 27:24, I Peter 1:19). When they nailed Him on a cross, He became a "cursed" man (Deuteronomy 21:22, 23). And under the curse, He paid the price that justice demanded and — at the same time — showed the whole universe to what extent God's love goes. What more could even God do to reveal Himself to us?

LET'S PRAY: Jesus, I have a difficult time thinking about You on the cross. My nature recoils with the thought of Your pain and suffering. All those things are so new to me that I often wonder if I'll ever be able to comprehend it fully. All I can say now is: Thank You, Jesus, for paying the price of my sins! Help me not to willfully disobey You. Help me to learn how to love You and others! Amen.

ABOUT PRAYER

15. We Talk to God

Prayer is our spiritual breath. The more regularly we learn to breathe (pray) the more it will be well with our souls (Luke 18:1).

Prayer has many functions. With it, we worship God publicly in church and prayer groups. Such prayers usually keep to a certain "form" that begins with addressing the Father and ends with asking in Jesus' name. Why? Because Christ gave us a perfect example of such a prayer: the Lord's Prayer (Matthew 6:9-13). And in John 14:13 and John 15:16, Jesus tells us to pray to the Father and also to ask in His name.

In our private prayer-life, however, we may talk to God as we talk to our best friend. Remember that the Father has given all the power, honor and authority to Christ (Matthew 28:18). And in Christ we see the Father, so we come to the Son. Thus, you may pray directly to Jesus as you talk with God — babes in Christ often find this easier, simply because they can visualize Jesus more easily, and thus feel more comfortable.

In other words, don't worry too much about the "form" of prayer — just learn to pray as naturally as you breathe. For a babe in Christ, prayer first becomes a way to get acquainted with God, to learn to speak and communicate with Him as a Father and Friend, to receive from Him what is needed for growth. Just as a natural baby must use communication to "know" that he or she belongs to the family, so must a babe in Christ communicate to be fully aware of belonging to the family of God.

An earthly child who withdraws from its environment and refuses or is unable to communicate will never know the beautiful sense of belonging that comes with greater awareness. We refer to such a child as being "autistic;" to watch such a person is pure agony. Parents want to shower their child with love, words of affection and everything else they have to offer, but the autistic child has no way to receive such gifts. A blank stare, an emotionless expression, a monotonous rocking motion and an imprisoned self are the sad results of an inability to communicate.

Unfortunately, God has many spiritual children who are "autistic" too. What a tragedy that is! Surely, such a sad thing is not His will. So we *must* learn to communicate with Him — and to do so, it is important to observe some spiritual laws.

For our physical lives, God provided us with noses and airpipes through which to breathe — but unless we *choose* to breathe, we turn blue in the face and eventually die. Suffocation can occur spiritually as well physically if we don't "breathe." So the beginning of communication is our *wanting* to do so! We must *want* to talk to God as a Friend and Father (Romans 8:15).

The next step, of course, is to contact God. But which of our three parts (spirit, soul and body) does that? John 4:22, 23 and Ephesians 6:18 tell us that it is our spirit.

Remember, however, that you are a *babe* in the spirit, and babes need to learn to talk. So at first, your spiritual prayer can only be a babe's babbling. Too often we don't know how we should pray as we ought, but "the Spirit" (the Holy Spirit) "maketh intercession for us with groanings which cannot be uttered" (Romans 8:26).

So, since we don't know how to sense the three functions of our spirit (communication, conscience and intuition) very well in spiritual babyhood, we must *begin* by praying with our soul. First we use our will, then we engage our mind and emotions to talk to God. The soul is often the nurse of the babylike spirit, and helps us reach deeper spiritual things and growth.

Paul says that he prays in the spirit *and* with his understanding — his mind — and both have their place (I Corinthians 14:15)!

Babes use their wills together with their minds and emotions to talk to God, and the Holy Spirit does the rest. So, with our understanding (our minds) we learn to grasp the principles of prayer.

Why is it that we have to *ask* God for things in order to receive? (Matthew 7:7, Luke 11:9). Doesn't God *know* — because He is all-knowing — what we need before we ask Him (Matthew 6:8)?

Yes, He does know, and He is eager to give us more than we ask or even dare think (Ephesians 3:20). But the fact remains that we must first come to Him and *ask*. The reason for that is important, and is tied into God's gift of freedom of choice to His creatures.

God's love gave us a free will, which is part of our souls. And with that free choice and will, we choose for or against God; we worship Him or the devil; we ask or we don't ask. And because God doesn't believe in force, He will not even force upon us what is *very good* for us unless we ask first (James 4:2).

That doesn't mean, however, that those who ask nothing receive absolutely nothing. God is love and — true to the nature of agape love — some of His gifts "spill over." With His perfect love, God cannot help Himself and He sustains life for both the just and unjust (Matthew 5:45).

Nevertheless, the *special* things that God has reserved for His children are available only when we ask.

Does that mean that we can go to God and ask for a million dollars, the mate of our choice or any crazy thing, and get them?

Well, remember one thing: God always answers every prayer that comes to Him, but He will never give you anything that could harm or destroy you. He loves you! Your mind will ask some foolish things before you learn to ask "in His will" (I John 5:14), but the Holy Spirit will immediately step in — in other words, make intercession (Romans 8:26) — and say, "Father, the babe doesn't understand better yet and I request that We say 'no'!"

God has four kinds of answers for His children: (1) "Yes, My child." (2) "No, My child, that is not good for you." (3) "Wait, My child, you have to grow some more first." And (4) "Try this, My child; this is better for you and you will like it better, too."

LET'S PRAY: Dear God, I don't know how to talk to You yet. I ask constantly for everything within my reach. I seem to think only of what I want. And I pout and yell when I don't get my way. Babies are like that, and I am glad You understand! How grateful I am that You give me only what is best for me! I love You, Father! Amen.

16. God Talks to Us

Does God "speak" to His children?

This is a sensitive issue among evangelicals. Some say that He does, and others argue that it is all a big self-delusion. A third group simply say they'd like to know how they can find such a new dimension in their prayer life, and ask how it is done.

I have many letters in my files in which people ask, "Hansi, you say and write in your books that God said things to you. Does He *really* speak to you in an audible voice, or is it just a thought or impression?"

Well, before I answer that, let's see what the Bible says about the subject.

We know that Adam and Eve heard the voice of God (Genesis 3:8).

We also know that God's voice spoke to Israel on different and often dramatic occasions (Deuteronomy 4:32, 33). And God spoke face to face to Moses, as with a friend (Exodus 33:11). In fact, Moses' great burden for Israel was that they would *listen* to God's voice and obey (Deuteronomy 4:12, 8:20, 13:18).

Other Old Testament prophets spoke about the voice of God (Psalm 29:3, Jeremiah 42:6, Zechariah 6:15 and many more).

Pharaoh refused to listen to God's voice (Exodus 5:2).

When Christ came to this earth He became the audible Word of His Father to this world (John 1:14).

Christ gave us clear teachings about who would hear His voice (John 10:3, 16, 27). Notice too that His sheep at the time of His earthly presence (who were then in His fold) heard His voice. Other sheep (of another time or place) would hear His voice also, according to John 10:16.

"Everyone that is of the truth *heareth* My voice," Christ said boldly to Pilate shortly before He went back home to His Father in heaven (John 18:37).

All these texts seem to give clear evidence that Christ has every intention of *speaking* to *anyone* who is one of His sheep and loves Him.

There are many voices in the world, however (I Corinthians 14:10). How can we distinguish God's voice from all the others?

Well, how long does it take for a little baby to recognize his parents' voices? Not very long, as we all know! Before the baby's gurgling and babbling sounds turn into recognizable words, his face lights up when mom or dad bends over his crib. Does a baby learn to understand words quickly? Of course—just ask a little tyke if he wants to go "bye-bye" and watch the smile spread big and wide as he raises his arms in anticipation!

Just as a baby knows a voice before it has learned to walk, so can we *know* and *hear* the voice of our Shepherd before we walk and talk maturely. Little lambs know the Shepherd too!

And what is God's favorite way of speaking? Let's read part of the story of Elijah (I Kings 19:9-12).

Elijah was ready for a great and new revelation of His God. He was ready for storm, earthquake and fire to teach that wicked Jezebel and all the children of Israel a mighty lesson — but as things turned out, Elijah had to learn a big lesson himself. God wasn't in any of the things Elijah thought were needed at the moment; God was *only* in "a still small voice."

Where does that still small voice dwell? In our spirit — in the innermost part of ourselves. It is deeper than our thinking and reasoning, it is removed from our stormy and fiery feelings, it is so deep and soft that we have to *learn* to listen that we may recognize it.

Unfortunately, we often drown out that still small voice with our own thoughts, or let Satan do it by allowing him to accuse us, torture us, tempt us, rationalize with us or fill us with guilt.

So how can you *know* that your most inner small voice is used by the Holy Spirit?

You must ask yourself two questions: (1) Are you following the Shepherd, or do you want to go your *own* way? Only if you are willing to let God lead you *all* the way will you be able to *hear* Him. And (2) did you *ask* Jesus to speak to you? Remember, you ask and you receive; if you have not received, it is because you have not asked.

Ask Jesus to teach you to recognize His voice in you! Ask Him not to let Satan or yourself confuse you, and *believe* that it is Jesus who speaks to you. It is best in the beginning to learn to *listen* to God when you set apart a quiet prayer time where other voices are hushed (I Thessalonians 4:11, I Peter 3:4). Once you learn to *hear* Him more clearly, you will be able to converse with Him anywhere — at any time.

Remember too that your spirit's communion with God is closely tied to your intuition and your conscience. If you did wrong, He or the Bible will tell you so. You must confess to Him first and ask for His cleansing blood; then everything will be harmony again in your spirit, and you may commune without fear and guilt. Also, don't confuse high and lofty or guilty emotions or elaborate, intellectual, new knowledge as something spiritual. Some of those things are an *aid* to your spirit, but you must learn to "hear in the spirit" (Revelation 2:7).

LET'S PRAY: Dear Jesus, I do want to hear Your voice through my innermost still small voice. Please show me if I am in the right position to hear You. Do You have *all* of me, or am I keeping something to myself? Do I insist on doing even a small thing my way? Help me to follow You! Please keep Satan and my own self away from Your voice, that I may hear You. Whatever You want to say to me, I am eager to hear, for I can trust You. Speak, my Lord! Your babe is listening! Amen.

(Now take time to listen!)

17. We Talk to God About Others

As you mature in Christ, you will come to learn — through the Bible and the Holy Spirit — many prayer dynamics other than the ones we've discussed so far—and that is as it should be. There is one more thing, however, that you must know right now, from the very beginning: how to pray for others (I Timothy 2:1).

Why is it so important to include others in our prayers? (II Corinthians 1:11). What can our little prayers do that God's power couldn't do anyway? (Revelation 5:8).

For years, I asked myself those questions. I *did* pray for others because the Bible said to, but I couldn't seem to see the reason for it. At times, your understanding will fail you, too. You musn't worry about it. Just do as God's Word tells you, and ask God for wisdom (James 1:5). God will give you what is needed (II Timothy 3:16, Colossians 1:10).

Eventually, as I began to understand the special role that our freedom of choice plays in the great conflict between God and the devil, I came to see the reason for *any* kind of prayer. It is this:

We have learned that God and Satan are right now displaying and demonstrating their plans (or programs) before the whole universe. God is doing everything in love, without force. He gives freedom of choice, and is perfectly fair, even with the devil. Satan, on the other hand, runs his kingdom in the opposite way: He and his demons sow hate, force anybody and anything that can be forced and enslave people with sin and evil habits.

Every human being is born in sin (Job 15:14, Romans 5:12, Psalm 51:5); therefore, every person on this earth is subject to Satan's dominion (Romans 5:21, 7:14). If you doubt the truth of this statement, just watch any little baby (either physical or spiritual) and see which tendencies dominate. From birth on, anger or temper tantrums come naturally; self-control and love have to be taught and implanted!

Satan claims every person on this earth as his, because Adam sold out to the devil (I Corinthians 15:22). Christ came to challenge Satan's ownership and bought the dominion back with His blood. Anyone who, by his free will and choice, now accepts the blood of Christ is bought by Christ out of slavery to be set free. Since force is strange to God's love, He says: "Whosoever will . . . may come!" (John 6:40, Revelation 22:17).

When Satan sees people coming to God of their own free wills, he becomes furious and more determined than ever to show the universe that God isn't really so fair and unselfish after all. So he accuses everybody (Revelation 12:10), including God Himself.

Of what does he accuse God? That He is unfair, that He bribes people into His Kingdom, that He plays favorites. (Only the devil himself does such things, of course, but Satan thinks he can put the blame on God.)

We read an example of Satan's unfair accusations against God in the story of Job. Satan accused God before His heavenly host that He was not staying on His side of the fence in the great show (Job 1, 2). And God said, "Satan, you have permission to show your side of the program for a while. You may do anything you wish except take Job's life."

Well, Satan left nothing undone in his efforts to prove his point. Job lost everything except his foolish wife and three self-righteous "friends." Job had no enemies for Satan to stir up, but "friends" such as Job had are sometimes even harder to take than enemies. Understandably, Job got very upset and confused and tried to figure out why everything had gone wrong, and why his friends were so sure that Job was being "punished" for his hidden sins. Nevertheless, Job *never* turned against God (Job 19:25, 13:15). He even repented before God for questioning Him at all (Job 42:1-6).

When Satan's show was over, God's program was justified again, and God proved before the universe that He had a *right* — even before Satan — to bless His faithful servant Job more than ever. Before He did, however, God asked (He didn't use force, of course) Job to *pray for his "friends."* Job obeyed, and God turned his captivity "when he prayed for his friends" (Job 42:7-17).

What did Job's prayer do? It gave God a right to say to Satan, "These three mealy-mouthed 'friends' of Job are not yours, even though they have sinned — for Job asked that I forgive them and bless them." And Satan had *nothing* more to say!

Truly, there are many people who are still under the slavery of Satan. They don't know how to use their freedom of choice because they are deeply in the devil's bondage. Satan claims them as his.

However, when we — as babes in Christ — use our newfound freedom of choice and go to our heavenly Father and *ask* Him to rescue them out of the camp of Satan, God *will* do it — and Satan cannot protest. God will never force people into His kingdom, but He loves to rescue people who are held in the devil's bondage against their wills.

Sometimes, God's children themselves are also heavily oppressed and attacked by Satan. Again, when we pray for each other, God is honored by our intercessory prayers and will do things He would not do if we hadn't asked. It's simply one of the rules of God's kingdom — we must ask — for ourselves — and for others who either don't yet know how to ask or are nearly overwhelmed by Satan's afflictions (Ephesians 1:16, James 5:16, II Thessalonians 3:1, 2). In Philemon 22, Paul tells his fellow believers that he would be given back to them by their prayers. God loves to answer prayers, so always remember to ask — for yourself, *and* for others.

LET'S PRAY: Dear God, I am aware that I still act like a baby, and ask mostly for gifts for myself. Help me to grow up enough that I may think of others, too. Teach me how to ask for others, and to accept a burden for my unsaved relatives and friends. May Your Holy Spirit give to my mind the names of those I should put on my prayer list. Help me to pray faithfully for them — I know that if

I ask, You shall do the rest. Thank You for hearing me. Amen.

(Now sit down and "listen" as God's Spirit gives you the names of people to pray for. Write them down on a separate prayer list — not in your regular notes — and pray for them daily!)

ABOUT WITNESSING, JOINING AND GROWING

18. Confessing Christ

Let's look once again at what makes us "saved" or "born again" people.

Romans 10:9, 10 tells us that when we believe in our hearts (spirits) that Jesus was raised from the dead by God, that belief is our righteousness. In other words, the moment we believe in Christ as our personal Savior, we are immediately saved and "justified." And at that very moment, when we believe and therefore receive salvation and justification, we are born again.

The second step, according to Romans 10:9, 10, is that we "confess" (declare our faith in) Jesus with our mouth. In other words, we must witness about our belief in Jesus to others. That, of course, is not something which is done only once, it is a lifelong process.

Confessing Christ is a part of something Christian philosophers call "sanctification" (I Corinthians 1:30, II Thessalonians 2:13 and I Peter 1:2).

Justification, which adopts us into the family of God, takes only a moment. Sanctification takes a lifetime.

There are different ideas and theological concepts of sanctification among various denominations, and — unfortunately — some can cause untold (and unnecessary!) agony and guilt feelings. Why? Because they teach that a true believer's sanctification comes from walking a torturous path of self-discipline, self-denial, penance, and other "soul cleansing" processes. For them, sanctification is a way of paying for their sins. But my Bible says otherwise; it says that we have already been sanctified once and for all through the offering of the body of Jesus (Hebrews 10:10). In other words, we have already been cleansed; there is no need to walk a path of self-imposed hardship (I Peter 2:24).

So what *can* we, as Christians, do in our daily lives to further our sanctification while we are here on earth?

We can tell others what Jesus has done for us, and what He can do for them. We can confess Christ.

A baby, from the day it is born, needs exercise in order to stay healthy and grow. Spiritual babes need spiritual exercise, and that's what confessing Christ is. We don't need to reach a certain level of "maturity" first; we don't need to learn special things. But we do need, from the very first day of our spiritual rebirth, to tell others what has happened to us since we came to know God. If we don't, our spiritual growth will be stunted.

I have counselled with many fine, devoutly religious churchgoers who have come to me in utter despair, and confided that they felt as though they were in a rut, that they weren't growing, that they were actually "backsliding" and felt powerless to fight temptation. In such cases, I always ask if they are fulfilling what is required of born-again people.

First, I ask, "Do you believe in Christ as your Savior?" They usually nod and say "yes."

Then I ask, "Do you confess Christ to the people around you?" They usually look down and shake their heads. Sometimes I get strange answers such as, "Well, I try to live a Christian life, and hope that others can see how I've changed," or "Oh, I teach a Bible study group, so I confess Him there."

I am convinced that no one can live a spiritual life of growth for very long without true verbal witness for

Christ. Words have power, and words have to tell others about *the* Word, Christ (John 1:1-3).

Keep in mind, however, that you — like many religious people I've met — can sometimes teach others about Christ without actually confessing Christ.

Jesus said, "Ye shall be my *witnesses*" (Acts 1:8, Luke 24:48). And what is a witness? One who can testify to the facts because he has observed *directly*.

I'm afraid that many religious people are so full of their own religious interpretations and doctrines that they teach others only what *they* think, rather than witness (confess) Christ. They are so busy declaring their own elaborate thoughts, so proudly wrapped up in their own head knowledge, that they don't understand what Christ expects of them. So many church people think that they witness when they only argue. We all love to be "right" and win an argument, but that can often drive a lost soul away. It is not witnessing!

I am always amazed at the answers I get when I ask people of different denominations to tell what they believe. More often than not, I get a lengthy discourse on the doctrinal "differences" between their denomination and those of others. It is such a joy for me when, instead, someone looks me straight in the eye and says, "I believe in Jesus Christ, my Savior and Lord, Who died for me that I may have eternal life." That is confessing Christ!

You don't always need a lot of words to confess Him; you don't need to be a Biblical scholar before you begin. In fact, too many words and too much prideful knowledge can lead to the sin of self-exaltation (Proverbs 10:19). But you need to declare your faith; it takes the confessing of Christ to be a Christian (Romans 10:8-11 LB). As a babe in Christ you won't have very much to say yet — all you can witness to is that you are born again. But it is by that very testimony that you shall overcome Satan and grow strong (Revelation 12:11).

LET'S PRAY: Dear Jesus, I am often afraid or embarrassed to be Your witness. You said that You would do what I cannot do, so please give me the words to confess You correctly. Help me to say it as simply as it is, and not to try to impress people with my new knowledge. Let my witness come from my heart, not from my head. Give me a chance to witness about You today. Amen.

19. About Doctrines

What is a doctrine? The Biblical term in Hebrew is "Legach" which means "teaching or instruction." In Greek, the term is "didaskalia" which stands for "act of teaching," "instruction" or "the thing taught."

Webster's dictionary gives all of those meanings, but also defines "doctrine" as "a principle" and "a view or set of opinions maintained by any person or persons."

I am afraid that many doctrines taught in various denominations are exactly what Webster calls them in that last definition: a viewpoint, a set of opinions. The founders of such denominations usually claim to have discovered "new truth" of some kind or another, and thus start a church based on their "findings" (opinions), and declare that what they have to say is the gospel truth.

If you don't have a church home yet and are looking for one, pray about it first. Then test the church that you visit by listening carefully, several times, to the sermons and teachings. Ask yourself two questions before you become a member:

First, does the church preach that Christ is the Son of God, who came in the flesh to save us (I John 4:1-11)? And second, do the members show love to one another and to visitors (John 13:35)?

If the answer to both questions is "yes," you might consider joining that church. However, let the Spirit within you confirm your choice first. Your heart will tell you if you are where God wants you to be — you need to *ask* God for guidance!

Remember too that Christ is love and that Jesus Christ and love must be the center of every other doctrine a church teaches. Love is the fulfillment of the Law (Romans 13:10). Love never fails (I Corinthians 13:8). So be sure that the church you are considering is based on God's love. If not, look elsewhere; it is important that you find the right kind of church fellowship. The Bible tells us not to neglect it (Hebrews 10:25).

I am often overwhelmed by the numbers of people from various denominations with whom I've talked who know every traditional church doctrine but *don't* know Christ and the joy of salvation. They are guilt-ridden and burdened by the many "do's" and "don'ts" of their doctrines; they try to live up to a standard, a way of life, and fail so often that many give up and turn their backs on both the church and God. What a tragedy!

Too many so-called Christians are guardians of doctrines, rather than witnesses of Christ. They are so eager to prove the "truth" of their doctrines that they forget that Christ did not come to defend their beliefs, but to save sinners.

In the name of Christ, church people condemn, judge and shoot their "wounded" instead of helping them. How much gossip is spread in the defense of a "just" God! How many hot arguments are fought and "won" while souls are lost all around us (Ephesians 4:14-16 LB)!

Nietsche, a famous German philosopher who perhaps influenced Adolf Hitler's thinking more than anyone else, hated Christianity. He once said, "Maybe I would have believed in a Redeemer if the Christians had looked more redeemed!"

When young people come to me and ask if it is "wrong" to do this or that, I tell them to test every so-called "wrong" on three points:

1. Does it deny the Lordship of Christ?
2. Does it annul love?
3. Is is morally wrong according to God's moral law (Exodus 20:3-17)?

Unfortunately, the doctrines of some churches don't do very well when put into the light of those three criteria. And confusion, especially among young church members, is the sad result.

If the people of a particular church worship tradition, legalism (according to their doctrine) or liberalism, and are fast and eager to judge others who don't "fit" into their exact little mold, avoid them. They will hinder your spiritual growth and discourage you. A harsh and judging church spirit usually comes from hidden sins (Romans 2:1) in the church members. There are churches and religious people who have only a "form of godliness" (II Timothy 3:5); stay away from them. Babies grow best in an atmosphere of Truth (John 14:6) and Love (I John 2:10).

LET's PRAY: Dear Jesus, I am already blown about by the winds of many doctrines. I get confused when people tell me what to wear or eat or how to talk in church cliches. Please protect me from the doctrines of men and show me the essentials of Christianity as You know them to be. Please, direct me by Your Spirit into the right church fellowship. Thank You that You are the center and Head of the true church! Amen.

20. Day by Day Growing Pains

So far we've talked about the things spiritual babes need to do to grow and stay healthy: We need to breathe (pray) regularly, we need to eat (study the Word) and we need to exercise (witness and join a Christian fellowship). Now we'll look at what happens when you do those things.

I Am But a Little Child

Since you accepted Christ, things have changed for you. I dare say that, with the new glow of your first love for the Lord (Jeremiah 2:2, Revelation 2:4), you suddenly have problems that you never faced before. These are growing pains permitted by the Lord (I Peter 4:12, James 1:2, 3).

In fact, all spiritual babes experience such pains. The devil doesn't like to lose a subject of his earthly kingdom, and always puts up a fight (I Peter 5:8). He uses people who are still under his power, and brings about circumstances that will cause difficulties and frustrations of overwhelming proportion (II Corinthians 4:8, 9). Many people have told me that when they first accepted Christ and were born again all hell broke loose in their lives.

I've often wondered why God permits Satan to attack Christ's new babies so viciously. They lose jobs, they are mercilessly teased, their cars break down, family tensions rise, they fail tests in school, their peer groups turn on them, they get sick — the list could go on and on!

I believe, however, that God has several good reasons for permitting such harsh growing pains. First, He is trying to teach us to trust Him from the beginning (Proverbs 3:5, 6). The sooner we learn that it is Jesus who takes care of us, not ourselves, the better off we are (I Peter 5:7).

God also lets Satan rage on so that — through our troubles — Christ can reveal Himself to us (I Peter 5:8). Psalms 50:15 and 86:7 tell us that we shall see His hand in our life as He *pulls us out* of our difficulties. As babes in Christ, we don't know very much about God yet, we cannot see or touch Him with our physical senses, so God wants to reveal Himself to us in the Spirit, as we perceive His external help (Psalm 91:14-16).

As long as everything goes smoothly, of course, we don't have any trouble being good little babies. "Good weather" Christians are plentiful. But what happens when the weather gets stormy and you can't have your way?

Do you throw a temper tantrum? Do you yell and say,

"Well God, if that is all You have for me, just forget it. You don't even take care of me!"

Remember, God always takes care of you; but He will not do it your way if it is not the best way for you. So wait for Him (Psalm 27:13, 14).

Everyone would love to have nothing but sunshine and roses, but some rain showers must fall in order to grow roses (Ezekiel 34:26, 27). Just sunshine alone makes a desert where nothing grows — especially babies!

Remember too that growing pains *always* accompany growth, both physical and spiritual. They are inevitable; if you run away, your growth will cease. And how sad that would be!

Don't forget, either, that growing up in Christ is not all pain and trial and tribulation! I can promise you that from my own experience, and the Bible tells you the same thing (Psalm 126:5, 6).

When difficulties come, don't try to handle them yourself. Let go — and let God (Psalm 37:3-5)!

A baby doesn't go out and earn his way — a baby waits for his parents to take care of him (Matthew 6:25-34).

In years past, when my own babies were hungry, I would heat some milk in a bottle. But before I gave that milk to my child, I would test it to be sure that it wasn't too hot. If the milk was, I would let it cool a bit. The baby would see the bottle and cry, and I would say, "It's too hot yet, honey, wait a little bit." But of course the baby wouldn't understand at first, and big tears would roll down. And sometimes a temper tantrum would follow that made the whole house ring.

Did I disown my child for his foolish behavior? Of course not; I would pick him up after the tantrum and love and feed him.

God will do the same (Jeremiah 31:3). He will never permit Satan to annoy you indefinitely. When you resist

I Am But a Little Child

Satan by trusting God, he has to flee from you (James 4:7). And Jesus will come and pick up His little lamb (Isaiah 40:11).

So smile, little baby — don't complain! Be still in God. Better days are ahead, and you shall see the hand of God as He delivers you and carries you and holds you by His hand and teaches you to grow strong (Psalm 116:5-7, Isaiah 30:15, Ephesians 6:10).

LET'S PRAY: Dear Father, I need You very much. I seem to be getting problems from every side, and I am tired of all my troubles. I feel like crawling into a hole in order to hide. Teach me to hide behind You instead. Father, You know that I can't handle life very well, but that is all right, isn't it? That's what I have a Father in Heaven for! Thank You, beloved Father, thank You, dear Jesus — just hold me tight! Amen.

ABOUT OUR SOUL

21. The Will

As you may remember, the three parts of ourselves — spirit, soul and body — are each again divided into three parts. We've already looked at the functions of our spirit (communion, intuition and conscience) and now it's time to examine the parts of our soul: will, emotion and mind. Let's look at the will first.

It's important to remember that each of the three parts of ourselves, and each of the elements which make up those parts, has a particular and designed function within us. As long as every part grows and develops in the manner that our Creator has ordained for us, we will grow harmoniously and things will go well for us. It is only when certain parts become underdeveloped or try to dominate us that we get out of balance.

In order to better picture the integral parts of your soul, think of a three-wheel vehicle with one wheel in front and the other two behind. If just one wheel is too small or too big or missing, the cart will not function well. That's why it is God's will for us to develop harmoniously under the nurture and teaching of His Spirit (I Thessalonians 5:23, I Corinthians 2:10-14).

The will, no doubt, is the front wheel of our "soul vehicle." It is *the* decisive part in us that decides *where* we are going (Revelation 22:17). It was your free will, for instance, which decided to accept Jesus Christ so that you could be born again.

Always remember how very special God's gift of free will (freedom of choice) is. It demanded the greatest gift

He ever gave earth beings: His beloved only Son Jesus. Next to Jesus, God's gift of freedom to decide for ourselves is, without a doubt, His most precious gift. In it, we were created in the image of God (Genesis 1:26, 3:22). Of course, the other two parts of the soul work very closely with the will, but it is the will itself which makes us what we are. Without it, we would be robots or automatons. No wonder God calls us in the Bible "living souls" (Genesis 2:7); for the soul, through the will, decides our lives, and often our deaths, characters, and personalities.

As we look into the Bible, we find many texts which show the function of the will in our souls (Job 6:7, 7:15; Deuteronomy 4:9; I Peter 4:19).

As long as a person is not born again, Satan will try everything in his power to enslave, seduce, deceive or weaken the will of that person. Satan hates God's gift of freedom of choice to us, and will do anything to limit that freedom, both externally and internally.

Look, for instance, at the Godless governments here on earth, such as communism and fascism. The very basis for their existence is the elimination of human freedom — even the freedom to think and do for yourself. We here in America can't even comprehend what it means to be forced to "live" under such tyranny.

Always remember, though, that — no matter where you live on this earth — nobody and nothing can truly take your freedom of choice away; it is God-given. No dictator, not even Satan can touch your will unless you *choose* to let it happen; and Satan knows that!

Thus, Satan will try to weaken and cripple your will, so that he might eventually gain power over it. In dictatorial countries, he carries out that task by ruling the ones who rule the governments. In a free land such as ours, however, he tries different methods: He tries to tempt us into over-indulgence and lusts of the body, and does everything he can to create an imbalanced development of our various parts.

As a result, our bodies (flesh), our emotions or our cold intellect often try to dominate our wills (Ephesians 4:22, I John 2:16, I Corinthians 2:4).

According to God's original plan, our wills (and every other part of us) were supposed to be subordinated to the spirit. As long as our spirits were dead in trespasses and sin (Ephesians 2:1-3), either the two other parts of our soul — emotion and mind — or our bodies would try to run the will. That's why our newborn spirits often struggle so hard with the "flesh" and our souls; our wills aren't used to listening to the spirit. It takes a while for the whole of us to catch on to the new order of command.

The body, of course, is usually the last to catch on, because it is furthest away from the spirit and is used to giving orders according to the lust of the flesh (James 4:1-5).

Satan remembers well how we operated before we were born of the Spirit, and will try anything to trigger the same sinful patterns that we've lived with for so long (Romans 7:15-23). Thus, our wills often give consent to the wrong things over and over again — even though we know better — and we become discouraged by the constant battle within ourselves. That is what Satan wants; he tries to weaken our wills by wearing us down. And he never gives up.

In fact, the Bible tells us that — even when we grow up and mature and become more and more "righteous" in the sight of men — we'll still fall often every day (Proverbs 24:16). It is going to be a *struggle* to bring your whole being into harmony with God's plan! And you and I might just as well give up if we try to fight the devil and straighten things out by ourselves; we can't do it alone. But with God we *can* (Psalm 51:10-12)!

LET'S PRAY: Dear Lord, my will is not doing very well so far. I never understood the important role my will plays in matters of life and death and everything else. Dear Jesus, make me willing to be made willing to obey Your will. I give You my will by my own free choice, so that You can straighten it up. Please, make me strong through the Spirit. Not my will but Your will shall be done; so please — take over right now! Amen.

22. Our Emotions and Feelings

Among religious people a discussion of emotions can become very touchy. Why? Because some church saints are convinced that emotions must be kept under tight control, and that it is a sin to bring any emotion into church worship or family life or any other interpersonal relationship. And still another group goes to the opposite extreme, and believes that feelings are the moving of the Holy Spirit. The more they shout or roll in the aisles of their church, the more they "have the Spirit!"

Both approaches, however, *are* extremes, and cause an imbalance of the soul.

What, then, are the real purposes of our emotions, and what role do they play within our souls?

The Bible tells us that we can express affection through our emotions in the soul, that we can desire, feel and sense.

The soul of Jonathan was knit to the soul of David, and Jonathan loved him as his own soul (I Samuel 18:1).

By our soul's emotions we can magnify the Lord (Luke 1:46). We can hate with the emotion (II Samuel 5:8). And our emotions can get vexed (Zechariah 11:8).

Also we desire God (or others) with our emotions (Deuteronomy 14:26, Psalm 84:2, Isaiah 26:9).

We feel hurt, bitter, happy, exulted, sorrowful, and have many other feelings in our emotions (Luke 2:35,

I Samuel 30:6, II Kings 4:27, Judges 10:16, Isaiah 61:10, Psalm 86:4, Jonah 2:7, Matthew 26:38).

Have you noticed something? Not one of these texts indicates that emotions are always wrong and should never be expressed!

Remember, the soul can be compared to the inner court of the Biblical temple. Only the priests could enter and present oil, incense and bread to God. With our souls, we draw near to God and offer our wills, emotions and minds. Meanwhile, our spirit dwells in the Holy of Holies and makes contact with God through the Holy Spirit. Anyone who believes that emotions have no place in the worship of God and in our relationship to Him is not in harmony with the Bible.

People who try to suppress their emotions at all times become insensitive and hard as stone. The Bible speaks about a stony heart and stony places (Ezekiel 11:19, 36:26; Matthew 13:5-20; Mark 4:5-16). Such cold hardness is undesirable; God is eager for us to exchange stone for something more soft and alive.

On the other hand, the opposite extreme — the type of person who goes only by feelings — is unbalanced, too. Such people make themselves and others around them miserable. And they judge their religious experiences completely on how they "feel" at any given moment.

If they feel "right" or "elated" or "excited," God is near; if they are "out of it" and are discouraged, upset or hurt, God isn't around any longer. But that's not true! God is *always* with us, if we feel Him or not!

Satan loves to play tricks with our emotions, to make us feel guilty, lonely, rejected, forsaken by God and man, hyperactive, overly-excited or anything else that will throw us off balance.

God, however, is eager to bring every part of our being back into proper balance. And He can do that, *if* we face ourselves in the new light of our turned-on spirit and find out what parts of ourselves have gone wrong or are missing.

Are you one of those cool collected people who is either afraid to show emotion or proud of yourself because you haven't cried in years?

Then you'd better ask God to take your stony heart and give you something softer. If you as a male feel that such a request would cause you to lose your rough, gruff Western-style image, remember that Christ is our example, not John Wayne! Jesus wept! (John 11:35, Luke 19:41). He was also very tender with children (Matthew 19:14) and sinners alike (John 8:11). You needn't "act tough" to be a strong man; you *can* also be soft and gentle. Jesus, on one occasion, became so consumed with zeal for His Father's house that he drove a whole group of influential businessmen out of the temple with a whip! (John 2:14-17). Strength and tenderness *do* go together!

If your feelings dominate your life, your will, and the people around you, ask Jesus to teach you how to control your over-emotional life. Make your will the front wheel of your "soul vehicle," and learn to act by that will, not by your feelings.

Also, learn to reason things out with your mind *first* before your mouth runs over with too many words (Proverbs 10:19). Let's face it: Some babies make too much noise, others withdraw and become autistic. Both groups need help — if you're among either one of them, remember that Christ is able and willing to put your emotions where they belong: in balance with your mind, and directed by your will, with all three faculties of your soul enlightened and guided by your spirit.

LET'S PRAY: Dear Lord, You know my emotions better than I do. All I know is that my feelings give me so much trouble that sometimes I hate myself! Jesus, please help me to accept my emotions as an important part of my spiritual development, so that I neither fight nor magnify them. Help me to magnify You with my emotions instead, and let me feel secure in Your love. Amen.

23. Our Minds

Intellect, knowledge and wisdom come from our minds, which are the instruments of our thoughts. Our soul's ability to use these things is made very clear in the Bible. Solomon tells us that a soul without knowledge is not good (Proverbs 19:2). David says that his soul knows well (Psalm 139:14). Wisdom and discretion will be life for our soul (Proverbs 3:21, 22). The soul can think (Lamentations 3:20). People may "lift up" their souls (Psalm 25:1).

Through our minds, we become rational beings; we can reason things out, and then our wills can decide where to go. As we have learned, our soul's three parts — emotion, mind and will — must work together harmoniously in order to function smoothly.

Just as some people allow too many or too few emotions to surface there are others who use too much or too little of their mind; and I'm not referring here to education and book learning. Those things don't necessarily make a good mind. A native in the bush who never sets foot in a classroom may have a very fine and balanced mind and soul; knowledge alone simply doesn't make a mind. In fact, sometimes education can actually destroy a mind (Ecclesiastes 8:16, 17). I know some people who are walking encyclopedias, but they don't show much wisdom or rational, sensible behavior.

God and His Word look at us and our abilities differently than the world does. The world honors earthly wisdom, book knowledge and fancy, elaborate thinking very highly, and shows it as desirable — but the Bible calls such things "vanity" (Ecclesiastes 1:12-18).

The wise of this world look at the cross of Jesus and it is foolishness to them (I Corinthians 1:18).

God Himself has made the wisdom of the wise and the understanding of the prudent foolishness in God's eyes (I Corinthians 1:19, 20).

What, then, *is* wisdom, and how does a person truly become wise?

The first step is to trust and reverence the Lord (Proverbs 1:7 LB). A simple peasant who never had a chance to get much higher education or a fancy degree, but who has learned to believe and trust in God may well be wiser than the most learned scholar.

That's not to say, of course, that it is wrong to go to school and work toward a degree. It isn't wrong — as long as the higher learning does not destroy the foundation to all true wisdom: our faith in God and Jesus Christ.

According to God's value system, a trusting little child who believes in God, a so-called "Simpleton's mind," who can grasp the steps to the born-again experience has *enough* of a mind — and often more of a mind than someone who is great in the eyes of the world.

As long as a person — no matter how smart — stays in his "natural" state of mind, and refuses to accept Christ, he is simply unable to understand the things of God — regardless of how hard he studies and tries (I Corinthians 2:14).

One of God's special delights seems to be in calling those people whom the world labels as "simple," "weak" or "insignificant" into His wisdom and knowledge. At the same time, interestingly enough, not very many of the "mighty and wise people of the world" ever make it (I Corinthians 1:26-28 LB).

Is God partial, then? Does He keep the "smart" people out of His program by choice? No, of course not. It isn't God who does the choosing; it's the people themselves.

You see, for some reason great amounts of learning and intellectual exercise often foster enormous intellectual pride — and pride is a tool of Satan to enslave people (Proverbs 21:4, I John 2:16, Romans 11:20).

It's important to remember too that intellectual pride is not just in "the world" (among the unconverted) — it can frequently be found in today's Christian churches.

Unfortunately, many religious people think that they are "spiritual" because of their great knowledge. They think that — because they are moral, learned, wise and strong — they've "arrived." But men can be all those things, and more, and still be "dead" in God's eyes.

We are not born again into God's family by our brilliant minds or moral conduct. We are born anew by believing, *as simply as a child,* in Jesus Christ. Strangely, that beautiful simplicity — just because it *is* simple — is an offense to many people — even church people (I Corinthians 1:24, 27). The fact remains, however, that a reborn child of God must not be controlled by his intellect, rationale or worldly wisdom — but by the *Spirit.*

When proud intellect is not willing to humble itself and be taught by the Holy Spirit, when a person wants to lean on his own understanding, he can present masterful ideas and theories; he can even teach and interpret the Word of God and be admired for it by many people. But God calls the practices of such a person "vanity of vanities." Anyone, regardless of how "smart" or "ignorant" he sees himself to be, has to begin all over at *God's* starting point. He must be born again as a babe in the spirit. It is a very simple, humble beginning, but it is God's way — and the only way to become truly wise.

LET'S PRAY: Dear Jesus, please help me to forget all the prideful things I ever learned and start all over again. I want to start at the beginning of Your wisdom. Help me not to be proud of my intellect, and help me not to feel stupid either. I am simply a child who is ready to learn from You. Teach me, Lord, by Your Spirit — I want to become wise in You. Amen.

ABOUT OUR BODY

24. Our Defense

Christian philosophers and theologians have always tended to ignore the third part of ourselves — our bodies. In times past, certain functions of the body were not even mentioned without embarrassment. The less said, some saints felt, the more "spiritual" they would be.

The Bible, however, says that the body has a very significant role in the sanctification of the whole person (I Thessalonians 5:23). Even though the body is the last in the order of spirit, soul and body, it is clearly cited as one of the three parts that needs to be sanctified by God.

We put the functions of the body into three categories: defense, nutrition and reproduction. Let's look at defense first.

Defense, as a function of our bodies, came as a result of sin. No survival or body defenses were needed when our first parents — Adam and Eve — came from the hand of their Creator. Everything was good (Genesis 1:31) and they knew nothing of death and harsh existence. The Tree of Life was available to them (Genesis 2:9) and its fruit and leaves were life-giving and healing (Revelation 22:2, Ezekiel 47:12). They lived in a perfect environment and in total harmony with themselves and God.

After the fall, however, the couple was sent away from the garden that God had prepared for them. An angel stood guard at the Tree of Life so they could not eat from it any more and live forever (Genesis 3:24).

Because Adam and Eve came perfect from the hand of their Creator, and most likely had already eaten freely from the Tree of Life, it took a long time for their bodies to deteriorate and die. Adam lived 930 years (Genesis 5:5), and some of his children and grandchildren lived as long as he did or even longer. Methuselah lived to be 969 years old (Genesis 5:27). It was only after the flood — when nearly all the offspring of God's original children were destroyed — that the lifespan of people on earth was drastically shortened.

The Bible does not give us the details why it was so, but we can assume that harsher living and weather conditions after the flood caused people to die earlier. A body wears out more quickly when it has to struggle for basic survival against hostile elements, wild animals and shortages of food.

In our society today, that basic struggle is not as severe as it could be — and has been for our forefathers and the pioneers. Statistics show that we Americans now live longer (on the average) than our ancestors did. Does that mean that our body's defense function is no longer needed?

No, it is still needed — but the emphasis has shifted. Now, instead of concentrating so much on protecting us from weather and hunger, our bodies' defenses have to fight our own foolish living habits.

God designed our bodies very wisely (Psalm 139:14) and in such a way that they would meet the demands of human life on earth. When God created His first earth children, He planned for them to be the "keepers" of a garden. That means that the first people on earth were farmers.

Am I saying that we should all go back to the country and begin farming?

Well, not exactly. For many of us, though, such a move would be the best thing that could happen. Why? Because our living conditions and our food have become so artificial that our bodies cannot defend themselves rigorously anymore. We don't "wear out" these days — we rust out. We live longer, but our bodies have to fight sickness and ailment from the time we are infants.

God designed our bodies to have physical exercise daily. We were made to move and bend and stretch — but how much of that is done by the average American? I still remember watching with amazement when our sponsor — the man who sponsored our family to come to the United States — would drive his car from the garage to his mailbox to get the daily mail. The distance was perhaps a few hundred feet! He didn't like to walk; he liked his soft chair in front of the TV. And probably as a result, he dropped dead of a heart attack before he could enjoy his retirement.

The body was designed to exercise, to be outdoors and receive sunshine, breathe fresh air, eat good food grown "just right" by God and to rest at night. And we also need peace in our souls, and quickened spirits, because all three main parts of us work closely together and need to be in harmony.

The further we go away from God's original design for us, the more we ail and suffer. The body can adapt itself well — but only if we give ourselves a chance, and see to it that our bodies are in the environment they were made for. If we sin with or against the body, we must face the consequences (Galatians 6:7, 8).

LET'S PRAY: Dear Jesus, You made my body and You know how I function better than I do. I never really understood that my body needs certain things to operate correctly. I am afraid that I've taken my body's wondrous performance for granted all my life. Please teach me how to treat my body properly. One of my greatest neglects is exercise. Please show me how I can bring more healthy exercise into my daily life. I know where there is a will there's a way. I have the will, and You have Your way in my body. Amen.

25. Our Body's Intakes

The body has to take in three basic elements from its external environment in order to function properly: air, water and food.

Our most urgent need is for air. Generally speaking, a person can live without oxygen for only three minutes — after that, severe brain damage and death are certain.

Our second most urgent need is for water. Few people have survived more than three or four days with nothing to drink. We humans thirst to death much sooner than we starve to death.

In fact, food is our least urgent need. Jesus ate no food for forty days in the wilderness (Matthew 4:2) and came back alive to start His special ministry. We have records of many humans fasting for a prolonged time.

Whenever the body is in need of any of the three basic elements, the whole person suffers. The body affects the rest of us at all times. If it is well taken care of, our soul and spirit can function properly with more ease. When the body is sick, however, we have a hard time thinking straight. The Romans of ancient times knew that, and said, *"Mens sana in corpore sano"* (In a healthy body lives a healthy mind.) The opposite is true, too: A sick soul (mind) can affect the body adversely.

So, always remember that the brain and its thinking suffer when the body doesn't have enough oxygen, liquid, or proper nutrition.

Satan is well aware of the divine principles that govern the human body, and tries to keep any human being as ignorant as possible about the laws of life and health. Sin, sickness and death came (and always have come) through Satan, not through God's will.

God, even after the fall, wanted His children to prosper and be healthy, so that the soul might prosper as a result of the body's prosperity and health (III John 2).

Often, when Jesus came upon scenes on earth where He found sickness and suffering among people trapped in sin, He would heal them. And after they were divinely healed, Christ repeated one admonition: "Go and *sin no more!*" (John 5:14; 8:11).

I have seen with my own eyes people who became healed through the power of God, and I know that it is the *same* power of divine healing that cures someone in a year that it is when someone is healed in a single moment.

Unfortunately, I have also seen divinely healed people return to the same or another sickness and more suffering in later years. Why? Wasn't the divine power efficient enough to heal them completely?

Yes, it was! When Christ heals, He heals completely. But many of us don't heed Christ's advice: "Go and sin no more!" Too many people forget that there is such a thing as sinning against the body!

Some people, for instance, argue that smoking is not a sin. But it is a scientific fact that we all need plenty of fresh air. And God will not keep our lungs miraculously healthy if we breathe poisoned air by our own choice. Such abuse *is* a sin; in fact, we also sin when we sit day in, day out in the stagnant air of our living rooms and offices without going out for fresh air.

Remember, too, that the body suffers when we don't drink enough water. I have counselled with many people who complained to me about all kinds of ailments, depressions and tiredness. And without exception, every one of those people simply wasn't drinking the water he or she needed. I have yet to see a person who doesn't feel better immediately once he or she learns to drink more water during the day. Health experts tell us that the body needs a glass of water every day for every ten to fifteen pounds of body weight, and that the water should be taken in between or before meals — *not with* the meal.

Because their bodies crave liquid, many people drink pop, coffee, tea, coke, or beer from morning to evening. And while it's true that the human system can use the water that is contained in such drinks, it's also true that the body has a hard time defending itself against the other substances in those concoctions.

I often smile when I listen to some Christians as they expound on the evils of tobacco and alcohol while they drink endless cups of coffee and overstuff themselves with fattening empty-calorie foods. How easy it is to judge the world for its "sinful" habits while we overindulge in what is "good" or "legal" or "proper"!

If we learn to listen to the Spirit, God will show us what is "right" or "wrong" for us. Personally, I always hesitate to tell anyone what to eat, drink, wear or do, because I strongly believe that the Holy Spirit can do a much better job of taking care of God's children than I can. I know only what *I* can and cannot do, or will and will not do. Though all things are lawful for me, not all things would be expedient for me (I Corinthians 6:12).

If we want to be taught, God will teach us. The Word of God gives us great insight into what is best for all three parts of us, including the body (Psalm 32:2, 62:1, Romans 12:1, 2).

In other words, God knows you best. He knows your weaknesses, your habits and even the addictions that you acquired while you were living under the deception of Satan (Psalm 139). God's Spirit — through your spirit — (your still small voice) — will tell you where *your* sanctification of the body begins. God is loving and understands our frames (Psalm 103:13,14). He will not suggest more than you can handle at any given time; He knows best where it is most urgent for you to begin. So *ask* your Heavenly Father what He wants you to do or not do, breathe or not breathe, drink or not drink, eat or not eat. He will show you, — one step at a time, precept by precept, here a little and there a little (Isaiah 28:9, 10).

LET'S PRAY: My wise and loving Father and Maker, I know that I need to make some changes in my physical habits. But I don't know where to begin. I am Your baby and still quite ignorant. I do want to learn, though, and obey as I grow in You. Please show me what is most urgent for my body at this very moment. And after You show me, make the change Yourself, for I cannot; I am too weak. You promised that You would sanctify me, so I trust You to bring it about in Your way, whatever it takes — I shall let You do it, and thank You for it. Amen.

26. Nutrition and Diet

When God created Adam and Eve, He gave them every fruit and herb-bearing seed for their original diet (Genesis 1:29, 2:9).

Once the couple had sinned, however, the earth was cursed and God told Adam that he would have to struggle with the ground, and sweat, and also eat the herbs (rather than just the seeds and fruits) of the land (Genesis 3:17-19).

After the flood, men received permission to eat the flesh of animals, but not the blood (Genesis 9:3, 4). Leviticus 17:10-14 tells us that God reserved the use of blood as a symbol of sacrifice and atonement.

Why did God allow man to eat the flesh of animals after the devastation of the flood? Perhaps because there was no longer sufficient plant life to sustain Noah's family; the Bible does not say. But we do know that — ever since that time — man's diet has been composed of meat, vegetables, fruit and grain.

Of course, in many parts of the earth people must adapt their diets to the limitations imposed by their environment. The closer man lives to the poles, for instance, the less fruit and vegetables he can find. Thus, Eskimos depend mainly on fish and sea animals for their physical survival. In dry, desert areas, people often suffer a very meager existence because there is not enough water, vegetation or animal life to support them.

We here in America, on the other hand, are truly blessed; just about every kind of food is available in abundance, and we can choose our diets as we please.

Satan, then, cannot do evil to our bodies through starvation and lack of water. So he tries to tempt us through overindulgence and the wrong kind of appetite instead. And I don't think I need to tell you what the result has been! Just about everyone knows that overeating is America's number one health problem; you don't need to be a Christian to feel conviction about that. But you do need to be a Christian to fully understand the devious ways in which Satan goes about destroying our bodies.

Remember, the first sin was committed in response to the lust of the eye and appetite. The fruit "looked" so good to Eve that she "wanted" to eat it. Of course, her soul's desire also played a part: Eve wanted to become wise by eating the fruit (Genesis 3:6). But it was her body that opened the door to her soul's desire by letting its senses lust after the forbidden food. So we know that the lust of the eye and appetite are two of the most powerful tools Satan uses to lead us into sin (I John 2:16).

Unfortunately, many Christians do not truly understand the nature of their runaway appetites; they do not realize that it is more than just Satan's tricks that makes them overeat. I have seen scores of Christians agonize and struggle in an attempt to "cut down" on their nibbling and overindulgence — all to no avail. They remain hungry. And it's simply because they think they're fighting Satan's temptations — and nothing else — when in truth their hunger is also caused by their bodies' *legitimate* cravings for *real* nutrition.

Some say, "I'm not skinny and undernourished; I'm overweight." But the fact is, a 200-pound body can be just as undernourished as a 90-pound body! When we eat the *wrong kinds* of foods — no matter how much or how little — our bodies don't receive useful nutrients. All they get is stuff that's stored away as fat.

What are "wrong" foods? The kind that God didn't prepare for us. The kind that we "civilized" humans have decided to "improve" upon so that we don't have to chew so hard or make any effort to prepare them for a meal.

America has refined, peeled and whitened nature's good foods to the extent that all minerals, enzymes, vitamins and roughage have been removed. As a result, the average American exists mainly on "empty" calories that put pounds on his flabby body but no nutrition into his blood and bones. The body knows what is needed and craves for it; but all we do is stuff ourselves with more and more bleached-out stuff from our supermarkets' shelves.

I don't think that saying it's time for people in the Western world to go back to natural foods, makes me a "health nut" or "food faddist." Such foods are the ones God in His wisdom gave to us for the best of our bodies! Why do we refine and bleach and grind what grows for us, to pure white nothingness — and then try to add "fortifiers" to make up for the loss of nutrients — when God puts everything (in just the right proportion) into every kernel of grain? I admit that eating and baking whole grains might require a change of habit and appetite, but it is a well-known fact among cancer specialists that people need enough roughage and fiber (whole grains, nuts, fruits — some with the peel intact, such as apples — and vegetables and raw salads) in order to keep their digestive tracts healthy and free of constipation. Years ago, at a conference on cancer in Sweden, every doctor attending reported that most of his cancer patients had a long record of constipation!

It's important to remember also that we can become as addicted to refined foods as others are to drugs, alcohol or tobacco. Over the years, for example, I've observed that many Christians are addicted to sugar. There are far too many "chocoholics" among God's children — and without exception, they all go around wondering why they feel so rotten most of the time!

God told us to be moderate in *all things* (Philippians 4:5) and to eat and drink to the glory of God (I Corinthians 10:31). Let *God* prepare your table and pick your diet. He knows best what we all individually need (Matthew 6:31, 32).

LET'S PRAY: Dear Jesus, I know that I need to learn more about sensible eating habits and nutrition. Not everything that tastes good to me is good *for* me, and I'm afraid I need to re-train my tastebuds to enjoy healthy foods. Lord, so far I've tried losing weight because I wanted to "look" better, younger and "sexier" — but I know that motivation is weak, and cannot last long. Now I want to "shape up" for Your glory, so I ask You to help me to live, eat and drink for You alone. Better yet, I ask that You do it for me, as I give You my permission and will for it. See to it, Father, that Your baby gets the right kind of food! Amen.

27. Sex and Reproduction

Sex is a word that embarrasses some church people rather deeply; they are convinced that the word, discussion of the subject, and perhaps even the act itself should be eradicated. If they had their way, they would even erase the topic from the Bible. They feel uneasy when they read about the many "begats" in the Bible (Matthew 1:1-17). They are firmly convinced that sex is "dirty" and equal to sin, lust and fornication.

But the Bible says that this is not so. The gift of reproduction was included in God's blessings upon His two earth children before they sinned (Genesis 1:28). Adam and Eve would have multiplied themselves in harmony and under God's blessings — and their children would have been born into God's sinless image — if they had stayed true to God and obeyed Him.

When the couple sinned, however, Adam's children were born in Adam's image rather than God's; they were like Adam and leaned toward sin and disobedience. And they had to die just as Adam and Eve did (Genesis 5:3).

The creation story tells us that God gave His newly created beings three instructions or "gifts." God told Adam and Eve to (1) eat freely, to (2) multiply themselves in order to fill the earth and subdue it, and (3) to give God allegiance by obeying Him and not eating from *one* special tree (Genesis 2:17).

Satan, of course, hates all gifts that God gives to His earth children — but the three gifts that God called "good" before sin came are the ones he detests the most. As a result, our freedom of choice toward obedience, our eating practices, and our sexual (reproductive) functions have become more perverted and misused through Satan's influence than any other human trait — just look at the long sad story of our history, and you will see that this is true.

Eating, drinking and sex are used by Satan to debase the human race to the level of animals, which have neither freedom of choice nor rational reasoning power toward good and evil. Animals act by instinct. Humans are supposed to be dominated by their spirits and will power. Instead, however, many people are totally dominated and enslaved by sex and appetite (I Thessalonians 4:3-5, Philippians 3:19).

God had to destroy mankind once, in the flood, because

eating, drinking and sex got completely out of control (Genesis 6:4, 5, Matthew 24:38).

Jesus tells us that the end of the world (when, according to the Bible, our globe will be destroyed by fire, not by water) will be "as the days of Noah were" (Matthew 24:37-39). So we know that eventually eating, drinking and sex will again overrule the reasoning power and will of men, and will bring about the earth's final destruction.

I do not think that it is necessary to go into detail about the moral corruption of our times and — in so doing — prove that the end of the world is near. What we need to know is how we — the babes and children of God — must relate ourselves to the wickedness of these times, and how we can keep ourselves undefiled and unaffected by it (James 1:27).

When is sex "good" and when is it evil? When is it God's gift and when is it Satan's perversion?

The Bible makes it abundantly clear that sex and marriage belong together (Hebrews 13:4). It takes marriage to "know" your mate, and Adam "knew" his wife Eve when she conceived (Genesis 4:1).

I wish I had the time and space to tell you here of the many couples who have come to me for counsel about their miserable lives. So often it all began because they rushed into sexual relations and marriage too soon, before they "knew" each other! Guilt, unwanted pregnancies, abortions, resentment, impotence, frigidity, estrangement, unfaithfulness and other heartaches result from hasty sex relations.

If a person wants to reduce himself to the level of animal instinct, he may respond to every arousal of his sex glands, and use anyone who's available at the moment. Dogs do that, too, when in heat (II Peter 2:20-22, Philippians 3:2)!

Over the years, I have observed that uncontrolled appetite toward food and strong drink very often go together with a strong and passionate sexual drive. Feasting, partying and drinking and sex sins often go hand in hand — which is why the sex sin is worse than some others. With it, we are led into additional sins, and we pull others into sin, too (I Corinthians 6:16-18, I Timothy 5:22, II Peter 2:14 LB).

God is very eager to restore in His children the proper place for His three gifts — gifts which He gave as something very special, something worthy of His children in the Garden of Eden. So always remember that, in God's eyes, it is "good" to have a free will, to eat and drink, and to have sex with your marriage partner. God wants us to enjoy what He gave to us. But the only way to enjoy God's gifts is to use them as He intended them to be used — if you do that, God will make them a blessing again.

LET'S PRAY: Dear Jesus, please help me to see my sex drives for what they really are — a gift of Yours to be used in Your way. Help me not to be afraid of them or use them indiscriminately. If I can't have sex because I am not married, help me to sublimate my desires into some beautiful friendships and spiritual relationships instead. Help me not to feel guilty because I have sexual desires. I shall acknowledge them as something normal, just like hunger pains. Give me self-control and guidance for both. If I eat, drink or have sex, let me do it in a way that will honor You and Your love. Amen.

GOD'S APPAREL FOR US

28. God's Best Robe

When Jesus walked on earth, He did not go around shabbily dressed, looking like a beggar. His garments were good enough that the Roman soldiers under the cross divided them into four parts — and his coat was so special (it was woven without seams) that the soldiers decided not to tear it into four pieces, but rather to gamble for it (John 19:23, 24).

Jesus is our example in all things. Some churches have much to say about exactly what a Christian should wear and how he should look. I, on the other hand — as I've mentioned before — have no desire to tell anyone how to look. But it's important to remember that — whatever we wear, or however we like to look — worldly people (and some church saints, unfortunately) judge us by first impressions. So I personally have a deep conviction to look my best — after all, I am the daughter of *"The* King!"

Anyone who wishes to honor God will not look sloppy, dirty, or ragged, or believe that worn-out clothing will demonstrate to others his frugality for God's cause. We only suggest by such a practice that God doesn't keep His word, and does not keep His believers well-clothed as He promised (Matthew 6:25-33).

On the other hand, God doesn't want us to be slaves to fashion, obsessed with chasing after every season's newest styles, either. Following the world's whims can be awfully exhausting to those who try! So remember: Let's be sensible, moderate in *all things,* and try to avoid extremes that will draw people's attention to ourselves. Who wants to stick out like a sore thumb and claim that he or she is doing it for the glory of God.

Remember too that God *is* very much concerned about our *spiritual* clothing, and is very explicit about that in His Word.

For everyday warfare (and life *is* a warfare from babyhood on, be it physical or spiritual), God provides us with an "armor." We'll discuss that protective cover in later lessons; it's important to look first, though, at the type of "clothing" which Jesus mentioned in two of the parables He told while here on earth. Let's study Matthew 22:1-14 first.

Here, Jesus told the story of a king's wedding feast for his son. The king had everything ready, and sent word for the guests to come — but they didn't want to come. So he finally sent word that anyone could attend the feast, and — as a result — the place soon became filled with guests. And the king gave everyone a special wedding garment appropriate to the fancy occasion.

One man, however, came in without the provided outfit; he preferred to wear his own suit instead.

The king approached him very tactfully, and gave the improperly dressed man a chance to explain or perhaps show that it was just an oversight. But it wasn't! The man had nothing to say for himself, and so was thrown out.

What was Christ trying to say with His parable? Well, no doubt, the king in the story represents His heavenly Father, and the wedding the marriage feast of the Lamb (Revelation 19:7). The chosen people symbolize His fellow Jews, who for centuries had been specially invited to attend Jesus' "wedding," but had refused to come (John 1:11). So God sent the "invitation" to the whole wide world, and we — the Gentiles — were permitted to fill the places that were first reserved for Abraham's seed (Romans 11:11, Galatians 3:28, 29). God Himself provided the "wedding garment" for everyone, because nobody else had a "cover" good enough to appear in the presence of the King.

In order to find out what that "cover" is, we must read what God has to say about the end of the world. That's when the wedding of Christ and His bride (the church) will happen (Revelation 21:1, 2). The book of Revelation tells us several times about the robes and raiments of God's redeemed people. Whatever we shall wear, it will be shiny white, washed in the blood of the Lamb (Revelation 7:14). God's provided robe is the righteousness of Jesus Christ (Philippians 3:9, Isaiah 61:10). Christ tells us quite plainly that we must accept God's plan for our salvation, not men's ideas (human "robes").

From the beginning of time, Satan has tempted people to try to work out their own salvation or "earn" their way to heaven. Cain did that when he refused to accept God's way of worship and the symbol of the slain lamb, and — instead — "grew" his own sacrifice (Genesis 4:3-5). But God cannot and will not accept us in any way other than if we cover ourselves with Christ and His blood (I Peter 1:18, 19).

On the other hand, the second parable — Luke 15:11-23 — gives us still more insight as to what God expects of us in the way of spiritual "clothing." In that story, the son (who was born into his father's family and carried his family's name, but ran away) is willingly accepted by his father when he returns dressed in rags. He is not thrown out, as was the man in the first story, but was given the father's best robe.

What is the difference in the two parables? Both individuals came to the king or father (symbolically, God) improperly dressed. But in the first case, the guest did not wear what the king offered. In the second story, the prodigal son *accepted* his father's best robe!

God will save to the uttermost (Hebrews 7:25), but

we have to do it His way. We cannot bypass Christ; He alone is our proper cover (Acts 4:12).

LET'S PRAY: Dear Father, please help me to understand that I cannot "earn" my way to Your wedding for Your Son, and that *You* are giving me my heavenly clothing. I don't need to buy or sew it myself here on earth. It has been ready for me since Jesus died; all I need to do is accept it. But I don't want to stay all dirty underneath, either, Jesus, so please clean me up all the way — my body, my soul and my spirit. In Your name and for Your sake I ask. Amen.

29. The Armor of God

God has two "covers" for us. The white garment is Christ's righteousness and He provides it for us (Isaiah 61:10). He also wants us to have another outfit, the armor, ready-made by God for us to wear here on earth. All we need to do is put it on (Ephesians 6:10-18).

In order to understand the nature of that second cover, we must realize that every child of God — even a babe in Christ — is fought by the devil from the very moment of spiritual birth. Thus, we need an armor — and that is the second cover that God provides. Paul refers to the war armor of a Roman soldier as an illustration to help us understand it better (Ephesians 6:13-17).

The war we must fight is not the kind we can win ourselves. Nor is it a sporty wrestling game that we can take or leave for the fun of it. It's a deadly battle. We are constantly and mercilessly attacked by an enemy who was a murderer, liar and deceiver from the beginning (John 8:44). The enemy is neither fair nor capable of abiding by any humane rules. He is out to destroy us, at any cost.

In strength, intelligence and experience, Satan and his demonic helpers are far superior to any human, for man is "lower" than the angels and even the spirit forces which were expelled from heaven (Psalm 8:5).

So, here we are, little babes of our heavenly Father, just learning to walk and talk in our newfound kinship — and along comes a roaring lion ready to devour us (I Peter 5:8). We are in no way a match for him — even when we have grown into mature Christians — and our heavenly Father knows it.

What does any good Daddy do if he sees his child attacked? He fights back, of course!

Our Father in heaven does the same thing. He hands us a perfect cover to protect us against the flying bullets and darts of the attacking enemy and says, "Put it on. All you need to do next, is to face the enemy — just stand still and watch the fight. I Myself will do the fighting for you. Your part is to put on what I have provided for you. You must never run, no matter what, for your back is not protected. So just stand firm in your armor and don't be moved. You'll see something great happen if you do what I tell you — the enemy will not only stop fighting, he will run from you" (James 4:7).

The first thing we do when we get up in the morning is get dressed. We choose clothing that will meet the demands of the day ahead. And we wear clothing and shoes that fit our size — a small child does not wear his father's clothing, for it would fall off his tiny shoulders.

God, our Father in heaven, custom-fits our armor to our size too. The armor fits perfectly at all times, and the size is adjusted as we grow. There will at no time be an ill fit or an unprotected part *unless* we turn our backs or forget to put on the whole armor; then we leave certain parts of us wide open to the enemy's attacks. Satan sees our uncovered parts before we remember that we didn't keep ourselves covered properly, and we end up wounded — it happens often! Then we turn to God and say, "Why did You let that happen to me, God? Aren't You keeping Your promises?"

Well, of course He is. It's just that we forget too easily what we must do as well. Remember, God is always fair — even to the devil. Satan follows no rules or war agreements, but God does. God has clearly laid out what He does — and what *we* must do — to be victorious over *any* enemy.

He provides everything and fights for us (Zechariah 3:1-3, Exodus 14:14-25, I Samuel 12:16, II Chronicles 20:17). We must accept His ways, put on what He provides, and "resist" or "withstand" by standing our ground and not turning our backs to run!

In Israel's time, one of the greatest shames to befall anyone came if a soldier got panicky and turned his back to the enemy. That was a sign of defeat (Joshua 7:8). Even if a soldier had to retreat for a while, he would always do it by walking backwards while facing the enemy. Why? Because you must know and see the tactics of the other side in order to be prepared for his attacks.

Satan has wily ways, and many plots and schemes against us. Quite often we don't recognize him or his attack, for he comes as an angel of light if he cannot scare us with his wild-lion roaring (II Corinthians 11:14). So remember: He *can* be subtle and will study our weak points carefully so that he can plan the most effective attack possible. He uses the sins of his own rebellion in the heavenly places (Ezekiel 28:17, Isaiah 14:12-14) to tempt us. His sins, as you know, were pride and jealousy — and those are the very temptations we so often struggle with, in physical as in spiritual babyhood! Thus, it's important to understand and know your defense — and how to put it on. Our entire well-being — as well as that of others here on earth — depends on it. If we learn to fight God's way, we don't have to really fight at all, for His victory is ours (II Corinthians 2:14).

LET'S PRAY: Dear Father, I am so glad You do the fighting for me. Every time I try to do it with my own strength, I fall flat on my face and the devil batters me. Help me to understand and remember what my part of the battle is. I always panic and do the wrong thing. I either fight or run and come pouting to You afterward, when I am bleeding and in pain. I am so glad You know me and understand me, for I am your ignorant child and we both know it. I am so glad that I don't have to be strong or smart to win the battle with Satan — all I need to remember is to hide behind You in my new outfit of armor. Thank You for it — please help me now to put it on. Amen.

30. Getting Dressed

Each morning, before we put on our physical clothing, we should "put on" our spiritual gear for the day's coming battles. And, just as we must reach for our dress or suit with our hands, so must we reach for our inner cover with our prayers. We begin by *asking* God for it, piece by piece. The Holy Spirit will hand it to us (Ephesians 6:18).

First comes the "belt" or girdle of truth to hold our "tunic" in place. In Roman times, the tunic was a long, straight type of undergarment. A belt was cinched around the waist and buckled tightly, so that a soldier could pull it up and "tuck in" his tunic and keep it out of his way while he walked or marched. Without the belt, the tunic would not stay in place — it would interfere with the soldier's movements, and make him stumble or fall.

Who or what is our belt of truth? Jesus Christ is the only Truth with a capital "T." Every other "truth" must point toward that center Truth, or it will not encircle us correctly, and as a result we may stumble. The Bible tells us that He was yesterday, He is today and He will be forever (Hebrews 13:8). It also says that other important truth and nearly everything else will be done away with someday (I Corinthians 13:8-10). Christ is the great "I Am" —"I am the Truth" (John 14:6, 17:17).

Whenever we "loosen" the Truth as it is in Jesus (John 8:31, 32) we begin to stumble (Jude 24). And whenever we begin to tighten that "belt" too much and try to "improve" Truth — with legalism, liberalism, or any other man-made theology — we end up with short breath after a while; we might even turn pale or blue in the face!

The one Truth cannot be improved upon. In order to keep ourselves (our "tunics") together, we must use God's belt for us; our own meager strings are too weak, or cut too deeply into our vital parts! In Him we stand in comfort.

Over our belt we then put the "breastplate" of righteousness. The breatplate in Paul's time covered the entire trunk, from the shoulders to the beginning of the legs. All the vital organs of the body that sustain our existence are in that area. A blow to the heart, lungs, stomach or groin can incapacitate an unprotected man.

Thus it is with our spiritual life. Christ's breastplate of righteousness sustains us, for He *is* our righteousness (Jeremiah 23:6, I Corinthians 1:30), and His blood protects us.

Unfortunately, many people put on their *own* righteousness every morning. They just know they are "right," and mercy on anyone who doesn't agree. Such "righteous" saints can hardly wait for a fight — in fact, they'll often start one themselves, and hurl some of the many chips on their shoulders at others. And all in the name of Christ our Righteousness!

We all need God's breastplate — our own is of little use, and gets "bent out of shape" constantly. His righteousness alone can cover the sins of our "flesh" — sins which usually take the form of overindulgence and lust, and come from within our unprotected torsos. We also need Him to cover our "righteousness" which — being of the Law — is self-righteousness and as bad as wickedness in God's eyes (Isaiah 64:6).

Next we need to cover our feet with God's "shoes" of the Gospel of peace: *God's peace* (Ephesians 2:14, John 14:27). In the days of Rome, the only parts of the body which a soldier could touch the ground with were his feet. If he fell down, he was shamed. If he crawled on all fours, it was assumed that he was either wounded or a coward — or both.

Likewise, this world should always be under our spiritual "feet" — the peace of God should be between us and the world. If we walk with bare feet, the ground can hurt us. The world does not and will not change; it remains hot, cold, stony, thorny, dirty, covered with broken pieces of pointed glass to cut us. That's why God provided protection: His peace! In Christ is our peace (John 16:33).

Truly, peace without Him does not last long. Satan will try his best to irritate us. As a result, it is not so often the big calamities that disturb and cut us as it is those little "gnats" and "ants" of Satan's that try to bite us. Bare feet also pick up dirt, fungus and splinters — and then we limp with little hurts and pains that aggravate our whole being. Doctors tell us that aching or wounded feet affect the entire body. Anyone who has to stand all day on his feet can testify to that. And any woman who puts on the wrong shoes for a day of walking and shopping knows better the next time!

So, it is important that we put on the right shoes — the ones provided by God — to take us along our spiritual walk. If we wear shoes that do not truly fit, we get blisters; if the heel is too high, our vanity might be served, but it throws our backbone out of kilter and we feel pain.

One of my sons, I remember, used to love to take his shoes off when he was small. Oh, the hours I spent hunting for one lost shoe and taking care of his stubbed toes! I would always try to make him look for his own shoes, and — without fail — he would look for a while, and then present just a single shoe proudly, as though his mission had been accomplished. It took him a while to understand that just one shoe wasn't enough — only both shoes would do the job. And so it is with spiritual babes. Sometimes we put on only one shoe, or wear shoes only when we go to church or religious meetings. We put on the peace of God for a few hours, or when things go smoothly for us, and then take them off. But God's shoes were given to us for nothing less than day-to-day battle — so we have to learn to wear them *both, all* the time.

LET'S PRAY: Dear Jesus, peace isn't my natural state of mind. I cause much commotion and trouble, and there is much turmoil both around and within me. You never said that You would make the world around me peaceful, and it isn't. You did say, though, that You would make me peaceful with Your peace. That's good — I need Your help. Lord, babes have a hard time learning how to put their "shoes" on and how to tie the laces correctly. I am not there yet, and I'm afraid I'm losing my peace — the peace that You gave me — rather often. I know things will get better as I learn to put them on right, though — and I love to wear Your perfectly fitting shoes more and more. Amen.

31. A Shield, A Helmet and a Sword

The shield was by far the largest part of a Roman soldier's armor; it was as tall as the man who carried it, and he could hide behind it for complete protection. And because the shield was moveable, he could use it any time, in the place he needed it the most.

God gives His children a "shield" of faith that protects them in the same way. We can't "manufacture" faith, we can't just "try hard" until we produce it, we don't have the capacity to make it ourselves. God gives us faith as a "birthday gift" when we are born again (Ephesians 2:8). And just as human arms learn to hold a shield, so our wills learn to hold and move the faith that God gives us so freely. We decide to believe, and He gives us the rest! Our faith does not depend on our feelings or the amount of knowledge we have; our faith is based strictly on the One who gives it to us — the One in whom we trust.

The Roman soldier didn't trust his own arms to protect him, but he did trust his shield. He held one because he could place his trust in it far more than he could in his own self. We embrace God's faith for the same reason.

Some people, unfortunately, have too much faith in their *own* faith in God, and believe that they can use it like a magic button to push and receive anything they want. But we are shielded by *His* faith, not ours! Nor can we live by another Christian's faith or shield!

You see, God custom-makes our armor; He fits it to our own size and arm length. When we try to hide behind somebody else's shield it doesn't fit — it's either too short (in which case our head and feet stick out unprotected) or too big (so that our arm gets tired holding it, and we let it fall). God gives each one of us our own shield of faith, and — as we grow — He adds just the right amount to it Himself (Romans 1:17, Ephesians 4:7).

Significantly, the Bible uses the word "faith" only in relation to God, never in reference to our relationships with people. And God knows the reason why, for we are very foolish if we ever put our faith in any human being (I Corinthians 2:12, Psalm 118:8). We are simply too human to be trusted completely; we cannot even trust our own hearts until we give them to God (Proverbs 28:25, 26, Jeremiah 17:9).

What *is* faith, then, as it was given to us by God? It is the faith of Christ which He shares with us (Habakkuk 2:4, Galatians 2:20).

What kind of faith did Jesus have? Christ trusted His Father so completely that He could go to the cross and not question His Father. He did not base His faith on any promises of God, but on God Himself — and therefore He acted on the promises of God as an *exercise* of His faith in God.

Faith is *active*, and moves. "This *is* the victory that overcometh . . . even our faith" (I John 5:4). Faith is also passive, because we don't ever use it as a weapon to hit someone over the head with, not even Satan. We move the shield or hold it still, as need be. We never fight or show off with it.

So let's not try to grow, produce or manufacture our own faith based on our knowledge or high and flighty feelings. That kind of shield will break and burn up in the attack of Satan's fiery darts. Let's ask God to give us *His* shield of faith, and hide behind it!

Another vital part of the Roman soldier's armor was his helmet. It covered his entire head; he could even pull down a plate that protected his face. In battle, it was his physical "salvation."

David knew a lot about salvation, and knew where it came from (Psalm 68:20, 98:2). The Lord was his salvation (Psalm 27:1). Thus we know that salvation is a Person — the Lord Jesus Himself — rather than a belief in a creed or the religious practice of the law or a high and mighty feeling.

Christ Himself has to cover our heads — our thinking, our wills and our senses. If He doesn't, we are in deep trouble. Doubts and guilt feelings torture us. We are constantly tempted by our senses (such as the lust of the eye toward food, sex, pride and vanities). We want to hear the wrong things, say the wrong things, and — most of all — work out our own salvation. But if we do that, we worry constantly over whether we will ever make it to heaven.

When God's helmet covers us, however, we *know* that we will make it — because Christ is in heaven and we have Him as our salvation, rather than our own works and thoughts.

So, after we are all dressed and have our shields and helmets in place, we reach for the Sword of the Spirit, which is the Word of God (Hebrews 4:12, Revelation 1:16, 19:15).

The Word of God divides us into spirit, soul and body — but it is not used to fight. It is used to defend. We are simply not called by the Word to attack; that is God's job.

We Christians use the Word of God to "resist" and "stand firm" and "withstand" Satan's fiery darts of temptation and doubt. In fact, the Lord Himself showed us how to use the sword. Satan tempted Him fiercely in the areas of appetite, pride, exaltation and disobedience toward the Father's plan and will (Luke 4:1-13). And Christ used His sword to parry Satan and answered every temptation the same way: He said, "It is written . . ." The Word of God was His and it is our defense that will put Satan to flight.

So let's not neglect our sword or use it improperly and let it become dull. Every morning we should get dressed in God's armor. We should pick up the shield and the helmet and the sword before we face the day — and we do that with prayer. If we forget to pray, Satan finds us the way he wants us — in our undergarments, unprotected. How embarrassing and dangerous that is!

LET'S PRAY: Dear Lord, I am only a babe and don't know how to dress myself completely every morning yet. Will You give me a hand, and help me to put it *all* on, so that I don't forget one of the parts? So often I put the shoe on the wrong foot! Lord, You are my cover, my helmet, my breastplate and shoes — so teach me how to put and keep You on for my protection. I am not too much to look at when You don't cover me, Lord — and I am so easy to attack! I am Your vulnerable child, Father, and need to hide behind You — I feel very secure in that spot. How good You are to have thought of everything I need for protection! You provide it all because I have nothing on my own but "bare me" — and with You, that's enough. Amen.

ABOUT GOD'S SCHOOL

32. God's Three R's

If parents truly care about their children, they begin teaching them as best they can from babyhood on. Only neglectful parents let their babies grow up to "do as they please." Mature adults know that such an upbringing would produce children that are wild, selfish and hard to live with.

God is a perfect Father and would never neglect His children or let them grow up untrained and undisciplined (Hebrews 12:7, 8). He sends each of us through His school in life to learn and prepare for something very special: our service for Him on this earth, and our position in eternity.

It's important to understand one thing very clearly: God's school does not *make* us His children. Rather, we come *as* His children to be trained for Him.

We do not become His children by way of a lifelong training process. He does not kick us out or disown us if we don't learn quickly. He teaches us so that we might live a happier, fuller life, and so that we can do more for Him and bring sheaves with us into eternity (II Timothy 4:7, 8).

Remember too that we don't "earn" our positions by fast learning. Even if we fail our lessons over and over again, we are still His children.

We *have* eternal life already (John 3:36); we *are* His children by His name (Acts 11:26).

God gives us two kinds of promises. The first — His promises of *love* — are for the most part unconditional or based on one condition only and are not affected by our human behavior.

"He that believeth on the Son *hath* eternal life," Christ announced.

Notice that Jesus did *not* say, "He that believeth on the Son will someday have eternal life after he learns enough and proves himself." God's promise of love and eternal life asks only that we take and accept what Christ did for us. He did it *all* — we accept and take it. And for that we receive positions as children in the family of God (Romans 8:16).

So when God trains us, it is not to *make* us His children. Rather, it is to "polish" us and help us develop ourselves into His likeness (Ephesians 4:15). He wants us to "look" more like Him (I John 3:2).

The second kind of promises that God makes — the ones He uses in His school — *are* most often conditional.

He says: "Look, my child, if you practice, learn, and follow my advice, you shall have in return a happier life, more personal rewards and more honors in heaven (Matthew 25:23, Revelation 3:21).

Unfortunately, some of God's children don't learn very fast — as a matter of fact, they don't get much further than "kindergarten" for most of their lives. They remain His children, of course, but instead of enjoying happy, fulfilled lives — instead of having something to "show" when they enter heaven — they come empty-handed, with nothing to show but their own bare lives (I Corinthians 3:11-15).

Yes, and some of God's children will be like a brand plucked from the burning (Zechariah 3:2, I Corinthians 3:15). At the last moment they will be rescued — they will not have much time in God's school at all, but they shall be in heaven nevertheless.

The thief on the cross, for instance, was in God's school

only from the moment he accepted Christ to the time he died. We don't know how many hours that was, but we do know that he was still living when the executioners took Christ off the cross and broke the legs of the two thieves to hasten their deaths. Through the final hours of his physical agony and darkest loneliness, the penitent thief had one bright spot that he could cling to: Christ's promise that he would be with Him in heaven (Luke 23:43).

What faith that thief must have had, to trust completely in the words of a dying, condemned man beside him who had been forsaken by so many others! The thief learned in just a matter of moments what some people take a lifetime to learn!

So God's school *can* be long or short — but in any case, He will *always* try to teach us His three R's of learning: the right relationship to God, the right relationship to others, and the right relationship to ourselves (Luke 10:27, 28). Note that the Bible does *not* try to teach us relationships to things or possessions, or even to the earth itself (Luke 12:15, Philippians 3:19).

When Abraham's descendants slowly formed themselves into that special nation that was to show the true God to the heathen nations, they failed to learn God's three R's thoroughly. They *did* give God several names to show His might, His power, and His frightening majesty. They called Him Elohim, Adonai, El Shaddai. But all those names related only to His Creation, and to the respect for Him, the Lord of hosts. They did not give him a name which depicted their relationship to God, because they did not fully understand that relationship.

When Christ was announced and came to this earth, however, He tried to show the Jews and the rest of the world a side of God they didn't know. Christ Himself bore a name that represented a relationship (Matthew

1:21). And He revealed the *Father* God (John 8:58, 14:8-10).

LET'S PRAY: Dear God, I am a bit scared to begin in Your school. You see, I am one of Your very dumb kids and everything I've learned so far I've had to learn the hard way. God, I am not sure that I know much about relationships yet, but I certainly am willing to give it a try. I am so glad that You are my teacher! I trust You because You love me! Amen.

33. Relationship to Ourselves

Why should we begin our study of God's three R's by looking at the relationship to ourselves? Doesn't the Bible point toward our relationship with God as the most important "R" to learn?

Yes, it does, but the Bible also says that our love of our brother is the measuring stick toward our relationship with God (I John 4:20, 21). And Jesus said to love our neighbor *as* ourselves (Matthew 22:39). So before we examine our relationship to others and our relationship to God, we'd better look first at what it means to love ourselves!

That phrase, "love ourselves," might sound strange to some people — particularly those who have been raised within a religious environment. More often than not, such people have been taught at home and in church that we must crucify ourselves — despise ourselves, put ourselves down, and deny ourselves.

Well, let's make one thing clear: The Bible *never* asks anyone to crucify himself! Paul says in no uncertain terms that he is crucified with Christ (Galatians 2:20), and that our "old man" (Romans 6:6) is crucified with Him. And that means exactly what it says: We all went to the cross when Christ did. He did it *for* us, and now it is *done!*

I Am But a Little Child

What part of us was crucified and had to die on the cross with Jesus? Our "flesh" and the works of the flesh (Galatians 5:19-24). Must self (the soul) die to follow Christ? No, self has to *deny* itself (Matthew 16:24-26).

What does it mean to deny yourself? It means to say "no" to self interest, — to renounce yourself — whenever the Spirit tells you to do something that your self doesn't want to do. In other words, we learn to say "no" to our self because we know we are better off obeying God than obeying our own self's wishes.

Christ said that we must love our neighbor as ourselves. And if we put that statement in a negative sense, it tells us that we shall *not* be able to love our neighbor (and consequently God) unless we learn to love ourselves first.

So where do we begin? Well, first of all we must learn to accept ourselves as we are — what we are, and where we are.

I had an extremely difficult time learning that lesson. It took me years in the school of God to get that concept through my head. My background was such that I had a very crippled self-image. I grew up as an orphan, and knew that I was neither wanted nor needed. I didn't "belong" to anyone — at least not in my own mind — until Adolf Hitler claimed me as one of "his" youth. So I gave my life and affection and devotion to him and his cause.

As a Nazi, I was taught that the individual is of no importance whatsoever. Only *das Volk* (the people) was everything. So at the end of World War II, when Hitler's regime and all the things I believed in shattered into a thousand pieces, my already crippled self-concept shattered with it. I didn't know who I was, why I existed or where I was going.

Thus, when I finally found my way to a church, I quickly picked myself some "models" in the church fellowship and tried to become like them.

I was told to try to be like Jesus, but I didn't really know Jesus for years, even as a church member. "How can I make Him my model?" I thought.

Over and over, day after day, I tried as hard as I could to change myself — to become ladylike, composed, cool and collected, always calm and sweet. I had always admired such traits, but didn't seem to have them myself. I tried to get rid of my impulsiveness, my temper and my "unladylike" behavior — but I never succeeded. Oh, I managed to put on a good front ever so often — but as a famous American showman once said, "You can fool some of the people all of the time and all of the people some of the time, but you can't fool all of the people all of the time!"

Eventually, though, Christ became real to me and we became friends. He began to show me how to accept myself. And it was so easy, once I saw the Truth!

After all, He made me and formed me in my mother's womb by His design and choice! I was not an accident thrown together by the sexual desires of my parents. He *knew* me in my mother's womb even before I was born (Psalm 139:13).

When we think of ourselves as valueless we accuse God of making "junk" when He formed us!

Christ made something very special when He made you — something so unique that it never existed before, and will never be made exactly the same way again. Every human being is a unique individual, never to be repeated. God is so creative that He never makes two snowflakes the same, never a leaf exactly as the next on the same tree. God doesn't believe in putting anything or anybody into the same form or mold. God delights in our individuality; He accepts you as you are, where you are and what you are — so why not do the same?

Do you think you would like yourself more if you had a different nose or less oily skin or a more shapely figure or were taller or shorter or more outgoing? People who have plastic surgery on their noses, or attend modeling school in order to be more ladylike, may improve their appearance — but they don't solve the *real* problem! You still have to learn to *like* yourself!

So let's remember as we start out in God's school: God wants us to be ourselves, to accept ourselves and to develop ourselves. We need to be polished, not re-built! We want to look more like Him, but we have to do it within ourselves by our own individual blueprint. We're not supposed to become somebody else; we need only be content in being God's child as He made us!

LET'S PRAY: Dear Jesus, this is a new and confusing thing to me, and it will take me a while to digest it. You know that I dislike myself rather than the wrong things I do. And I can see how dumb that is, but it will take me a while to sort it all out. Jesus, I told You before that You have a very dumb child in Your school. I know that You have all the love and patience of a perfect Teacher, but I can't seem to find a way to be patient with and love myself. Teach me how to do that — if I follow You and do what You do, I will *have* to love and be myself! The thought overwhelms me! Thank You for teaching me such new and wonderfully exciting things! Amen.

34. Our Relationship to Others

As we have just learned, our relationship to others is strongly influenced by our attitude toward ourselves. It is a proven fact that we dislike in others what we dislike in ourselves, and like in others what we accept as "good" in ourselves. And it is also a well-known psychological fact that parents often reject the child that is most like them. Furthermore, children who hate their parents almost always grow up to be parents who treat *their* children in the same hateful ways! What a vicious circle!

Another example I can give you — one which I am very amused about at the present time — is my youngest son. He has quite a temper, and tries hard to overcome it with the help of Christ. Right now, though, he is terribly annoyed at one of his former high school principals, who also displays a very fiery temperament. The man bugs my son to no end, and I hear a lot about it — but I can't help but think that the situation would be considerably better if only *one* of them had a temper!

How human we all are, and how hard it is to accept that "human-ness" in ourselves and others! (Romans 7:19, 20).

Considering our nature, then, how do we begin to love someone else? By beginning where we began with ourselves: with acceptance!

Accept others for what they are, how they are and where they are. Don't try so hard to change *them* just because you're frustrated over the same things that you can see — but have a hard time changing — in yourself (Romans 7:24, Jeremiah 13:23, Matthew 6:27).

Remember, we must all *learn* and be *willing* to do so; we must all deny ourselves in our relationship with God and others, but it is only God who has the right to change people within their own blueprints. *He* made those blueprints — it is not our place to try to change them.

Interestingly enough, when a person comes to me for counsel I can usually tell how that person feels about himself by listening to what he has to say about others. If an individual is down on the whole wide world, I know that the person hates himself most of all.

There is no question that — as individual personalities — we have to accept the fact that we're going to find some people easy to get along with, and others rather hard to take. Some people are simply incompatible, and personality clashes will develop between them. Even the Apostle Paul had that problem (Acts 15:36-38).

So what should we do? Should we seek out only the compatible people and ignore, fight with, and gossip about the others?

Well, remember: God doesn't say "Love thy neighbor if you like him!"

As you mature in Christ, you will learn much about the concept of love. But before you can even begin to do that, you have to start with one very basic lesson — you must learn to accept all people as individuals that *God* made because it pleased Him to make them *the way they are*. It is not your calling to change them.

Remember too that Christ died for every member of the human race; *anyone* who accepts Him is your brother or sister in the family of God, and — as a result — you shall spend eternity together. So you'd better try to get along with each other — eternity is a mighty long time!

And, just as you consider one who lives in Christ as your "brother" or "sister," so must you consider the one who hasn't yet found Christ — and needs help — as your "neighbor." He might be nasty, filthy, rude and cantankerous, but don't forget that there may be a reason. He might be hard to live with because he has fallen into the hands of a robber and is bleeding from the beatings of the enemy (Luke 10:33, 34).

The robber and murderer, of course, is Satan. You were in his power once, too, until someone helped you find Christ. So now *you* need to be the good Samaritan to help your neighbor!

Please notice, however, that I said "help" your neighbor, not "manipulate" him. One of the sorest spots in our interactions with others is our natural tendency to manipulate people. But whenever we try to do that, we hurt ourselves and others — and God. You see, manipulation is opposite to God's great gift to His beings: freedom of choice.

It is amazing how often we try to manipulate people in the name of Christ! We try to trick our neighbors or relatives into going to church with us, to believe as we do, to see things our way — and then we feel insulted if everything doesn't work as planned. So we blame the other person, and wash our hands in innocence over the "lost" souls.

The Holy Spirit will *never* ask you or help you to manipulate the free will of anyone — not even your mate's or your child's. Neither trick nor force, temper tantrum nor tears will do the work, little babe; you must learn to accept *both yourself and others*. You must respect everyone's freedom of choice, and love them, and have the patience to wait for them to choose *by their own free will* to join the family of God. Then, with Christ's help, you can learn to help each other as all brothers and sisters do. Don't get too discouraged — babes *do* quarrel, and God knows it! That's part of the learning and maturing process.

LET'S PRAY: Dear Jesus, Your school is rough right now and I am not so sure I can advance very fast. It is hard enough to live with myself, but to accept everyone as my brother, sister or neighbor is nearly impossible for me to learn. I am not so sure I can do that, but I know You can do it for me! So will You do it as I *let You do it?* Thank You, Jesus, for giving me the love I don't have either for myself or for others. Next, will you show me how to share what You gave me? Amen.

35. Our Relationship to God

In order to have any kind of relationship with someone, we must first know or at least be acquainted with that person.

Likewise, we cannot relate to or love God unless we know Him or at least are acquainted with Him. The Bible tells us to "know" God (Hosea 13:4, John 17:3).

He is even generous enough to say to some people who have strong reservations about Him, or who sin deliberately against God, "Come, let us reason together!" (Isaiah 1:18).

We know God best through Jesus, when He was on this earth. When Jesus came here, He became a human being (Hebrews 2:18). Satan tried his utmost to make Jesus sin, and He was tempted in all points just as Satan tempts us (Hebrews 4:15). Christ also *learned* obedience through His suffering for us (Hebrews 5:8).

But just the fact that He became human for us doesn't mean that He ever stopped being God. He laid His divinity aside by His free will while He was on earth (Philippians 2:5-7), but once in a while a flash of that divinity shone out of Him.

One of the names of the almighty God is "I Am" (Exodus 3:14). Jesus Christ knew who He was, and He would announce without fear:

"I Am the Good Shepherd" (John 10:14).

"I Am the Living Bread" (John 6:35).

"I Am the Way, the Truth and the Life" (John 14:6).

He also said, when He rose from the grave and talked to His disciples, *"All* power is given unto Me in heaven and in earth" (Matthew 28:18).

Sometimes, we study and see the human side of God in Christ so much that we forget that there is another side to our Big Brother (Jesus) and to God our Father.

When a baby is born, it doesn't realize what type of family he or she has been born into. Its parents are just smiling faces, cooing words, a secure arm, warmth, and food and care.

As children grow older, however, they become more aware of the kind of families into which they have been born. After a while, for instance, a youngster knows if he is a child of a peasant or a child of the governor.

Similarly, as babes in Christ mature, they come to know God as more than a babe in a manger and the dying or risen Christ of the cross.

The Christ we belong to has the most majestic, magnificent, awe-inspiring glory and power in the universe. He is the King of kings (Revelation 17:14, I Timothy 6:15). He is the Ruler above every ruler and His majesty is so overwhelming that angels cover their faces when they worship Him (Isaiah 6:2).

God is so mighty that the earth is only a footstool for Him (Isaiah 66:1). However, we are told by Jesus that we may come boldly into His presence (Ephesians 3:11-13, Hebrews 4:16). We are also told that we can ask the Father in Christ's name and He will hear us gladly (John 15:16).

So, we may do as Jesus told us, but we must *never* approach God without reverence, respect and admiration.

It's important to understand that the more we see God for what He really is, the more He will show us who *we* are. When we are born again, we are sons and daughters of the mighty King of the universe and we call Him Father. We are sisters and brothers of our Creator and Big Brother, Jesus Christ. We carry within us the spark of eternal life and the Holy Spirit Himself, and all of it because we *accepted* God's gift to us.

A baby of any royal family on earth is taught from infancy to behave like a child befitting his father, the king. Likewise, it is just as important that babes in Christ learn how to behave in our royal Father's presence. We also learn how to represent Him to others, and how to relate ourselves to the overwhelming fact that we are royalty through Jesus Christ (Revelation 1:5, 6).

What splendor and glory eternity will bring to us, we cannot even comprehend yet (Revelation 22:1-5). What our eyes have never seen nor our ears heard, our Father has prepared and it is already waiting for us (I Corinthians 2:9). But even on this earth He wants to glorify His royal name in His royal children.

So let's be careful not to act like children of a beggar! We have a sure promise for everything we need on this earth, given to us by our Father, the King. He owns the cattle on a thousand hills and all the silver and gold (Psalm 50:10, Haggai 2:8). He dresses up the lilies of the fields. So don't go around complaining for your needs — all you have to do is ask your Father!

LET'S PRAY: Almighty King and Heavenly Father, it is hard for me to comprehend how great and majestic You are. I think of You as my Friend and Father, and I keep forgetting how great You are, and what a great universe You handle. I can't even understand why I have the privilege and honor to belong to Your royal family. It's nothing that I did or have that made me worthy — but Your royal Word said so and here I am, Your child, the child of The King! May I always bring honor and respect and joy to You, my Royal Father! In Jesus' name. Amen.

CHILDHOOD PROBLEMS

36. Loneliness

Nearly all babes in Christ experience a wonderful, warm feeling of love and security at the time of their conversion. But sometimes, after a few weeks or months, they lose that "glow" and feel lonely, depressed and fearful. Sometimes they even wonder if God has abandoned them.

Well, it is very typical for a little child to be afraid of the dark or of being alone. Don't worry about it — such feelings are only natural. But you *do* have to learn to overcome them, and the only way to do that is to understand the nature of those feelings. Let's look at loneliness first.

I shall never forget a prayer meeting I once attended, where I sat and listened to a young woman — a newborn babe in Christ — sob her heart out. We had formed small prayer groups and were sharing our personal thoughts and spiritual needs with each other.

"Please," the woman said under her tears, "pray for me because I have lost contact with God. I have searched my heart, I have reached out to Him, but my prayers don't seem to get past the ceiling!"

"Honey," I asked quietly, "when did you accept Christ into your life?"

"Just a few months ago," she replied. "At first, I could feel Him within me, all around me — I glowed inside. But now the glow is gone and there is nothing — I can feel nothing!" She sobbed some more.

"My friend," I said, smiling, "you haven't lost God. You are just growing up. You see, God permits some new babies in Christ to have a very deep emotional experience when they are born again. And those emotions can glow for a while, sometimes for as long as several months, but eventually there comes a time when God says, 'Now it's time for my baby to have the emotional lights turned off during the night. She has to learn to trust Me in the dark.' "

One of the most important things we need to develop in order to mature in Christ is faith (Hebrews 11:6). Hebrews 11:1 defines faith as "the substance of things hoped for, the evidence of things not seen." So we know that faith — which is a gift of God — cannot truly be experienced by us when we can *only* see, touch, or feel Him. The only thing required of us is that we *believe* Him, we experience trust in Him without the evidence of our senses, our emotions or even our understanding.

God does not build His Word and the fulfillment of His promises on senses, emotions and understanding. He builds everything He said or did on Himself. Because He said so, it *is* so, regardless of whether or not we can "feel" Him. The only thing required of us is that we *believe* Him, for God cannot operate in and for us as long as we don't believe (James 4:2, Hebrews 11:6).

So, when you cannot "feel" a thing, you must never forget one of the basic principles of faith: *God said it, you believe it, and that settles it!*

One of my favorite stories is a modern parable about three women who came to their church's altar to kneel and pray. As they did so, Jesus stepped into the church and walked down the aisle toward the three praying women. He bent down and hugged the first woman; He touched the second woman on the shoulder; and He simply passed by the third woman.

Someone who saw the entire incident touched the Lord on the sleeve and asked, "Lord, did You love the first woman — the one you hugged — the most?"

Hansi

P.O. Box 552

Huntington Beach, Ca. 92648

YOUR STAMP HERE HELPS TOO

(Please print your address)

Name _____
Address _____
City _____
State _____ Zip _____

☐ Jesus Christ is my Master and Lord.
☐ I want to do something for God and my country.
☐ I request your prayers for:

_____
_____
_____

☐ I will pray for the HANSI Ministries.
☐ I want to be put on your mailing list.
☐ I want information on your SPARC Program.

Comments: _____
_____
_____
_____

ALBUM: LEST WE FORGET TWO
messages on freedom and prayer......$8.00 *(New!)

(Continued on other side.)

NAME _____
ADDRESS _____
CITY _____ STATE _____ ZIP _____

Hansi MINISTRIES, INC.
P.O. Box 552
Huntington Beach, CA 92648

YOUR
STAMP
HERE
HELPS
TOO

"No," said the Lord gently, "the last one, whom I passed by, is very special to me, for she is able to live by faith and that glorifies Me the most!"

Our heavenly Father *has* to turn off the lights of our emotions and understanding once in a while to teach us to walk by faith (II Corinthians 5:7). But He will *never* turn off the lights of our spirit and the Holy Spirit — that's why it is so important to learn to "walk in the light of the spirit" (Galatians 5:16-25, I John 1:7).

As we learn to "listen" to God and to our still small voice that the Holy Spirit uses, as we ask Jesus to cleanse us whenever we do foolish things or doubt Him and His love when it gets dark, as we learn to obey the intuitions of the Holy Spirit instead of our own fickle feelings, God will fit our hearts perfectly together with others who belong to the family (body) of Christ (Ephesians 4:16).

You might "feel" lonely, but you are *never* alone. God is near, even in the darkest hour (Hebrews 13:5).

Perhaps, as a babe in Christ, you feel that the people around you — friends and neighbors and others — have suddenly become unfriendly to you since your conversion, and exclude you from their activities. On the one hand, it might just be your imagination; have you taken the time to communicate with those people — to tell them that you feel left out? On the other hand, it might be true. Your family and friends may well have reacted with hostility to your conversion, and think you have "gone off the deep end." That has to be expected in many cases; the Bible tells us so (Matthew 10:34-37).

Remember, though: It takes time to form new friendships and to grow into your new family. You are going through a period of transition, and will certainly experience emotional lows in the process. Don't fight it or run from it; face it as something that God permits to help you grow closer to Him. God has promised that He will never let any temptation or hardship come to you that is greater than you can bear; He will make a way of escape for you (I Corinthians 10:13). If you can wait upon the Lord, even when you feel alone, He will give you the desires of your heart (Psalm 37:1-7).

LET'S PRAY: Dear Lord, I feel so lonely so often, even in the biggest crowd or when I am invited to be with others. Nobody seems to understand me, Jesus. I have nobody I can really talk to without being misunderstood, nobody to confide in without being laughed at or rejected. Lord, I hate to be alone and in my own company. Could it be that I don't like myself and don't want to be with myself? Now Lord, You have promised not to leave me alone, ever! Thank You, God, I am so glad I found all three of You. Amen.

37. Depression

Depression is like a dark cloud over the sun, like frost on pink apple blossoms, like mildew over the soul. It is a sorrow in the heart that affects both body and soul — and can also break our spirits (Proverbs 15:13).

When we get depressed, we always remember one thing — a fact that is easy to forget: *Everybody* gets "the blues" once in a while. It's not just females who have "mood cycles" — men have them, too!

We must accept the simple reality that depression is a normal thing — that we cannot always sit on top of a cloud or a mountain, that the sun cannot always shine, that some rain must fall in order to nurture growth and life. When we accept that, we have won half the battle.

Unfortunately, some people believe — and tell others — that the perfect true Christian will always be happy, always smiling, never sad. But the Bible tells us this is not so. Jesus said to His disciples, before He departed, that they would have many troubles and tribulations. And Ezekiel 13:22 tells us that other people can make righteous people sad.

Then what about all the rejoicing the Bible tells us to do?

Well, keep in mind that joy is different from constant bubbling, smiling happiness. We can have the "joy in the Lord" while tears stream down our faces.

The American ideal — the kind of carefree, always-a-happy-ending life that comes to you in wide-screen color from the phony world of Hollywood — is totally unrealistic, and has done untold damage to millions of people all over the globe. It puts people into a dream world, makes them want things they can never have because such things simply do not relate to real life.

So, if you find yourself frequently depressed and blue, pray about it, and let the Holy Spirit show you where the *real* root of your problem is.

If you're unhappy about where you are, what you are, and how much you have—if you're dissatisfied about yourself or your environment — your blues are a result of being covetous. You believe that more money, more clothing, a fancier home would make you "happier"? But the Bible tells us that "more" things don't make God's children happier, and that they often bring with them many sorrows (I Timothy 6:6-10).

Why should two closets full of clothing make you happier than one closet full? Any person, rich or poor, can eat only until his stomach is full. The body can wear only one outfit at a time. So if we have enough clothing to cover ourselves properly, and are not missing any meals, let's thank God for it. After all, millions of other people all over the globe are starving, and have neither a bed to sleep in nor sufficient clothing to protect themselves against cold and heat. So, thank God for what you *do* have!

Some people feel that anger — like sadness — is something which should always be suppressed, or kept within them. Everyone gets angry once in a while. The Bible recognizes that fact and in Ephesians 4:26, 27 gives us good advice on what we can do with our anger. We learn that if it is directed toward the right cause at the right time and used correctly, anger can become something positive. Suppressed anger creates depression.

Abraham Lincoln, before he became President of the United States, once took a trip down the Mississippi to New Orleans aboard a boat full of produce. After taking care of business, he and a boatman wandered through the city and came upon a slave market — the first that Lincoln had ever seen. Abe watched for a while, aghast, and became very angry. Eventually, he turned to his companion and said with deep seriousness: "If I ever get the chance to hit that thing, I'll hit it hard!" I thank God for Lincoln's anger, for later on he *did* hit that thing hard, and abolished the evil practice!

The Bible tells us of an angry Jesus who cleaned out His Father's house on earth with a whip and a voice that everyone could hear (John 2:13-16). And we know that Jesus never sinned. So anger does have its right place in life.

On the other hand, if anger hits the wrong "spot," watch out! One of the worst places your anger can go to is your subconscious. People who rarely show their temper are not necessarily cool and collected personalities — they might just be afraid to spoil their "well balanced" image, or perhaps they're too inhibited to express how they really feel. So they "swallow" their anger.

In any case, the result can be at least as bad as if they went around "blowing their tops." Suppression of anger is extremely harmful to the whole person — physically, emotionally and spiritually. Ulcers, high blood pressure and other bodily ailments — even severe mental illness and a broken spirit — are the terrible effects of suppressing anger and the resentment that goes with it.

You say you can't think of very many people you're angry with? Well, one is enough — and perhaps that one person is yourself. Maybe you get so uptight with yourself because you still can't stop doing "stupid" things even though you are now a Christian and know better. Is that the case?

Then you are forgetting something! Rejoice, little baby, even if your heart condemns you, for God is greater than your heart (I John 3:20)!

Ask God to put your anger toward a righteous cause, and to help you accept your "mood swings." Let God sit in the swing with you!

LET'S PRAY: Dear Jesus, I know that I am moody and blue too often. I have a habit of feeling sorry for myself, and when things don't go my way I withdraw and feel depressed. Would You show me where the root of it is? Am I angry inside or discontented? If my depression has a physical cause — such as low blood sugar or thyroid troubles or any other problem with my metabolism — please make me aware of it and send me to the *right* doctor. I want to become a well-adjusted person, Jesus, for Your sake. Amen.

38. Anxiety and Fears

Those who study the Bible carefully will learn that the Word of God repeats the phrases "fear not" or "don't be afraid" ninety-six times. God knows His earth children well, doesn't He?

God knows that Adam's sin and disobedience brought fear of death, fear of being or getting hurt, fear of being left alone, fear of fear itself, and hundreds of other fears.

But is fear wrong?

No, not all fear! There is such a thing as healthy fear — the kind that helps us avoid calamities.

A baby, for instance, must be taught to fear fire, or he will eventually burn himself. A child must learn to fear the dangers of water — and thus learn to swim — or he may someday drown. Such a tragedy happened to some friends of mine once, when their toddler innocently jumped into a swimming pool and died.

Spiritual babes need to have a healthy fear, too. The Bible tells us to fear God. But you must remember that the original meaning of the word "fear" was "to reverence." So the word does not imply that we should be afraid of God, but — rather — that we should come to God in reverence, awe and total loyalty (Revelation 14:7, Deuteronomy 4:10).

Jesus also warned us to fear him which is able to destroy both soul and body in hell (Matthew 10:28).

Some people, unfortunately, think that they need to fear absolutely nothing — that they can do just as they please, dare what they want to dare and "get away with murder." But they're wrong! They should learn quickly that those who don't fear (reverence) God now will have to fear Him in a different way when He comes to judge the earth (Hebrews 10:29-31, 12:29).

It is too bad that people, by their very nature, tend to put their fears in the wrong places. If we "fear" God, we don't need to fear anything else. But Satan loves to torture people with fears. In fact, there is even a "spirit of fear," which the Bible clearly states was *not* sent by God (Romans 8:15). There is no fear in love (I John 4:18); therefore our loving Father sends no fear to His children.

Fear caused a battle in my soul for many years, even after I became a Christian. The memory of a horrible war and the nightmares of time spent in a communist labor camp after that war haunted me mercilessly. My only antidote for those fearful memories was prayer. For years I prayed myself through one fear after another, but I was never able to truly "triumph" over it (Psalm 27:1). I knew that God had the key that would help me conquer my fear — rather than just "keep it under control" — somewhere, so I kept searching. And I eventually found it!

One day a woman came to me for counsel. She told me that she was afraid of a certain something that was happening to her, and seemed to be obsessed by that fear.

"Well," I said to the woman, "why don't you just pray and say, 'Yes, God, if that is Your will, if You *want* that to happen to me, then I shall accept it.' Say 'yes, God' to your fears, for if that is what God thinks best for you, you wouldn't want to fight it. If you could see the end from the beginning, as God does, you would see that His love lets only what is best for you happen."

The troubled girl prayed until she could say it: "Yes, God, Thy will be done . . ." And what she was afraid of *never* happened.

By now, I have learned the same thing. Whenever the devil comes and tries to torture me with worries of what could happen to my children, or that I may die of cancer, or how I might end up penniless, since I have no savings account, I just say to him: "Satan, get lost! If that is God's plan for my future, He knows best and He will see me through. I don't need to take care of myself, He does!" (I Peter 5:7).

The strange thing about our fears is that they almost never really happen. In fact, I've observed that the bad things that do happen to us are often *caused* by our fears. And psychologists agree; they say that we humans *do* bring things upon ourselves simply by fearing them.

What is the opposite of fear? In human terms, we call it courage — but God calls it love. Love drives out fear

(I John 4:18). Love begets love (I John 4:19), and fear begets fear.

Fear also creates anxiety and cowards. The Bible takes a dim view of our anxieties, and tries to show us the foolishness of them (Philippians 4:6, 7). Our worries won't change things — they'll just make things worse.

We know, for example, that anxious people invite physical and mental illness upon themselves and others. Neurotic mothers often produce anxiety-ridden, neurotic children. And the nervous breakdowns that frequently come as a result of constant, needless worrying don't do anybody any good — but they do please the devil. Satan is forever eager to wear down God's children with fear, worries, and anxieties so that he can accuse them before God and the universe of being cowards or worse (Revelation 12:10; Job 1:9-11, 2:4, 5).

We should never let Satan poison us with his spirit of fear! Anxieties and worries can paralyze not only our souls and bodies, but can blind our spirits and block our communion with God as well. Fearful people dishonor the God of love more than any other kind of people, for they proclaim by their fears that they cannot trust God, and that He cannot help.

If we by choice remain fearful, we will not see God. Those who want to be fearful and not trust Him will go where all unbelievers and murderers and liars go — into the fire and the second death (Revelation 21:8). Notice, when you read that passage from Revelation, that the "fearful" go first, before all the other evil and depraved sinners are mentioned — whereas God's children "triumph" with God (John 14:1-3, Revelation 21:23-27).

LET'S PRAY: Dear Jesus, I know that I am a coward — even though I put up a good front. I am afraid of so many things, not only physically but mentally and emotionally too. I worry about what other people think of me, where

I will go in life, what will become of me if I am ever alone, and if I would be true to You, God, if things ever got really tough. I worry myself sick with foolish fears, Jesus, even to the point where I cannot talk to my friends about You because I am afraid they will laugh at me. I know that it is normal for babies to be afraid, but I *do* want to outgrow it — very quickly. You promised to help me and to do *for* me what I cannot do. I am counting on that, Jesus, for I want to tell my spirit of fear to get lost — in Your name. Amen.

COMMUNICATION SKILLS

39. Talking

Every mother knows that it takes the first few years of a baby's life to teach a child how to speak properly; the rest of its life is required to teach him or her when to be quiet.

Words began with God. In the beginning was the Word (John 1:1). Words were one of God's gifts to men, for God and Adam and Eve "talked" to each other. It is obvious that Adam didn't need to learn or develop his language because, right after he came from the hand of his Creator, he "called" every creature by a name he chose for that particular animal (Genesis 2:19, 20).

Communication between God and the couple was "good" and perfect until sin came. Sin clogged communication between God and man, and between people themselves. One of the very first things Adam said after he had eaten the fruit was, "The woman You, God, gave to me, she gave me the fruit" (Genesis 3:12). In other words, the moment Adam disobeyed and sinned, he began to "pass the buck" and tried to put the blame for his own wrong decision on someone else—yes, even on God Himself. I've often wondered if Adam and Eve had the first quarrel that evening, after God had left, by trying to put the blame on each other.

It's important to understand that efficient communication skills are not so much a matter of *knowing* words as they are, but of learning how to *use* words *correctly*. It is a rare case that someone is not able to talk — and for such people other ways of "communicating" are usually found. Most people, though, do have a basic vocal vocabulary with which they can express themselves.

It's true that some people — the introverts — are shy and inhibited and say almost nothing while others — the extroverts — talk on and on, non-stop. But *both* types need to understand that just a few words — used effectively — are all that's really needed to communicate as much or more than a torrent of idle talk (Matthew 12: 36, 37). It's not how *much* we say, but *how* we say it and *what* is said (Colossians 4:6, John 9:25).

I have five children, and all of them learned to talk before they learned to walk. However, as they grew older, some became more outgoing while others tended to be more on the quiet side.

I myself am an extrovert, and have learned many things from my shy teenage daughter. For instance, I've noticed that — although she always had a much harder time making friends than her outgoing older sister, the friendships she eventually did make lasted longer.

One summer I sent my quiet seventeen-year-old girl (well, maybe I coaxed her) to a mountain camp in Colorado to learn survival skills. Little did I know that she would learn a lot more than just how to climb rocks and identify edible plants!

She told me later that she cried herself to sleep every night. Alone in her little pup tent, she felt sorry for herself and refused to mix with the other young people because she didn't think they liked her.

One evening, however, the camp director — a warm and motherly woman — crawled into my daughter's tent and said, "Honey, why don't you come and visit a bit with all of us? The kids *like you*. It's you who apparently don't like them — at least, that's the way it seems when you isolate yourself and act like a snob. How can we get to know you unless you're willing to mix with us?"

Fortunately, my daughter is the type of person who can be reasoned with. She crawled out of her tent, smiled a frightened little smile and joined the group. They began to talk, and — to her amazement — she found out that most of the other kids had the same problem she had. They were afraid that their peers wouldn't like them, that they would say the wrong things, that the opposite sex would find them stupid or foolish or laugh at them.

At the end of that summer, my girl came home from Colorado a different person. She had made many new friends, her self-confidence had begun to blossom, and she had learned some basic rules about communication.

"Mother," she said, "you know what a person has to learn in order to communicate? You have to know how to *listen!* I thought I knew it just because I never talked as much as some others did, but I never *really* listened. I was so preoccupied with myself, I felt so sorry for myself, I was so defensive that I never truly heard what others had to say. I would just wait for a chance when I could spill out my woes to others about *my* loneliness, *my* insecurities, *my* fears and desires . . ."

Now in college, my shy girl is still struggling ever so often with her natural tendency to be introverted. She still hates to begin "all over" in a new place where everyone is a stranger; she still has to force herself to get out of her shell and mix with others. But she *makes* herself go out and smile and show a genuine interest in other people's needs — and she listens better.

Her outgoing sister is trying to learn similar things, but from the opposite end. She knows that she talks too much when she isn't very sure of herself. So she tries not to "smoke screen" people with her verbal abilities; she tries not to steal the show, and gives others a chance to say something, too.

Words are a very great and precious gift from God. We all need to understand the power that is given to us when we make use of words, and we all must also learn to listen to others when they use that power. Let's *communicate* with words (I Timothy 4:12)!

LET'S PRAY: Dear God, I know I have a problem when it comes to talking to others. I manage to say either too much or not enough. And it's the same when I talk to You, dear God; I either forget to pray or I talk all the time and do not take time to listen to You. Father, teach Your baby to get out of baby talk and foolish prattle; teach me to communicate. I know that whenever communication breaks down anywhere, it results in big trouble. You said You will be with me in my troubles, so please, save me from my foolish tongue. In Jesus' name. Amen.

40. Listening

Listening is an extremely important communication skill for any child of God. So let's study it more closely.

Our communication has to go three ways: toward God, toward our sisters and brothers in God's family, and toward the people "of the world" (those who have not yet entered God's family or never will).

Any little child has to learn to listen to his parents first; even little animals know that! One warning sound from a mother hen, and her little chicks run for shelter under her wings!

Jesus thought of the importance of listening when He mourned over Jerusalem and His Jewish fellowmen: "Oh, if you would only listen," Jesus cried (Luke 19:41, 42).

Think of it, my friend: God *cried* because people He loved wouldn't listen! Throughout the entire Bible, we find God again and again telling people on earth to listen to Him, to *hear* what He has to say and live! (Isaiah 45: 22, 23, 55:3; John 5:24, 6:63).

How can we listen to God? There are many ways. He speaks to us through the written Word of God. He may also speak to some of us through His creation and the beauty of nature. God wants to speak to His individual children through the Spirit in order to establish a very personal relationship — but we must *let* Him.

How are your listening skills coming since we began to study the subject in our prayer lesson? Are you still *really* listening, or have you gone back to the old "one way communication" where you talk to God, say "amen" and run?

How long do you think your friendships with others would last if you called them on the phone, rattled off everything you had to say without a moment's pause, and then said "Bye!" and hung up? That's what we do when we pray to God but don't take time to listen to Him!

The longer I walk with God, the more time I spend listening to Him and others. I've learned to talk less, too, even to God. He is so much more qualified to talk than I am! He has the wisdom, the love, the insight; if I can only be quiet long enough, He teaches me and guides me with His written and spoken word every moment of every day.

God's Word becomes a bright lamp that lights the path we walk; we can "see" and don't trip or stumble or fall down if we just listen (Psalm 119:105).

The more we listen to God, the better we learn to listen to others, even our fellow believers. We do not need to interrupt others so often to show off our own great "knowledge of the Bible" or any of our other "accomplishments." And we argue less often about small doctrinal differences that sometimes seem important to *us* but are not really matters of salvation — they're mostly just our own efforts to be "right!"

We even learn to hear someone out completely before we begin to draw conclusions or judge what is being said. That does not mean, however, that we have to listen to a person for hours on end (it seems that way sometimes in prayer meetings, when one verbal church member prays or talks forever without really saying much. Matthew 6:5-7 tells us about such people).

Certainly, I have learned by my counseling and talking with people that listening *is* the most important part of communication. However, there comes a time when a person has said it all and then begins to repeat himself. That's the point at which I do both of us a favor and say, "I think we have said enough to see the problem. Now let's see how we can find a solution."

Letting people go on and on and on can do great harm to them; they get deeper and deeper into the misery and confusion within themselves.

There's another thing you should learn to avoid when listening to others, too: Don't project your own interpretations into their words!

How often we hear what we want to hear, and try to fill our own needs with the words of others!

To listen the way God wants us to listen means to deny ourselves and show a genuine concern toward the other person. We must look the people who talk to us right in the eye, and show in *our* eyes genuine, warmest interest and love and kind understanding. We must bite our tongues, if need be, to avoid interrupting and giving unsolicited advice. If people want advice, they will ask for it. And if they do, send a little prayer up to heaven before you answer. God knows the heart of the person you're trying to help — you *don't*. Well-meaning advice can do untold harm if it is the *wrong* advice for a particular situation.

Remember, things are not black and white, but in various shades of gray. Don't feel that you know it all. Don't look "down" on anybody (Philippians 2:3, 4). Stay humble when people come to talk to you. On the other hand, don't feel unable to help them. God can use *any* child of His to help others, if we are willing to listen to Him *first*. And — no matter what your education or background might be — *never* feel that you are "too dumb" or ignorant to talk to God or other people!

The greatest influence in my life came from a little peasant woman — my foster mother. She had only an eighth-grade education, lived most of her life in a tiny mountain village, and was so shy she didn't dare talk to her neighbors about her faith in God. That's why she took me in, so she could "share" God with one little orphan girl.

She did a lot of listening! She listened to God, and she learned patience by listening to me! I was so talkative I even talked in my sleep!

That humble little woman taught me with few words, but what she had to say was important. Many of the things I share in this book I learned from her — and my mother learned it from God, because she knew how to be still and "listen" to Him.

LET'S PRAY: Dear Jesus, I have to admit it: So far I have been a poor listener. Even when I don't talk, my thoughts wander and I think "my own thing." It's obvious that I am still too much of a selfish baby to listen to others and I am glad You understand. Please, help me to learn how to listen — first to You and then to others — with the heart! I am listening, Jesus . . .

41. Sharing and Receiving

As we have just learned, words play a very important part in our interactions with God and each other. But communication involves more than just the use of words — it also involves our body, soul and spirit.

Sometimes however, we underestimate the power of words, and try to use only our minds. We think that people should "know" how we feel without our actually *saying* how we feel. I've talked with many people who — for some reason — assume that others can read their minds. So they never say, *"I love you,"* and then wonder why relationships go sour. Even God loves to hear His children say "thank You" and "I love You;" it honors Him before the angels and the universe (Psalm 50:23; I Peter 1:12, 2:12).

Other times we *overestimate* the magic of words and believe that they alone can convince and communicate. I remember several occasions on which my children, when they were small, tried to sell me on something that wasn't completely true. But their guilty faces spoke louder than their words!

We often do the same kind of thing as spiritual babes; we say something, but our behavior says just the opposite!

"Body language" is more than just a current fad; man has conveyed messages with his body, soul and spirit ever since he came from the Creator's hand. Adam's hiding spoke of sin before he opened his mouth to admit it (Genesis 3:8).

When I speak before a group, I often find myself smiling as I watch the people in the audience. If I see someone sit with crossed arms over his chest through the whole meeting, for instance, I have a pretty good idea that the person is having a struggle inside and is not very eager to "listen willingly" to what the Holy Spirit is trying to say to his heart.

When a person speaks to me but doesn't look me in the eyes, I know that the person either comes from another culture — one in which people are taught to look down as a sign of respect — or that he has deep-seated emotional problems with inferiority, fear, lying or hidden resentments.

Our physical bodies aren't the only parts of us that send signals to others, either. Our souls and spirits shine out of us, too (Luke 6:45, 11:34-36).

When we are in love, for example, we don't need to speak about it all the time — every move we make gives us away. When we dislike a person, we can talk to that person with nothing but sweet, kind words — but he or she knows that we are being phony. Our behavior gives us away.

Christ had some very revealing things to say about people who do nothing but put on a good front (Matthew 23:27, 28).

So, if we want to *truly* communicate and share with other people, we must be genuine and converse from the inside — particularly from the heart (spirit), which is in touch with the Spirit of God.

Furthermore, if communication really comes from the heart, we don't share just to get things in return (Matthew 5:42-48). We give as God gives (Luke 6:38, II Timothy 2:13).

Man is the only creature on this globe who wants to give selfishly — nature teaches us the principle of God. The sun shines upon both righteous and unrighteous people; the rose blooms and fills the air with its scent regardless of who will admire its beauty and appreciate its aroma. The bird feeds its young without worrying about whether or not the babies will repay it some day. Nature shares in the great circle of coming and going, living and dying, giving and receiving.

We too must learn to fit ourselves into God's grand pattern of give and take. It is not enough to do just one or the other; we must learn to give *and* receive.

I know many Christians who are forever up and around

doing things for others, sharing, handing out literature, working from early morning until late at night on their jobs and in many church activities — but they have absolutely no ability to receive. If someone tries to do something for them, they try to return the favor in an even bigger way; they have a hard time simply saying "thank you" and letting it go at that. They can't even accept just an honest compliment.

When people tell such a person that they like what he or she said or did, for example, the person says, "Oh, no, that wasn't really very good at all," and feels that such an answer is very Christlike and humble.

Well, there is nothing "Christlike" or "humble" in such an answer! It reveals hidden pride, and tells the person who gave the compliment that he had very poor judgment in doing so.

I had to learn and ask for wisdom from God before I was able to handle the kind compliments I receive from many people when I do public speaking. I know that some listeners don't mean what they say, but most people are truly speaking from their hearts when they say kind things to me that I honestly don't feel I deserve. I've learned to accept such kindness, however, in the way it is given. I thank people for it and often say, "Praise the Lord," for the praise must go to God, the Giver of all good things (James 1:17).

Corrie ten Boom taught me something once when she said to me, "I take the compliments of people as though they were handing me flowers. I savor the beauty and the lovely scent, put all the flowers into a big bouquet and hand it on to God."

You see, if we don't *let* people share with us, we are being more than just too proud — we are depriving others of the blessing that they will receive from God when they learn to give (Acts 20:35).

LET'S PRAY: Dear God, I think I have a hard time with love, with giving and receiving. I like to "exchange" gifts just as little kids "share" toys, and that's about all. Even when I do share with the poor strangers, I like to do it so that I can give a good report in church. I am pretty selfish, Lord, and I am glad You are not that way, too — otherwise I would be in bad shape. Teach me to give and receive in Your Spirit, Father, the way Jesus taught us -— and to glorify You, not myself. Amen.

ABOUT GOD'S FRUIT

42. Abiding in the Vine

When Christ created the earth, He gave every living thing the ability to reproduce its kind and bear fruit or seed. This is important for a babe in Christ to know, because — as Romans 1:20 tells us — God's visible creation carries symbols of the invisible and spiritual kingdom of God. And Christ used the things of nature to teach us great and basic spiritual principles.

Thus, we can see that God's gift to all his creatures — the ability to reproduce and to bear fruit or seed — holds great significance for us.

In fact, one of the most vital lessons that any "babe" must learn is that God wants us to grow His fruit in our spiritual lives (John 15:5). This is particularly important for an "infant" in Christ to understand, because the fruit-growing process itself begins long before the actual fruit appears (Mark 4:28). When a tree, bush or grapevine is still very young, it sets the beginning for future yields. If a plant is not nurtured or fertilized and produces no blossoms, it will not be able to bring fruit at harvest time.

So, we'd better know from the beginning what kind of fruit we need to grow in the future, and how we must prepare for it!

Paul tells us *what kind* of fruit God wants to grow in us through His Spirit (Galatians 5:22, 23).

Christ Himself taught us *how* it could be done (John 15:1-14).

It's important to notice right away that the Spirit of God grows the fruit—it is not our fruit, it is God's! Notice too that the word "fruit" is singular, even though the Bible tells us that it includes nine different Christian graces: love, joy, peace, longsuffering (patience), gentleness, goodness, faith, meekness and temperance. The word is used in a singular sense because when the Spirit of God grows His fruit He grows all of the graces in the same cluster of grapes, or none.

If a person does not permit the Spirit to grow all of Christ's fruit or tries to grow it in his own strength, just one grape at a time, that person will find his efforts to be of no avail — it cannot be done. Every one of us either produces the fruit of the Spirit as a whole, all at one time, or we produce the works of the flesh (Galatians 5:19-21).

It's also significant that the word "works" in that passage from Galatians is plural, for it shows us that evil has many forms in which to express itself. One does not need to have all the "works" — just a single "work" is enough to hinder the growth of all of Christ's graces in us.

How is the growing of the fruit accomplished?

Christ is the Vine, we are the branches. The branch is the connecting link between the stem and the fruit. It allows the fruit to grow as long as it is connected with the vine — separated, it withers, dries up and dies. So the secret of growing lies in what is called "abiding" in Christ. The original meaning of the word "abiding" is "to remain in a place as opposed to going away" — but in a spiritual sense there is even more to it than that. In the Bible, Christ gives us clear directions as to how we abide in Him.

"If you keep My commandments, you abide in My love" (John 15:10).

And what are Christ's commandments? "This *is* My commandment, that you love one another as I have loved you" (John 15:12, 13:34).

So, in a spiritual sense, abiding means deciding to obey

Christ's principles of interaction with Him and others (Matthew 22:37).

John used the word "abide" often, and in much the same way that Paul used the phrase to "be in Christ." John gave us Christ's teaching of the vine; Paul named the fruit of the Spirit. Both Biblical writers knew by experience what it meant to "abide."

All humans stay, come and go by their own *wills*. So we must use our *wills* to abide! It is significant that — in the Bible — John uses the word "abide" in the present tense, not as some future attainment. We learn therefore that we must abide from the beginning, *now*, long before the fruit appears and ripens — we don't even need to worry about the fruit at all! That is God's role and His concern. He grows it stage by stage. The Father sends the sap, the flower, the pollen, the little green beginnings; and finally — someday — the juicy, sweet grapes will be ready to be used by the Heavenly Gardener (Mark 4:29).

So we must always remember that our Christian graces grow gradually. Babes often get very discouraged because they don't seem to be coming up to the ideal fast enough — they see no fruit. And maturing Christians — whose tiny fruit is still in the green stage and thus tastes terribly sour — also get discouraged easily!

The problem is that we are frequently unwilling to wait for God to grow the fruit fully — so we try shortcuts to grow our own "early varieties." Or we hang out phony, plastic imitations to cover the bare spots on us. But such practices can only fail and stunt or hinder the growth processes of the genuine fruit of the Spirit.

God knows no haste. Step by step, day by day, in sunshine and rain, after purging, He does His work (John 15:2). We have nothing to do with it — except for one thing. By our will and wish we must *abide* — we must stay in our one abode: Jesus Christ. Outside of that single, simple requirement, God does all the rest. We don't need to squeeze, pull, force or even "hang in there" by our own strength.

Frequently, we try *too hard* to abide. So always remember: A branch grows relaxed and naturally out of the vine — even if it should get bent or cracked by the storm of life or attacked by pests or disease, it's the husbandman (gardener) who takes care of the problem, not the branch itself (John 15:1, Jeremiah 30:17).

In other words, "to abide" means to let go and let God do His thing while we stay willingly where we belong: in Christ! (Acts 17:28).

LET'S PRAY: Dear Father, You are the Gardener, and can see if I am growing on the vine or "hanging loose" because Satan is trying to tear me away from Jesus. I can't do a thing about it, God, but ask You to do Your thing: Protect me from being bent or cracked while I am yet a very tender twig, and please *do* begin the growing of Your fruit even though I can't see or feel it yet. Jesus, hold on to me. I don't know yet how to abide and obey You but I surely *want* to stay with You; I have no other home to go to! Amen.

43. Love

Love — the first of the nine parts of the fruit of the Spirit mentioned in the Bible — has many meanings, ideas and descriptions. The Greeks, for instance, had three words for the idea of love: *agape, phileo* and *eros*.

Eros is the passionate, sensual "love" of the body; it is physical infatuation, and the word is not found in the New Testament.

Phileo is brotherly love, kindness, tender affection, human sentimentality built upon feelings and impulses and likings. Because phileo is based on something that can change very rapidly — as our feelings and impulses often do — it is unpredictable, human, and can come in conflict with the love the Holy Spirit is growing in us: agape love.

Before we look at agape — God's love — let's look more closely at the two forms of human love.

Nearly every human being is capable of loving with body (eros) and soul (phileo). We all have a great need to love and be loved. And, in our normal (earthly) sphere, that love is based on trust. In a friendly environment, we "react" with love. If someone is unkind, however, and treats us cruelly, we don't "love" any more. Human love can die if it receives no response, and can turn into resentment and hate.

On the other hand, God's love (agape) — which the Spirit longs to grow in us — is born and nurtured in the Spirit. Only a born-again person can grow that kind of love; when we are "of the world," we have no capacity within ourselves (souls) to ever develop such perfect love (I John 4:7).

Agape love is the explicit nature of God, and is based on the principles of His character. God loves by principle, and He *acts* — He never "reacts." If He did, the human race would be in big trouble! If God loved only when He could trust, He could not love you or me — for we are not very trustworthy yet (Romans 5:5, 8).

God's love always *acts*, regardless of how "worthy" or "unworthy" the object of His love is. God's greatest action of love was the gift of His Son Jesus, which He "gave" by deliberate choice. He had no other cause for it but the love that was in Himself; God's greatest gift was based on His own nature, and nothing else. God always loves for love's sake, and because He is true to Himself (Deuteronomy 7:7, 8, I John 4:10).

Likewise, the love that He wants to grow in us cannot be based on our own human reactions and feelings; it can *only* be based on Him and His principles.

When the Holy Spirit opens up God's principles of love to us, we are overwhelmed by them. I shall never forget the first time I read I Corinthians 13. That passage staggered my soul and body, and I knew I would *never* be able to love in such an unselfish, noble and constant manner. Lucky for me that God didn't expect *me* to do so — for He knows that I don't have it in me! God offers His own love to you and me just because we *want* to have it (Ephesians 3:17-19)!

Our wills say "yes" to God's way of loving regardless of how we may "feel" about it. His kind of love goes against our natural inclinations to judge and condemn, against our resentful impulses, perhaps even against our religious feelings. It is not spent only on those we look upon with our eros or phileo love. When we love in God's way, we can love those whom we don't like or who hate us and treat us unkindly or even cruelly (Matthew 5:44-46).

By feeling and human reaction we might never learn to "like" certain people, but — as Christians — we treat them as God would—and we pray for them (Luke 6:27, 28, 35).

We learn by our *wills* to obey the Spirit of God and to *act,* before our "selfs" (especially our emotions) have a chance to *react.* Such a thing takes time to learn, and the fruit of love often grows slowly, but grow it must in order to give the rest of the graces a chance to develop, too. The other eight parts of the Spirit's fruit seem to be based on the first part — God's agape love. If agape doesn't grow, neither does anything else!

Agape is the *only* kind of love we can present to God. He does not want our sentimental, spontaneous, emotional love — the kind that worships Him happily one day and pouts at Him the next. Our love to God must come out of respect, reverence, and our total willingness to completely obey, trust and serve Him by loving one another in the way Christ loves His Father and us (John 13:34-35, 14:31, 15:9).

We look at ourselves and we know that we shall *never* have such a heavenly fruit within us — we look at God and we know that His love can do the impossible! He *will* do it if we do just one thing: abide in Jesus Christ.

LET'S PRAY: Great God of Love, I get pretty excited when I think of what will happen to me if I just let You grow in me what I don't have so far. God, I am not very loving by nature and You know it. I can't stand what I do or what others do most of the time, and I show how I feel! God, remind me to act right regardless of how others react to me. I am so glad I don't *have* to love by my feelings anymore — it's misery! I *want* to love You right, God, and the others around me. Please, love through me! I simply can't! For Your love's sake. Amen.

44. Joy

What *is* joy? Doesn't it mean the same thing as "happiness?"

Well, sometimes, in order for me to understand a concept fully, I try to "see" it in my inner eye as a picture. And that's what I do for each of the nine words of God's fruit. I "see" love, for instance, as a shepherd, holding a little black lamb securely in His arms (the Shepherd is my Jesus and I am His little black sheep).

Joy, on the other hand, I "see" as a deep, deep well filled with cool, crystal-clear water. When I "look" at happiness, however, I "see" a bubbly, murmuring flat brooklet running busily down a mountain. When drought or wind storms come, the brooklet dries up; the wind plugs the spring with dirt and sand and the nodding flowers beside the stream bed die. But the well remains deep and filled with cool, refreshing water. Thus, I can easily visualize the difference between joy and happiness.

The Bible does not carry a word that depicts happiness; that concept is human, created in places like Hollywood and in unreal, fictional dream stories. It is a *feeling* brought on by pleasant *circumstances,* and lasts only as long as those two factors remain — which, of course, never seems quite long enough! (Ecclesiastes 2:1, 2, 9-11, 25, 26).

But joy — the joy of God, the kind the Spirit wants to grow in us, the kind He wants to give to us — depends neither on feelings nor on circumstances (I Peter 1:6). It is a principle and attitude, like agape love. In it, we act instead of reacting; we *know* — and when storms hit or drought parches our environment, our deep waters of joy are not affected (Psalm 63:9-11, 30:4, 5, 16:11).

Before I truly understood the meaning of God's joy, I couldn't see why the admonition to rejoice and the word "joy" seemed to be on nearly every other page of the New Testament, and throughout the Old Testament as well — all together, they are mentioned more than four hundred times in the Bible! But why?

Why would God ask us over and over to rejoice when life seems to be so full of frustration, sickness, heartache and hardship? (Acts 5:41, I Peter 4:13, Matthew 5:12).

How does joy show itself in a Christian life? Do we run around with pasted-on pin-up smiles from morning to night — and thereby turn other people's stomachs because they know we're being phony? Or do we always run around with sour, long faces to "prove" that our joy and religion are so deep that no one — sometimes not even ourselves — can find it?

Well, either way would be a "reaction" or a "response" of our human ways, and not God's fruit for our lives.

God's joy, just like His love, begins and ends in Him — for God *is* our joy (Psalm 43:4). The foundation of it lies in our trust and knowledge that God controls our circumstances, and that He will never let anything come to us unless it is for our best. We may not be able to understand the "why" of our problems, but we can know that we would ask for the *same things* if we could see — as He does

— the end from the beginning. Our hope in the Lord and our faith in God are the source of our joy (Romans 15:13, Philippians 1:25; Romans 5:2).

Joy does not always smile, but it *can* always glow — even through our tears. Experiences of sorrow often prepare us for or enlarge our capacity for God's joy (John 16:20, Romans 5:3, 4, II Corinthians 7:4, Hebrews 10:34, James 1:2). Sometimes life isn't all fun and games, neither for the non-Christian nor the Christian. But as I've said before, our lives *must* have both sunshine *and* rain; all sunshine and no moisture will only produce a desert where nothing can live or grow!

When the rains and storms come, we have a choice: We can either murmur and complain and turn bitter (which is what many non-Christians do) or we can let the Spirit of God have His way — we can let Him dig a deep well within us.

Yes, often that well is filled with the crystal-clear water of our tears! Tears of sorrow, tears of repentance when we sin, all become the waters of joy. The sky above will always change. Sometimes sunbeams will dance on top of our waters; sometimes the heaviness of black thunderclouds and storms will darken the surface of our joy-wells in both color and appearance. But the depth of our joy cannot be affected by outer circumstances — we are still and content in God (Psalm 27:1-6)!

Even though joy doesn't always smile, it can *always* praise and thank God (II Corinthians 12:10, I Thessalonians 5:18). As we learn to thank God in *everything*—even the hard things in life—the Spirit will grow a new joy in us — something we never had before, something the world will never know! Only God's children receive it as a special gift from God: the joy in and of the Lord!

LET'S PRAY: Dear Jesus, You are my example of joy. You didn't have a very easy or happy life from a human standpoint, did You? You were so poor all Your life! From the manger to the cross You lived with hardship and sorrow — but You never lost Your joy, did You? You always knew that the Father was with You — and so can I. Father, I want to trust You, too. Please, grow the joy in me, even if it takes some tears to water Your fruit. I want Your love and joy and I know they must grow together while I hold still in Jesus! Amen.

45. Peace

If someone were to ask you to describe a scene or a mental picture that would portray your idea of peace, what would you say?

I've often asked young people the same question, and their answers have almost always been very similar. Some described a peaceful mountain scene with a quiet, deep-blue lake reflecting sunshine and sailing white clouds; others would see a dark-green, flower-filled meadow with grazing deer and stately trees. Still others had different ideas — but they were all scenes of total serenity and calmness.

Personally, I have seen too much turmoil in my life to be able to associate peace with perfect harmony and rest. I once read, however, about a famous picture that I would certainly like to see someday. The artist portrays a bird's nest built into the crevice of a steep cliff high above the ocean. A little bird sits on her eggs in perfect ease and rest, while below her roars the big stormy sea. Angry waves foam, froth and break, and fine spray reaches up for the mother bird's tiny fragile abode. The painting is called *Peace*.

That's the kind of peace God wants to give to His children — the kind He wants to grow in us.

Once in a while life grants us the peace of mountain meadows and unrippled smooth-as-glass lakes, but that is the exception rather than the common rule of life.

Satan is the prince of this earth, and he will see to it that we are upset or in turmoil throughout most of our lives. He might give a false smoothness to the ways of the wicked in order to bribe them and make God's children envious, but those who are deceived only find terror and desolation in the end (Psalm 73).

Satan knows that he cannot destroy us (Job 1:9, 10), but he will try to annoy God's children as much as God or we permit him to (Job 1:11).

Jesus knew that He left His disciples and all of God's children in a world that has troubles (John 16:33). But He didn't ask His Father to take us *out* of all troubles (John 17:15). Why? Because He knew we need to learn from our experiences how to go *with* Christ through troubles while receiving His gift of peace.

Peace, like all the other Christian fruit, needs to go three ways: We must have peace with God, we must live in peace with others and we must be at peace with ourselves (Romans 5:1, I Thessalonians 5:13, II Thessalonians 3:16). The Greek word used in the Bible for peace has much the same meaning as the Hebrew word "shalom," which is used as a greeting. "Shalom" wishes the person to whom it is said wholeness — well-being and salvation. And that is the kind of peace God gives; it affects the "whole" person. The *spirit* is in a state of reconciliation with God (I Thessalonians 5:23). The *soul* is at rest, emotionally and mentally (Philippians 4:7). And even our *bodies* will learn to handle the stress of life without falling apart, which in turn will keep us from uptight nerves and many diseases (II Corinthians 13:11, Hebrews 12:10-14).

Whenever we have a lack of peace with God, others, or ourselves, we can usually trace the cause down to a breakdown in fellowship and communication. When we have no peace with God, it is most likely because sin is clogging the channels between us and Him (I John 1:6, 7). So we must confess our wrongdoing and ask for forgiveness, and peace is restored (I John 1:9, Philippians 4:6, 7).

In our relationships with others, we can find our communication channels clogged from either or both ends — we can wrong our brother and neighbor, or they can wrong us. But in both cases, the result is the same: Our peace with one another is destroyed.

If we wrong someone, we had better make it right (Matthew 18:32-35). If we have been wronged, we do not need to wait until the other person comes to us to apologize; we must *forgive* — and forgiveness restores peace (Matthew 18:21, 22, Romans 12:17, 18).

Oh, the unrest, confusion and strife we so often force upon ourselves and others just because we feel the right to hold a grudge and carry an unforgiving spirit! None of God's fruit can grow when we hold on to our resentments and hurt feelings (Matthew 6:14, 15).

We also need to be at peace with ourselves. Maybe you do many dumb things — all humans do. Perhaps, sometime in the past, you messed up your life (and maybe even the lives of others as well). So now you wonder what would have happened if you had "done things differently," and you torture yourself with guilt feelings from day to day.

Well, "shalom," my friend, God wants to make you whole. His peace will heal you if you let Him (Hebrews 13:20, 21). He can even make your miserable, confused past a blessing and give you total peace about it. He did that with me, and He wants to do it for you. Will you *let Him?* (Isaiah 61:1-3, John 14:27).

LET'S PRAY: My Lord of Peace, You came to this earth to bring peace and rest for our souls. I need peace badly — I lose it so easily! I get uptight, resentful, embarrassed, anxious, and so nervous when things don't run smoothly! Will You show me how to hold on to Your peace — I can't! I lose it like a baby loses its shoes. Teach me to walk and grow in peace. Amen.

46. Longsuffering

"Longsuffering" is another term for "patience." The original words for the phrase in Greek are *macros* (long) and *thumos* (temper); thus, we know that the Spirit of God wants to grow the fruit of "long temper" in us. Truly, such a grace is needed in all of us!

I have yet to meet a person who was born with the gift of patience. Yes, some people are more easygoing than others, and don't blow their temper fuses very fast. But we all have our boiling points!

Some people are able to keep "still" on the outside as they boil inside. Others have to endure frustrations for a long time by necessity — due to demands at their jobs or personal lives — while things eat them up inside. But in any case, maladies such as ulcers, high blood pressure and nervous breakdowns are some of the prices we pay for suffering if we do not nurture the fruit of God's longsuffering.

When the Spirit begins to grow God's fruit, it comes out of agape love (I Corinthians 13:4). When we love others (or even ourselves) as God does, we have hope — and because we have hope we can wait, as God waits, for the sinner (John 6:37-39).

God's way of dealing with the unbeliever, as Christ has shown it to us, sets the pace for our "long temper." God wants everybody to be saved — so His love waits, calls, pleads and reaches out in the face of rejection, rebellion and disobedience (II Peter 3:9).

Nothing can reflect the nature of God more completely to the world than when we treat people with God's patient love. Such treatment overwhelms people, and brings them to their senses — they long to have what we have. So we can lead them to the Giver of such fruit — and then *they* can begin to grow it too. God Himself went even one step further than "long suffering." Christ's patience is rendered in another Greek word — *hupomone* — which means "an abiding under undeserved affliction as coming from the hand of God" (I Peter 2:20, 21, 3:17).

That's exactly what Jesus did — He suffered obediently unto death (Philippians 2:8), and never opened His mouth to protest His execution (Isaiah 53:7; Mark 14:61, 15:5). And He prayed for those who killed Him (Luke 23:34). Such behavior is more than "long temper" — it is God's highest glory!

God wants us to learn at least the basics of His kind of patience.

Keeping "still" on the outside when we are angry inside is not enough; we must obey the Spirit and "see" things with God's eyes. God sees all of us for what we are: fallible and in need of tolerance. We *all* err because of our human weaknesses; nobody is perfect. So we need a true insight into every situation before we jump at it feet first. In other words, we must not act by feeling but by principle, just as we do when we grow God's love, joy and peace. Sometimes we endure quietly, other times we must speak up when our feelings tempt us to be still. Some Christians mistakenly consider indulgence to be patience, and in so doing bring great harm to themselves and others.

When we allow our children or others to do wrong — and give consent to it with our silence — we do not show longsuffering as given to us by God. When we stand up for what is right in God's eyes, we show our patience and love by *how* we act, not *if* we act!

Even words of correction and reproof should be given in the Spirit of Christ, in a loving way, which leaves the door open to hope.

True patience never overlooks or covers up sin, not even for the sake of reputation. Paul had something to say about that to the Corinthians (I Corinthians 5). Longsuffering calls sin by its right name, but in such a way that the spirit of the sinner may be saved in the day of the Lord Jesus (I Corinthians 5:5).

When we are reproached for wrongdoing, we must learn to take it humbly, without rationalizing and being defensive. When we are accused or provoked for no good cause or reason, our "long temper" must learn not to retaliate but — rather — to restrain self from punishing others in anger. We musn't let circumstances run us; we musn't give up when the trials of life get heavy. If you combine —in your spirit—agape love with the deep joy that comes from faith in God, and add the peace of Christ to it — that will provide enough endurance and strength to keep your temper from breaking. Give your irritability and defensiveness to God; He is eager to exchange it for something beautiful: His patience!

LET'S PRAY: Dear Lord, I feel like saying, "Give me patience and give it to me right *now*" — but patience, even developing patience, waits! Jesus, I see more and more why You have to grow the fruit — I couldn't, even if I tried! I simply am not a patient person, and life rubs me the wrong way so very often. I want a longer temper, I really do — and only You can bring about the change and the fruit. God, please begin by giving me more patience with myself — for Your patience's sake. Amen.

47. Gentleness

The original word for the fruit of gentleness is *chrestos,* which means "kindness." There is another word for gentleness in the New Testament — *epieikeia* which conveys the idea of "fitting," "fair" and "not insisting on the letter of the law" as it "looks humanely and reasonably at the facts of a case." But *chrestos* goes beyond the meaning of that word; it comes from the same root as the word "grace" (*charis*).

Grace is a favor and a gift that one does not deserve. God's grace sets us free from the debt we owe Him; it paid the price for us on the cross and graciously gave us everything we didn't earn or deserve.

Gentle kindness is an *action* which comes out of favorable, warm understanding of the individual (you or another person). Those who can be gentle and kind to themselves can treat others the same way.

Agape love carries that trait of kindness. One cannot love God's way and be deliberately rude, harsh or unwilling to understand (I Corinthians 13:4).

People who do not have a desire to know God cannot help their own harshness. Their understanding is darkened, and they often carry much bitterness within themselves. They are unable to remove that root of bitterness by their own strength, so they are intolerant, brash and unkind.

When God's Spirit begins His work in us, He has to pull out *any* root of bitterness *first* before He can begin to grow the fruit of gentle kindness. Letting God start that growth is one of the hardest things for many Christians — particularly babes in Christ — to do. Little children are often not gentle by nature; they fight, argue and grab. Others — the quiet, timid children — cry, pout and withdraw.

But withdrawing or pouting in silence is not gentleness either; neither toward God nor toward others or ourselves.

Our "grace-ious" attitudes must express themselves in kind *actions* in order to become the fruit of gentleness. To think kindly toward someone is not enough; we must *act* upon the thought. This not only holds true toward those who rub us the wrong way, but also to those we favor. Just think how many homes would become little heavens on earth if people would only learn to *show* their kindness in word and deed! Unfortunately, many people are afraid to show their gentleness — some husbands, for example, fear that doing so might ruin their masculine "image."

Well, remember: Christ was not afraid to be gentle! Gentleness is not strictly a feminine trait; it does not come out of a weak, demure, fearful nature that doesn't dare to "stand up" against people. On the contrary — the stronger and surer a person is, the more he or she dares to be gentle. Only weak people have to be harsh and cruel, because they are so often on the defense (Matthew 11:29).

A child of God doesn't need to be defensive — God defends us; we don't need to do it ourselves.

Some people are afraid to be gracious and gentle because they wonder if people will take advantage of them. But they're putting the cart before the horse! If we are gentle and kind to others, people can't take advantage of us because we willingly do for them — by our own free choice — what they would otherwise try to manipulate out of us! (Matthew 5:38-48).

It is also the fruit of gentleness that protects Christians from becoming religious snobs. When we witness for or define "truth" for others — both believers and unbelievers alike — we need God's gentleness to keep the proper balance of righteousness in our spirits.

How angry, impatient and caustic we can become in the name of Christ! How judgmental we can be if we live only in our "better" morality and our "new knowledge" without the fruit of the Spirit! Having knowledge alone leads to pride and intolerance (I Corinthians 8:1-3). But gentleness in love will give us the right perspective — and it will also give us something else: charisma.

One of the greatest goals most people long to achieve is to become a dynamic individual with personal charisma, or magnetism. And it's within the reach of *every* person who lets God do His work! No, it is not even a matter of take or leave, maybe or maybe not — we *shall* have charisma if we walk in the Spirit! It will not be just a winning front, a phony friendliness; we shall have genuine, gentle kindness toward *all* men!

LET'S PRAY: Dear Father in Heaven, You sent us Your Son to show us what kindness means. Lord, if I didn't know that You are going to grow all of the fruit in me, I simply would give up. I just don't have what it takes. It's not only that I have a tendency to be short and curt, I actually get embarrassed to be too kind. I don't want to appear to be a "softy"; I love my rough front — I love it when people call me "tough." So where do I start, God? You know best what to do with me; do it, please! Amen.

48. Goodness

Whenever I read the word "goodness," I think of a story in the Bible. I see Jesus walking along a dusty path, surrounded by His disciples and other people, when a very well-dressed young man runs to Him, kneels down and asks: *"Good Master, what good thing shall I do that I may have eternal life?"* (Matthew 19:16, Mark 10:17, Luke 18:18-23).

In order to see the real conflict presented in that story, you must understand the Jewish culture of Christ's time — the culture with which both Jesus and the rich young ruler were well acquainted. The Jews believed that God alone was the source of *all* goodness (James 1:17). The word "good" was, out of respect toward God, *never* used in normal Jewish life except to address God or to speak about God's attributes.

A Jew would never say, for instance, "My *good* friend, your food tastes *good*; you are so *good* to me . . . " And no person was ever addressed as *good*.

The well-dressed man and Jesus both knew that fact, so Christ asked him for a public explanation of his question by saying, "Why callest thou Me *good*?"

Thus, the young man was forced into a position where he had to commit himself. Did he believe that Jesus was God, or had he used the word carelessly?

We shall never know exactly what he thought, for the young man left Jesus sorrowfully without saying, and we have no record that he ever returned. Notice, however, that the rich ruler started out rather confidently. After all, he *did* keep all the laws Jesus quoted — and most likely all of the 613 additional laws of the Jewish faith as well. So he called Christ *good*. But perhaps he saw himself as rather *good*, too, without actually saying so.

Christ had to teach the young man something. First, He had to point out that the fellow had not kept *all* of the commandments. By his love for wealth, he worshiped a god other than the Lord God. Remember, it was *because* nobody can keep *all* of the Law and live without sin that Christ came to do it *for us!* Jesus was trying to make the young man see his need for salvation through Christ, and the error of trusting his own "goodness" to "earn" him eternal life.

There is nothing good in any of us until God begins it in us when we are born again (Philippians 1:6). That fact is hard to take for some people. The "bad" sinners usually have no trouble recognizing their need for Christ's goodness and redemption. But the "good" sinners — the ones who live exemplary lives and try so hard to "earn" their way to heaven — have a much harder time acknowledging their need for a saving Christ (John 8:31-37).

God cannot begin to grow His goodness in us until we recognize our attempts to live a "good" life in our *own* strength are futile! Let's face it! We are *all* charity cases in God's eyes — even the best of us! Only when we take our plastic fruit down off our phony fronts can the Holy Spirit begin to grow Christ's goodness in us.

Knowing how hard people try to be good by attempting to keep the Law or by many other human devices, Paul tells us over and over again in the Bible that goodness can only be obtained as a *gift* from God through Jesus Christ (Romans 3:21-24, 7:18; Philippians 3:8, 9).

What happens when God gives us His goodness?

God gives *only* good things (Matthew 7:11). He will never give anything evil or bad. There are times when He permits evil to have its way, or when our foolish behavior invites some bad consequences, but God Himself never gives bad things such as sickness, sorrow, death or even temptation (James 1:13). He *permits* them, but God *gives* only *good things.* So, if we want to know if something is good or bad, we need only ask ourselves: Would God send it; would Jesus approve of it if He were on earth right now?

Does the story of the rich young ruler and Jesus mean that we all need to go out and sell everything we own and give it to the poor? In other words, is material wealth bad?

Well, if we study God's principles carefully—even that story — we find that money and riches are not bad — but that the love for such things is *not "good."* Gold or silver or any other earthly possession cannot be bad because God made it all, and He called it "good" in the beginning (Genesis 1:31). Furthermore, *God* is the final owner of all the precious metal — He owns the cattle on a thousand hills (Psalm 50:10). But when we make a god of material possessions, when they become the center of our lives, our hope and our security, we shove God aside and earthly wealth becomes bad for us because it competes with Christ.

Even "good" things such as laws and doctrines become bad for us when we make them a substitute for Christ (Galatians 2:21, Romans 7:1-6, 8:3, 4).

When God's goodness works in us, He doesn't just give us a "good" facade — He longs to make us good right down to the core. His goodness will teach us to do *more* than just act right. His Spirit will lead us past right and wrong *actions* to right and wrong *motives*. And that's where our wills come in to aid our goodness.

Suppose, for instance, that two of us could go to Jesus today and ask Him the question the rich young ruler asked. Christ might point to one of us and say, "Go and sell it all," and to the other say, "Keep it and use it the way you have used it so far!" Or, as another example, two Christians might stand up at a meeting to give their testimony. To one the Spirit might say, "Speak," and to the other, "Sit down and be still!" In each story, are not both people involved doing something *good*? Yes, *we* see it as good, but the Spirit knows whether a person is prompted by his will toward God's goodness or by his own human kind of spiritual pride — perhaps that person is actually boasting or even attempting to "earn" favor in God's eyes.

Satan hates for us to grow God's goodness. He knows that nothing will make us more like God, and put us back into the image of God, than to be good the way Jesus was and is. So the enemy of all real goodness will try to deceive us into being "good" by ourselves and in our own strength. Don't be fooled into doing so — it is not enough! Let *God* be good in you!

LET'S PRAY: Father God, You giver of all good things, I thank You for every good gift I have ever received. I have a problem, Lord: I don't even know yet how to let You be good in me. I don't know if I am trying, or if You are trying to do the good in me. Remember, I am your very dumb kid, but I *do* want to be good Your way, Jesus. Amen.

49. *Faith*

Time and time again, people come up to me and say, "I wish I had the kind of faith that you have!" And that statement always takes me by surprise, because I keep forgetting that babes in Christ don't undersand the dynamics of faith at all. I fail to remember that I, too, once thought that — to *have* faith — I had to *make* myself believe, and squeeze and push and try in order to have more faith and thus please God, for without faith we cannot please Him (Hebrews 11:6).

But faith is a gift that God *gives* to us (Ephesians 2:8, 9). He Himself grows the fruit in us (Luke 17:5). Therefore, the first thing we must do is *ask* our heavenly Father for His gift of faith (Mark 9:24).

Next, we must learn the way in which God has ordained to give us His gift. Paul tells us that faith cometh by hearing, and hearing by the Word of God (Romans 10:17). In that particular verse, "hear" means "to be persuaded" or "to receive a message without contradiction." So that passage simply tells us that as we study and understand the Word of God more clearly, God creates and grows more faith in us.

Faith comes custom-made, just like everything else God gives. He gives to each of us individually, and according to our needs, desires and our willingness to trust and obey Him. God deals to every person his own individual measure of faith (Romans 12:3). We don't need to wish for someone else's faith; we don't need to be covetous or feel superior. We get the faith that "fits" us personally. As we "grow" from babyhood into our full stature in Christ Jesus, God "matches" and grows His gifts right along with us (James 4:6, Galatians 3:22-26, Philippians 4:19, Romans 1:17, II Thessalonians 1:3).

Once we understand where faith comes from and how to get it, we must understand how to use it.

The use of faith is as important to its growth as is physical exercise to an infant. If we don't use our muscles, they deteriorate. If we don't use our brains because we are lazy thinkers, we lose the ability to think clearly. And if we don't use God's faith in us, it shrivels and dries up before it can ripen into a luscious, juicy-sweet fruit (I Corinthians 16:13, Matthew 14:28-31, Hebrews 11:6).

"Faith," as God gives it to us, is "trust in God" — a total belief that God *can* be trusted at *all* times and that

He is always faithful and hears us *whenever* we call (II Thessalonians 3:3, I John 5:14, 15, Jeremiah 33:3).

When we believe in God's promises, we do so because we put our trust and faith in God. Our faith is not based on His promises; it is based on God Himself. Because we *have* that faith, we *can* trust His promises.

We also need to know that we cannot base our trust in our *own* faith in God, but only in faith *in* and *from* God. Ask the Holy Spirit to show you whenever you make this mistake, for it is easy to do. Perhaps that is because the idea can be difficult to understand.

When I woke up this morning thinking about this lesson, God gave me a simple example of the concept that should help you to understand better.

It was still dark outside; the dawn hadn't come, but there was a faint shimmer of light. I heard a bird twitter in a tree, and I knew that my little friend sang to greet the new day.

The day hadn't come yet, but the bird never questioned that it would come; he simply got ready for it. The little featherball didn't sing *in order* to bring the new dawn about — he sang *because* it was coming.

Too many Christians put their trust and belief in other good things besides God Himself. They believe that *if* they pray the right way or *if* they use God's Word as medicine or *if* they fast or do certain rituals, they will bring certain things about. They try to "believe more," but they don't understand that their belief is a *result* of their faith and trust *in* and *from* God, not the other way around.

We can sing our song of belief *because* God brings the dawn; we can't force the daybreak or bring it on by our belief. We *can* act, trust, obey and be steadfast even in persecution because we know in Whom and why we believe. But God Himself is our source of faith, not His gifts or our special experience or encounter with Him, nor can our trust in a good Christian friend be the cornerstone of our faith. We can believe in many fine things and good people, but our faith must be based *on God alone*.

He is the *only* foundation that will stand and never shake (Deuteronomy 7:9). Are you going through life's darkest hour? Does it all look hopeless, discouraging and forbidding? Well, start singing and praising God. A new day *is* coming. He *is* the light (I John 1:5)!

LET'S PRAY: Dear God, I am afraid that I too often present my own "homegrown" variety of "faith" to You in order to make You do my will. Please forgive me! You are not a universal bellhop who comes when I push my magic button of faith; You are the omnipotent great God of the universe and my wonderful Father who loves me. So I shall put my hand into Yours like a little child who trusts his parents and walks by faith in darkness and into dawn. Please, dear Jesus, give me Your living faith; mine is lifeless and plastic. Let my work for You be a result of faith in You, not a means to bring about my own desires, as good as they may be — and all the glory must go to You. Amen.

50. Meekness

A "meek" spirit is very precious in God's eyes (I Peter 3:4). He considers meekness a very great, special and Christ-like virtue (Matthew 5:5, II Corinthians 10:1).

Christ said of Himself that He was "meek" and "lowly in heart," and that because of it we could find rest for our souls (Matthew 11:29).

We Christians, however, don't use the word "meekness" very freely. We like to talk about love and peace and joy — but "meekness" makes us cringe. It sounds too much like "weakness" — and who wants to be weak? After all, aren't we supposed to be "strong" in the Lord?

Well, there is much to be said about both concepts, but let's get one thing straight first: "weak" and "meek" are *not* the same! In fact, they are opposites!

That doesn't mean, however, that it is wrong to be weak. Any baby is, by its helpless nature, weak and easily hurt. God gives us the assurance that His grace is sufficient for *all* our weaknesses, be they in our spiritual babyhood or when we mature and "grow up" as Christians but discover we have a "thorn" in our flesh. Paul was not a babe at all when he wrote in his letter to the Corinthians that God had reassured him that He would be strongest in the most weak of His children (II Corinthians 12:9).

Nevertheless, God does not intend to grow a fruit of weakness (which is a condition) in us, but — rather — the fruit of meekness (which is an attitude of the heart)!

The original meaning of meekness — which can give us a better insight as to how the word is used in the Bible — is very difficult to express by way of the English language. Words such as "gentleness," "humble" and "soothing" simply don't fit completely — they depict an outward action of an inner attitude which *springs out of* God's gift to us (Ephesians 4:2). Meekness, on the other hand, *is* God's gift; He *gives* it to us. And then we *show* that the fruit is growing in us with our gentle, humble, soothing behavior.

The German word for meekness is *Sanftmut*. *Sanft* means "gentle" or "tender;" *Mut* means "courage" or "bravery" and "fortitude."

The Greek word depicts "great strength under complete control" (which, as I've said, is exactly the opposite of weakness).

A very dear friend of mine who is a fine Bible scholar told me that she once did some thorough research on the origin of the word "meekness," and that her findings were very significant and revealing. And indeed they are!

She discovered that the term was *first* used in the days of ancient Rome to describe the horses in the famous chariot races of the Circus Maximus. (If you've seen the film *Ben Hur* you've seen the races of that time.) The "meekest" animals in Rome were the race horses — the best and strongest of their kind — that had not been trained by a whip. Rather, they were the ones that had learned to trust their masters and the drivers of their chariots so much that one touch or pull of the rein was enough to make them obey willingly and give their all to win the race!

No wonder Jesus is called "meek" in the Bible! The Son of God, even while He was on earth, had the infinite resources of His Father at His command — He had total power! He also had total self-control and willingness to obey and "run the race" to a victorious end on the cross! What submission in love!

Meekness does not make us weak — it's the fruit of the power controlled by God's Spirit!

Meekness begins with our attitude toward God. When we are willing to trust Him so completely that we stop struggling and resisting and arguing with God, when we begin to know that His dealings with us are always best (Romans 8:28), *then* God can begin to grow that special grace of a meek fruit in our spirit. We submit — He grows!

Out of our contentment, trust and willingness to follow His reins comes a new gentleness in us toward our fellow men — even those who are erring (Galatians 6:1, II Timothy 2:25, Matthew 5:10-12), or who try to harm us.

In the Old Testament, Moses is called the most "meek" man on the face of the earth (Numbers 12:3). Certainly, his life story proves that he wasn't a weak man in any way. But he was patient, longsuffering, tender and forgiving toward his people because he *first* trusted God.

Christ showed us all what meekness is. He trusted His Father completely. He never tried to go His own way; He never needed to be "tough." He considered others more important than Himself; He took upon Himself the punishment that we deserved. So let's behold and learn from the meek Lamb of God! (Isaiah 53:7).

LET'S PRAY: Dear Jesus, help me to understand the nature of meekness. I have had a completely wrong concept of it up to this point. I know if I *let* You grow that fruit in me, my life will be easier and much happier, and so will the lives of those around me. Most of the arguments, tensions and fights that I have, come out of my unruly, temperamental spirit and the self that does not want to be run by Your reins. Lord, I do want to run a "meek" race and be victorious through You. Please, win for me through Your gift of true meekness in me. Amen.

51. Temperance

Here in America, the concept of temperance has been limited by its past history to mean abstinence from intoxicating drinks and tobacco. The Biblical word for "temperance," however — *enkrateia* — says a lot more; its root means "strength," "power" or "lordship" which one has over oneself or something. And in German, the word is *Keuschheit,* which connotes purity, modesty and virtue, as well as innocence and abstinency.

The closest English synonym would be "discipline" or "self-discipline." And the opposite would be "undisciplined" or "without control."

In I Corinthians 9:25, Paul tells us to be "temperate" to win a crown in the race of life. Does that mean that we need only exercise our self-control?

Well, since God is growing the fruit of temperance in us, there has to be more involved, because there has to be a God-control on every power of our life — be it body, soul or spirit.

No wonder the Bible lists temperance last in its list of Christian graces! Surely, it is the hardest of all to let God grow within us!

We always think of *self*-control as the battle with our fleshly desires — our appetites, our lusts of the flesh in sex, our materialistic hunger for things. But it is *God* who desires to control these things in His Spirit of love.

Nevertheless, we often put the buggy before the horse — we try to do it all ourselves. But God does not begin to renew and change us from the outside toward the inner man — He begins in the inner man (Philippians 2:13).

Temperance, then, begins in the spirit. God directs us toward new and better goals, and our self (soul) learns to submit to God's wisdom. We understand that every control He lays on us is for our own good, for we know that He is not an unreasonable tryant. He never takes anything away unless He gives us something better (Luke 6:38). He never restrains us unless He knows something would harm us (Psalm 91:11, 12). He is a perfect Father. He is our Creator and He knows how we are put together and what we really need (Matthew 6:6-8).

If we could see the end from the beginning, we would gladly ask for every control He ever brings upon us, and would respond and obey willingly (Psalms 25:20, 21, 141:3, 4).

The body is always the last of the three parts of ourselves to "catch on" to His will; therefore we can sometimes understand the blessings of temperance long before the body is actually brought under complete control. We get discouraged and weary as a result, and wonder if we shall ever be victorious over that stubborn, overpowering flesh of ours. Paul wondered about it, too! (Romans 7:22-25).

That's why it's important to remember that we simply don't have enough self-control to do it all ourselves; even the most disciplined ascetic person will never accomplish total control over evil habits and things.

God, however, will grow the fruit of His control in us if we give Him our wills and *abide* in Christ. He will not grow a fruit in us that is geared *only* toward the negatives, either — His fruit must ripen toward positive expression and right use of our life's power.

God's temperance means control and moderation in *all* things, not just the evil temptations of body and soul (Philippians 4:5). And that means that temperance is applicable to good things, too. But why should we be moderate in good things?

We need God's control to *love* His way and not turn it into overindulgence and the "spoiling" of a person (I John 5:3, 5; Psalm 19:12-14).

We have to learn to grow our *joy* amidst the storms of life and not go overboard with our "happy" Christian facades — otherwise, we would seem phony.

Our *peace* could lead us to seclusion and into a shell if God's control was not at work.

Our *longsuffering,* if left unbridled, could encourage us to never take any action at all, or could keep us from speaking up when we should — or we could run ahead of God's timing. Our *gentleness* might turn into cowardice, so that we would not call sin by its right name. And our *goodness* could become eagerness to seek acceptance from *everyone*. (Those who follow God will be persecuted by others — John 15:18-25).

Our *faith* could become nothing more than an outer display of our blown-up Christian self-image. Our *meekness* might degenerate into a spineless crawl, and our work for God would thus actually dishonor God in the end.

Many servants of God forget these possibilities — they forget that we must be moderate and God-controlled in *all* things! They toil and run and never stop until they have killed themselves, all in the name of God's cause! Will they receive a special award from God for their intemperance in working for Him?

Hardly! God is honored the most when we obey Him in *all* things! The fruit of temperance grows best when God is our loving Moderator in everything!

LET'S PRAY: Dear Father in Heaven, will I ever learn to do anything right? Here I thought I was pleasing You if I ran and worked for You day and night. Or was I doing it for me after all? I know I am a very insecure person and have a great need to be accepted. I have a hard time saying "no" to anyone, and I often feel resentful because even the church people take advantage of it. Lord, show me the whole scope of temperance and moderation, please. It's overwhelming! I have my hands full watching out for evil temptation, but when we can do good in excess, too — that staggers my understanding. I just have to remind You again, Lord, that I am Your dumb kid, so control my life all the way. I can't control it — neither the good nor the bad. Take over, my Lord! Amen.

GRADUATION

52. Finals

Welcome, little babe in Christ, to the graduation exercises of your first class in God's school!

It is no small achievement that you stuck with all the lessons in this book — I know very well that some of them were awfully difficult for you to understand. Learning the fundamentals of living in Christ can be as hard and confusing as learning to read for the first time! It's not easy — just as it isn't easy for a youngster to memorize the alphabet and multiplication tables!

I hope you *did,* incidentally, memorize some of the Bible texts that have come up again and again in the various lessons. And I also dare to hope that — at this point —you've learned to breathe and walk and talk a bit more naturally in your spiritual life.

You say you're still not sure that you understand all of the lessons? Well, how about going back and starting the class all over again? This time, you might really go into it by teaching the lessons to other babes in Christ!

Yes, I realize that you probably don't think you know spiritual matters well enough to teach others. But let me tell you a big secret: The very best way to learn anything is to teach it!

I've been a teacher by profession for many years, and I know that the principle works. For instance, I once had a terrible hang-up about driving — I was sure I could never learn. So what did I do? I offered to teach theory of driver's education at a summer camp! And by the end of that summer, I knew enough to take my driver's test and get my license. I've been driving — and loving every minute of it — ever since!

Every school term, of course, ends in a final exam — and it's time now for you to take yours. Let's review and summarize what you have learned long before you begin to teach others:

FINAL "EXAM"

1. Are you still sure of your personal salvation? Paul asked the Corinthians the same questions (II Corinthians 13:5).

2. Remember, you shall never grow spiritually or in your understanding unless you are utterly sure that you *have* eternal life already in you! (John 3:15, I John 5:12, 13). If you wonder about that, read Romans 10:9 and check yourself once more:

    a. Do you truly believe that you are a sinner (Romans 3:23) and that Jesus Christ is *your* Savior? (John 3:16).

    b. Do you accept His finished work on the cross as your sole salvation, or do you try to save yourself? (Titus 3:4, 5).

    c. Did you invite Christ into your heart, and do you know that by that act of your will you were born again in the Spirit? (John 3:3-16).

    d. Did you confess with your voice that Christ is your Lord? (Romans 10:9).

If you can say "yes" to all those questions, you passed the test! And now, because that is settled, you can consider yourself a graduate of "beginner's class," and can turn your spiritual eyesight toward higher learning — *and* service.

Remember, I am not asking you to "earn" your salvation now that you have matured a bit. Salvation is God's gift to you — it's free, you *have* it and it is *all* paid for. God does not believe in giving you a gift and then asking you afterward to pay for it on an "installment plan" for the rest of your life.

But maybe He does want you to ask yourself another question:

3. What are you planning to do with your life?

You see, when you invite Christ into your life and are born again, you give God your heart (John 3:8, Acts 15: 8, 9, Ephesians 3:17). As a result, there comes a time in your life when you must decide what you plan to do with that life.

God has your heart, but are you willing to live a life consecrated fully to Him alone?

"What about *my* future plans and dreams?" you ask shyly. "Must I become a preacher or missionary or nurse in order to serve in His cause?"

God forbid — professional Christian service does not always spell consecration to Christ. If you feel a need to become something other than a preacher, by all means be sure and do it. Too many people preach the gospel for human reasons and not because they *cannot help* but preach the gospel of Christ (I Corinthians 9:16, Acts 4: 18-20).

Someone once said, "Salvation is God's gift to you; your consecrated life is your gift to God in return." And that leads to another, final question you should ask yourself:

4. Do you want to give your life as a gift to God?

If you do, you will discover something both wonderful and puzzling. God is debtor to no one (Mark 10:29, 30).

So, as you give Him the gift of your willingness to live for Him alone, He will take your life and give it back to you richer, fuller, deeper — and you shall bring trophies with you — prizes far more valuable than any earthly possessions could ever be — when you enter into heaven (John 10:10, Ephesians 3:14-21, I Corinthians 3:12-14).

Remember, God will not force you to live for Him alone! I know some people who have never gone past drinking their first glass of spiritual milk — even though they have carried a Christian label for many years. They make their own lives and the lives of those around them miserable. They will be saved like a brand plucked out of the burning (Zechariah 3:2) and will stand before the Lord with empty hands, having helped no one, having saved only their own naked lives. What a tragedy, what a waste! They lived to follow their own wishes and dreams, and will pay the price of a wasted life (I Corinthians 3:15).

Only what we do for Christ will last; everything else is perishable; fame, material riches, worldly power, honor before men — all is lost and forgotten a short time after a person's funeral (I John 2:15-17, I Timothy 6:7).

You ask *what* Christ wants you to do for Him? I can't tell you — but if you ask Him, He will show you step by step, moment by moment, day by day. He will take your life and make it the best, the most fruitful — and He *will* give you the desires of your own heart as well (Psalm 37). Wouldn't you like to talk to Him about it right now?

LET'S PRAY: My great loving Father in Heaven, thank You for sending the Holy Spirit into my life to convince me that I was a sinner who needed a Savior. Now I have Jesus in my heart and You are my Heavenly Father, and I am Your child. God, I want You to take not only my heart but also my life under Your control. I know better than to try to run it by myself. I don't know yet what your plans for my life are, but Lord, I trust You completely.

I am a bit scared, Jesus, I wonder about so many things. Lord, You *know* my weaknesses and strong points. I wonder if I can do *anything* for You even if I am not called into the Christian professions. All I can say is: I am Yours and though I don't have too many abilities, I have two things — availability and consecration. Take both and use me as You see fit and may all the honor and glory and the credit for it go to You alone. I ask and praise You, God, in Jesus' name! Amen.